D1453543

EMIGRANT ENTREPRENEURS
SHANGHAI INDUSTRIALISTS IN
HONG KONG

Sketch Map of Cities and Provinces of China

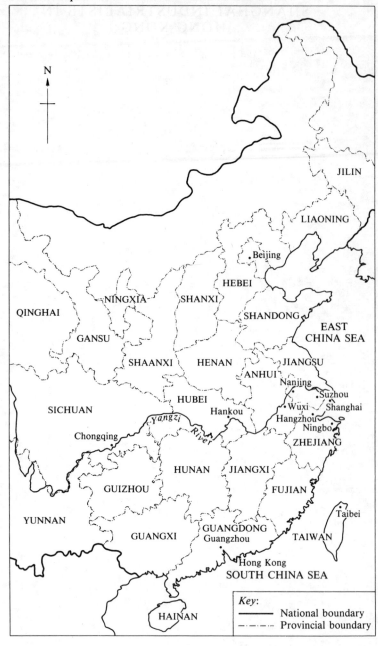

N

JILIN

LIAONING

Beijing

HEBEI

NINGXIA   SHANXI

QINGHAI

SHANDONG

EAST
CHINA SEA

GANSU

SHAANXI   HENAN   JIANGSU

ANHUI

Nanjing

SICHUAN

HUBEI

Hankou

Suzhou

Wuxi   Shanghai

Hangzhou

Yangzi   River

Ningbo

Chongqing

ZHEJIANG

HUNAN   JIANGXI

GUIZHOU

FUJIAN

YUNNAN

Taibei

GUANGDONG

GUANGXI   Guangzhou   TAIWAN

Hong Kong

SOUTH CHINA SEA

Key:
— National boundary
-·-·-·- Provincial boundary

HAINAN

EMIGRANT ENTREPRENEURS

SHANGHAI INDUSTRIALISTS IN HONG KONG

WONG SIU-LUN

HONG KONG
OXFORD UNIVERSITY PRESS
OXFORD NEW YORK
1988

Oxford University Press

Oxford New York Toronto
Petaling Jaya Singapore Hong Kong Tokyo
Delhi Bombay Calcutta Madras Karachi
Nairobi Dar es Salaam Cape Town
Melbourne Auckland

and associated companies in
Berlin Ibadan

© *Oxford University Press 1988*

First published 1988
Published in the United States
by Oxford University Press, Inc., New York

British Library Cataloguing in Publication Data
Wong, Siu-Lun
Emigrant entrepreneurs: Shanghai
industrialists in Hong Kong.
1. Hong Kong. Cotton spinning industries.
Role of Shanghai industrialists
I. Title
338'.4'76772122
ISBN 0-19-584213-8

Library of Congress Cataloging-in-Publication Data
Wong, Siu-lun.
Emigrant entrepreneurs: Shanghai industrialists in Hong Kong/
Wong Siu-Lun.
p. cm.
Bibliography: p.
Includes index.
ISBN 0-19-584213-8: $34.00 (U.S.)
1. Cotton yarn industry—Hong Kong—History. 2. Cotton spinning—
History. 3. Chinese—Hong Kong—History. 4. Entrepreneurship—
Hong Kong—History. 5. Shanghai (China)—Emigration and
immigration—History. 6. Hong Kong—Emigration and immigration—
History. I. Title.
HD9889. Y3H858 1988
338'.04'08995105—dc19 88-25160
CIP

Printed in Hong Kong by Nordica Printing Co.
Published by Oxford University Press, Warwick House, Hong Kong

Preface

THIS is a book about a group of Shanghainese entrepreneurs who dominated the cotton spinning industry in Hong Kong. The idea of writing about them was suggested to me in Oxford in 1975 as I was completing my B.Litt. thesis on the economic enterprise of the overseas Chinese in South-east Asia and was about to return home to teach. It was my supervisor, the late Professor Maurice Freedman, who made the suggestion during a discussion of my research plans. The idea appealed to me immediately as a logical extension of my B.Litt. research. Furthermore, the success story of the Shanghainese had an intrinsic appeal to someone like myself who grew up during the industrialization of Hong Kong. In his essay on 'A Chinese Phase in Social Anthropology', Professor Freedman wrote that '[students] of Hong Kong and the Overseas Chinese know something of the way in which Chinese commerce and industry can thrive outside the framework of the Chinese state, and, with a friendly push from the economists, might succeed in describing how Chinese entrepreneurs manage their affairs (the account would certainly not be dull) and in throwing light on the factors which have favoured and retarded Chinese economic innovation.' It was apparently in this belief that, shortly before his sudden death, he gave me a gentle push to encourage me to apply for the research grant from the Harvard-Yenching Institute which enabled me to carry out the study.

In the summer of 1978 after I had been teaching in the Department of Sociology in the University of Hong Kong for three years, I took the plunge, not without trepidation, and started to conduct the interviews. I was pleasantly surprised, however, by the openness of my respondents which made the field-work both enjoyable and educational for me. Numerous persons helped me in the course of my investigation, and I am very grateful to them. I would like in particular to thank Professor Frank H. H. King for providing me with a letter of introduction in his capacity as the Director of the Centre of Asian Studies, University of Hong Kong, and for suggesting many improvements to the interview schedule; Miss Judy Kwok for accompanying me to the interviews and contributing to the successful completion of the field-work; Mr C. S. Lai for putting his knowledge of management and business administration at my disposal and collecting the company records for me; and also Miss Laura Cheung, Miss Belinda Law, Mr Tong Kin-sang and Mr Wu Kwok-lai for their research assistance.

In 1979 I obtained study leave from the University of Hong Kong and spent three terms at Wolfson College, Oxford with the support of a Harvard-Yenching doctoral scholarship to write my D.Phil. thesis on the Shanghainese spinners. That year was a productive one. I owe an intellectual debt to my supervisor, Professor J. C. Mitchell, who kept me on course by reminding me patiently and firmly that I must not become so engrossed in the field-work material as to lose sight of the broader theoretical issues. I hope his intellectual subtlety and craftsmanship have rubbed off on me and found their way into the book. I also derived much benefit from stimulating conversations with Dr Mark Elvin who read part of the thesis for me. The beauty and serenity of Wolfson College and the Oxford meadows refreshed and sustained me during the solitary pursuit of thinking and writing.

After completing the thesis and returning to my teaching duties, I thought further about the subject and wrote several articles which are listed in the bibliography. But I did not have the time to carry out a thorough revision until 1985 when I was fortunate enough to receive yet another award from the Harvard-Yenching Institute to spend my year of long leave at Harvard University. During the course of making the revisions, I imposed the manuscript on a number of scholars, including Professors Marie-Claire Bergère, Sherman Cochran, Parks M. Coble Jr., Gary G. Hamilton, Y. S. Hu, Dwight H. Perkins, Ezra F. Vogel, and Frederic Wakeman Jr. I wish to thank them for their comments and encouragement. Parts of the manuscript were presented as seminar papers at the Center for Chinese Studies, University of California, Berkeley, and the Department of Sociology, University of California, Davis in April 1986. I am grateful to Professors Joyce K. Kallgren and Gary G. Hamilton for the invitation. Finally, I have to thank Mrs Hilda Chan, Mrs Grace Li, Miss Linda Cho, and Mr Robert Chung for their assistance in preparing the fine copy of the manuscript for publication.

WONG SIU-LUN
University of Hong Kong
September 1987

Contents

Tables

Figures

Abbreviations

AJS	American Journal of Sociology
ASR	American Sociological Review
DGB	Da Gong Bao (Hong Kong)
EDCC	Economic Development and Cultural Change
FEER	Far Eastern Economic Review
HKCSA	Hong Kong Cotton Spinners' Association
RQS	Shanghai Academy of Social Sciences, Institute of Economic Research (ed), *Rongjia Qiye Shiliao* (Source Materials on the Rong Family Enterprises) (Shanghai, People's Press, 1980)
SCMP	South China Morning Post

Romanization

CHINESE terms and place names are transliterated by the *pinyin* system in the text. But Chinese personal names are romanized according to individual preference, if known. A list of the romanized terms and names and their corresponding Chinese characters is provided in the Glossary.

1 Introduction: Industrialization and the Shanghainese

IN many societies entrepreneurship and ethnicity are intertwined. Individuals with common biological or territorial origins are often found to congregate in particular spheres of economic activity, giving rise to a phenomenon variously described as cultural division of labour, ethnic monopoly, or ethnic specialization. The archetype of this phenomenon is of course the Jewish merchants in Europe. And they have numerous counterparts in different places, for example, the Antioqueno industrialists in Colombia, the Hauser traders in Nigeria, the Parsi and Gujarati weavers in Bombay, the Armenian merchants in Iran, and the Italian home-owners in New York City.

In South-east Asia, the term 'Chinese' is often regarded as synonymous with traders and middlemen. Yet among these overseas Chinese themselves there are different 'speech groups' or 'sub-ethnic groups' with their own distinctive occupational divisions. In Bangkok in the early 1950s, for instance, the majority of the rice millers were Teochiu (Chaozhou), the sawmillers Hainanese, the leather workshop owners Hakka, and the machine shop proprietors Cantonese.[1] Such an occupational clustering by regional groups looks like a replica of a familiar feature of the traditional urban economies in China itself. In Hangzhou at the turn of the century, to cite just one example, it has been recorded that '[practically] all the carpenters, woodcarvers, decorators, cabinet makers, and medicine dealers are from Ningpo. The tea and cloth merchants, salt dealers and innkeepers are from Anhui. The porcelain dealers are from Kiangsi, the opium dealers from Canton, and the wine merchants from Shaohsing.'[2]

In Hong Kong, which is essentially a Chinese city, such a pattern of occupational clustering is also evident. Among the various regional groups there, the most conspicuous, both for their economic significance and their degree of concentration, are the Shanghainese in the textile industry. They figure prominently in academic as well as official assessments of the post-war economic performance of the territory. In an attempt to account for 'the ability of the Hong Kong economy to create a great export trade in manufacture out of next to nothing', E. H. Phelps Brown emphasizes the fact that '[at] the outset there was a powerful injection of capital, know-how and enterprise from Shanghai'.[3]

This analysis has become the basis of policy formulation within the Hong Kong government. In a document on industrial land policy prepared in 1973 by the Department of Commerce and Industry, Shanghai entrepreneurs were singled out for praise. It was stated that because Hong Kong had had the good fortune to receive 'the injection of Shanghai experience and capital', it had been given 'ten to fifteen years' start in industrialization over many other Asian countries'[4] even though they had the same essential economic inputs to offer.

Yet for all the importance attributed to this Shanghainese group, its story remains largely untold. The purpose of this study, therefore, is to provide a detailed account of its industrial accomplishments to fill a gap in our knowledge about the process of industrialization in Hong Kong, one of the most prosperous newly industrialized regions of the post-war period. It is hoped that the account of the Shanghai spinners will help to answer two theoretical questions. First, why do people with common regional origins often congregate in particular economic spheres? Second, what are the distinctive features of Chinese industrial entrepreneurship? In view of these questions, the story of the Shanghai spinners in Hong Kong will begin with a brief sketch of the setting in which they operate.

The Setting

Hong Kong is situated at the mouth of the Pearl River on the southern fringe of the Chinese mainland. With a land area of 404 square miles, it consists of a peninsula with some hinterland and several islands. Part of it has been a British Crown Colony since the middle of the nineteenth century. After China's defeat in the First Opium War, Hong Kong Island was ceded to the British government in 1843 in the Treaty of Nanking. The colony was expanded in 1860 with the addition of Kowloon peninsula when China was again defeated in another war with the Western powers. Then in 1898, a large area of the mainland to the north of the Kowloon peninsula was leased to Great Britain. The lease of this area, which became known as the New Territories, is due to expire in 1997.

As Hong Kong is a colony, the civil service is dominated by British officials in the higher echelons and controlled by a Governor appointed by the British Crown. In the Legislative and Executive Councils of the Hong Kong government, there are a number of 'unofficial' members appointed by the Governor to 'reflect' public opinion. Until recently, the unofficial members were mainly drawn from the business community, which demonstrates the colonial administration's concern for trade and industry.

Since the beginning of British rule, Hong Kong had been an important entrepôt. But after the Second World War its economic role was altered by two major events. The victory of the Chinese Communist Party in 1949 brought a large influx of refugees into the colony. The population increased suddenly from 600,000 in 1945 to over two million in 1951.[5] Among their other needs, jobs had to be found for these additional inhabitants. Then in the wake of the influx, the Korean War broke out. In 1951 the United Nations imposed a trade embargo on the People's Republic of China. This had the effect of putting a brake on the commercial activities of Hong Kong which were heavily dependent on the China trade. In order to survive the colony had to find alternative means of livelihood. The government and the business community, therefore, began to direct their efforts to industrial production.

The subsequent record of Hong Kong's industrialization is impressive, for it has become one of the most productive economies in the region. Its gross national product per capita reached US$4,240 by 1980, ranking third in Asia after Japan and Singapore.[6] Throughout the post-war period, it has sustained a high rate of growth. Except for short periods of economic fluctuation following the Communist victory in China and the Korean War, Hong Kong's gross domestic product increased at the steady speed of around 10 per cent per year during the 1950s and 1960s. In the first half of the 1970s, the growth rate was still about 8 per cent and gradually levelled off to slightly less than 7 per cent by the end of the decade.[7]

This economic performance is accomplished by the production of industrial goods for other parts of the world. The manufacturing sector generates about one-quarter of Hong Kong's gross domestic product. Nearly half of Hong Kong's working population is engaged in industry. It produces mostly for export, and in 1978 the average export value per capita reached US$2,270.[8]

The Shanghainese

As mentioned above, it is widely believed that the prime movers of the process of industrialization have come from the ranks of the

Shanghainese. 'Shanghainese' refers to Chinese people who trace their origins to the 'core' areas of the Lower Yangzi region. In his study of urbanization in late traditional China, G. William Skinner shows that Chinese cities in the nineteenth century did not form an integrated, empire-wide system. Instead, they constituted several loosely related regional systems.[9] The boundaries of these urban regions tended to coincide with the major watersheds marking off physiographic units. Each region had a core area, usually river-valley lowlands, with a concentration of resources of all kinds. This phenomenon was a product of a special feature of the Chinese economy — the low cost of water transport relative to land transport. Therefore, a core or central area can be identified by the existence of a dense transportation network with intense economic and social interaction.

Skinner delineates nine 'macroregions' in nineteenth-century China, one of which is the Lower Yangzi region covering the fertile Jiangnan area as well as the basins of the Qiantang and other rivers flowing into Hangzhou Bay. This region breaks through administrative borders and incorporates territories of three provinces: the southern parts of Jiangsu and Anhui, and the northern half of Zhejiang.[10] The core area of this region is identified in the provincial maps published by the People's Republic of China as the Hu Ning Hang area. 'This is the general name for Shanghai, Nanjing, Hangzhou and the surrounding areas. On the whole, its scope extends eastward to Shanghai, westward to Nanjing, northward to the south bank of the Yangzi, and southward to the Ningbo-Xiaoxing Plain south of the Hangzhou Bay.'[11] An indication of the intensity of social and economic interactions within this area is that the inhabitants share the Wu dialect as their *lingua franca*.[12]

Thus the overlap between the Wu dialect region and the core of the Lower Yangzi urban system can be taken as the boundary for delimiting the Shanghainese. The salience of this boundary is reflected in the pattern of voluntary association among the immigrants from this part of China. In the 1940s they formed a regional association in Hong Kong called the Jiangsu and Zhejiang Residents' (HK) Association.[13] Later on, it became an overarching association when two new organizations came into being drawing their members from smaller localities. In 1967 the Hong Kong Ningbo Residents' Association was set up 'to complement the former as a sister association'.[14] Ten years later a Shanghai Fraternity Association was formed specifically for people from the city of Shanghai.

The office-bearers of the three associations overlapped closely. Of the ten advisers to the Ningbo Residents' Association in 1977, one was simultaneously the permanent president, another a permanent director, and six others advisers of the Jiangsu and Zhejiang Residents' (HK) Association.[15] Then three executive directors of the Jiangsu and Zhejiang Residents' (HK) Association became the founding president and deputy presidents of the Shanghai Fraternity Association.[16]

By contrast, immigrants from northern Jiangsu have their own organizations with a different set of directors. The funeral notices of Mr Zhu Jie-xuan showed that at the time of his death he was the deputy president of the Hong Kong Northern Jiangsu Residents' Association and the Hong Kong Jiangsu Residents' Association, as well as the deputy director of the Tsuen Wan Northern Chinese Sojourners' Welfare Society. Yet the fact that he held no post in the Jiangsu and Zhejiang Association indicates that two distinct groupings of regional association exist for people coming from southern and northern Jiangsu respectively.[17]

As to the number of Shanghainese in Hong Kong, the president of the Jiangsu and Zhejiang Association estimated in 1958 that there were 350,000.[18] When interviewed by the author in 1978, the leaders of the Shanghai Fraternity Association and the Ningbo Residents' Association put the figures at respectively 10 and 16 per cent of the population.

The Hong Kong census contains no detailed information on the ethnic composition of the population apparently because of a belief on the part of the officials that this demographic characteristic is of little practical significance. The only exception is the 1961 census in which the question of ethnicity is approached from three directions. Inhabitants were asked to record their birthplace, nationality, and place of origin. The last question would have perfectly suited the purpose of the present study had it not been for the inappropriate geographical boundary used for classifying regional groups. Since the focus of the census was on people from Guangdong, Chinese from other provinces were grouped together arbitrarily. An undifferentiated category of 'Shanghai, Taiwan and Central Coast provinces, i.e., Chekiang, Fukien and Kiangsu' was used.[19]

It emerged that 6 per cent of the total population originated from this area[20] but it was then necessary to determine how many were from the Lower Yangzi region and not from Fujian or Taiwan.

Fortunately, there are figures on the usual language or dialect of the inhabitants. People speaking the Shanghai dialect in their daily life amounted to 69,523 or about 3 per cent of the population. But this figure could not include all the Shanghainese, some of whom were born locally and had possibly adopted the daily use of Cantonese. Therefore it was necessary to estimate the number of local-born Shanghainese by cross-tabulating the place of origin with the inhabitant's usual language.

People claiming origins in the central coast provinces can be divided into four main dialect groups — those speaking Shanghainese, 'Hoklo', Mandarin, and Cantonese. The second and third groups were obviously from Fujian, Taiwan, and northern Jiangsu, and can be regarded as forming a sub-group separate from the Shanghainese speakers. Assuming that the offspring of these two sub-groups had equal chances of adopting Cantonese as their usual language, it can then be estimated that local-born Shanghainese amounted to 33,697 persons.[21] The total number of Shanghainese in Hong Kong in 1961 was thus 103,220 persons or about 4 per cent of the total population.

As immigration from the Lower Yangzi region to Hong Kong has been reduced to a mere trickle in the last twenty years, the percentage has probably decreased slightly. The above estimate is much smaller than those offered by the leaders of the regional associations. The leaders obviously had a greatly inflated image of the size of their potential membership: an image which is presumably a product of the strong economic power of the Shanghainese that is out of proportion to their numbers in the local population.

Employment Characteristics of the Shanghainese

In the 1961 census, ethnicity was not cross-tabulated with employment characteristics. Consequently there are no systematic data on the distribution of the Shanghainese in the various parts of the economy. To arrive at an estimate, three rough pointers will be used. The first is the impressions of the Shanghainese community leaders themselves. The president of the Ningbo Residents' Association maintained that about one-third of their members were engaged in the textile industry, followed by those in shipping and film production. His view on the prominence of textile manufacturing as an occupation for the Shanghainese was shared by the presi-

Table 1.1. Distribution of Officials of the Jiangsu and Zhejiang Residents' (HK) Association by Economic Activities, 1977–1979

Economic Activity	No.	Adjusted %
Textile manufacture	25	32
Banking and finance	13	17
Construction/real estate	10	13
Professions	9	11
Shipping	6	8
Enamelware manufacture	3	4
Other manufacture	7	9
Other services	5	6
Unknown	27	—
Total	105	100

Source: Derived from Jiangsu and Zhejiang Residents' (HK) Association, *Directory of Presidents, Advisors and Directors, No. 20, 1977–79* (Hong Kong, The Association, no date).

dent of the Shanghai Fraternity Association who also gave air transportation, construction and shipping as other important niches for his fellow regionals.

The second pointer is contained in the 1977–9 directory of presidents, advisers, and directors of the Jiangsu-Zhejiang Residents' Association. Unfortunately, the directory has no information about ordinary members. From the company names listed in the business addresses of these officials, these élites can be classified by occupation. As shown in Table 1.1, about 32 per cent are textile industrialists. The rest are associated with banking and finance, building construction, real estate, the professions, and shipping.

The third indicator employed is the advertisements published in the tenth anniversary commemorative volume of the Ningbo Residents' Association. According to its editor, the advertisements were solicited from fellow regionals. Excluding those items entered by individuals, Table 1.2 classifies the economic nature of the companies advertising in the publication.

Table 1.2. Distribution of Ningbo Companies by Economic Activities as Revealed in Advertisements

Economic Activity	No.	Adjusted %
Textile manufacture	14	34
Banking and finance	8	20
Plastic manufacture	3	7
Commerce	2	5
Other manufacture	7	17
Other services	7	17
Unknown	10	—
Total	51	100

Source: Ningbo Residents' Association, *Commemorative Volume on the Tenth Anniversary of the Ningbo Residents' Association* (Hong Kong, The Association, 1977).

These pointers are not of course a very accurate gauge of the actual distribution, but they are consistent in isolating textile manufacture as the major economic sphere of the Shanghainese. They all indicate that about one third of the Shanghainese are involved in the textile industry.

The 'textile industry' is a broad term embracing cotton spinning, weaving, dyeing and finishing, as well as garment-making. As in many other places, the textile industry has been the leading sector in Hong Kong's industrialization. By 1977, it produced 47 per cent of Hong Kong's export value and employed 45 per cent of the workers.[22]

The Cotton Spinning Industry

There are several reasons for choosing to focus on the cotton spinning industry in this study. From the practical point of view, the small number of just over 30 mills facilitates a comprehensive, in-depth investigation by an individual researcher. But more important is that cotton spinning constitutes one of the cornerstones of Hong Kong industry. On the one hand, it furnishes a solid basis for other textile manufacture to grow. As the Hong Kong cotton spinners themselves have asserted, 'the spinning industry formed a reser-

Table 1.3. Spindleage and Employment in the Hong Kong Cotton Spinning Industry, 1947–1978

Year	No. of Workers	No. of Spindles	Spindles/Worker
1947	100	6,000	—*
1950	7,400	132,000	17.8
1955	12,400	308,000	24.8
1960	15,600	502,000	32.2
1965	18,500	724,000	39.1
1970	20,000	900,000	45.0
1974	19,100	850,000**	44.5
1978	17,300	827,000***	47.8

Notes: *   Omitted as the mills were not yet in full operation.
      **   Including 32,000 rotors. One rotor is counted as one spindle although the former is more efficient.
    *** Including 61,204 rotors.

Source: HKCSA (1975), *A Glance at the Hong Kong Cotton Spinning Industry* (Hong Kong, The Association), p.40; *DGB*, 29 July 1978.

voir by becoming the dependable domestic supplier of cotton yarn which was the basic material for other segments of the textile industry'.[23]

On the other hand, it represents the modern large-scale sector of the economy. In 1978 the biggest spinning mill employed over 2,000 workers with a capacity of around 94,000 spindles. Average employment and spindleage per mill were about 500 workers and 25,000 spindles respectively. These figures may not be impressive by the standards of developed economies, but the great majority of the industrial establishments in Hong Kong are small. In 1977 out of 37,568 manufacturing concerns, fewer than 1 per cent had as many as 500 workers. Over 90 per cent were small units with fewer than 50 employees.[24] Thus all the cotton spinning mills are at the apex of the industrial structure in terms of size. Technologically, they are also among the most highly mechanized enterprises as indicated in Table 1.3. In the 1970s there were on average more than 40 spindles for each worker in these mills.

Since cotton is not grown in Hong Kong, the spinning industry has to import raw cotton from abroad, mainly from the United

States. At the industry's peak in 1960, the United States supplied slightly more than half of the raw cotton spun by Hong Kong spinners. Other suppliers include Brazil, Pakistan, and East Africa.

The majority of the yarn produced by the spinners is consumed locally. Exports were quite sizeable in the early years, then steadily decreased as the local weaving and garments industries flourished and used up most of the yarn. In 1955 about 40 per cent of the total yarn production was exported. By 1970 the figure was reduced to just 9 per cent. The chief foreign buyers of Hong Kong yarn, in the early 1950s, were South-east Asian countries such as Indonesia, Pakistan, Burma, Taiwan, Malaya, and the Philippines. As these countries gradually became self-sufficient by building up their own spinning operations, the Hong Kong spinners directed their exports mostly to the United Kingdom and the United States. After the United Kingdom and the United States imposed quotas on Hong Kong textile products, the spinners opened up new and significant export markets in Australia, New Zealand, Nigeria, and more recently, in China.

Though only a small proportion of the yarn produced is exported, the Hong Kong spinning industry is nevertheless heavily dependent on foreign markets through the local weaving and garment industries which are highly export-oriented. In 1970 about 60 per cent of the cotton fabrics and 80 per cent of the garments were sold to foreign buyers, principally the United States and the United Kingdom. In spite of the quota restrictions, these two countries remain the largest markets for Hong Kong fabrics and garments up to the 1980s.[25]

Interviewing the Spinners

Information about the industrialists in cotton spinning was obtained during face-to-face interviews conducted in 1978. The sample included all the 32 cotton spinning mills in operation at that time. Two directors from each mill were interviewed as this gave an opportunity to cross-check the information on individual companies from two separate sources, and also because this was the sample size that could be handled by one person with limited time for field-work. Indeed the correctness of this decision was vindicated as it turned out that typically the more junior directors were reluctant to talk once the chief executive had been interviewed. They would usually make the excuse that their opinions were the same as those of their seniors. Therefore had more than two directors from each mill been approached, the result would probably have been a diminishing rate of forthcoming responses.

The names of the 'principal officers' of all the mills were compiled from the 1977 directory of the Hong Kong Cotton Spinners' Association. When more than two directors were listed for one mill, those chosen were the chief executive who held the title of chairman or managing director and the director with the second largest shareholding as shown in the company record. After 64 industrialists had been picked as the sample, a letter explaining the purpose of the research as well as requesting an interview was sent to each of them in the name of the Director of the Centre of Asian Studies, University of Hong Kong. The spinners were then contacted by phone to arrange an interview appointment.

As is to be expected, some did not wish to be interviewed. They seldom refused directly relying instead on the evasiveness of their secretaries. In order to fill the quota of two interviews per mill, two methods were adopted to counter refusals. In several cases, directors who said they were too busy for a personal interview were sent the interview schedule to complete at their leisure. In fact none of the schedules was sent back even though the return postage had been paid and repeated follow-up phone calls made. The other method used was to ask the respondent to suggest another director who would be willing to be interviewed if his colleague had declined. This usually led to a successful second interview in the same company.

In the end, 40 interviews were obtained from 23 mills. These mills will be referred to by number in order to protect their identity. Nine mills were inaccessible, seven of which were Shanghainese-owned and two controlled by non-Shanghainese entrepreneurs. The pattern of refusal was not related to regional origin. But there were indications that the spinners would shun contact with outsiders if the company was in trouble. For example, at the beginning of the field-work, Mill 21 was going through a succession crisis in the wake of the consecutive deaths of two of the principal officers and the retirement of a third; in Mill 29, negotiations on a major change in ownership were in progress; and Mill 31 had just been taken over by one of the local textile conglomerates and was being reorganized. It is thus likely that the sample was biased toward those mills which were doing relatively well at the time.

In spite of the presence at each interview of a Shanghainese-speaking female research assistant, the respondents avoided speaking their dialect which seemed to have the status of a private language within their own regional circle. The older spinners preferred to use English, while the younger directors generally conversed in Cantonese. Mandarin was used on two occasions.

The length of the interviews ranged from 35 minutes to two-and-a-half hours. The norm was about one hour. Adjustments were made to suit each occasion with the result that the interview schedule was not kept to rigidly. The schedule was divided into four main parts. The first two parts dealt with personal particulars and career profiles of the entrepreneurs; the third was concerned with the internal organization of the mills and managerial practices; and the last part contained the forced choice items on business ideology.

Parts one, two, and four were covered as fully as possible. Then depending on the time available, some of the questions from part three were selectively posed. The questions designed to trace the respondents' social network were the most problematic, as most of the spinners would not name other persons. Direct questioning in an interview situation is probably not, after all, an effective means of studying social networks and other techniques will have to be devised and tried in the future.

How reliable were their responses? It goes without saying that the information gathered was the product of a particular form of interaction. The fact that I am a Hong Kong-born Cantonese must have influenced the way the spinners answered questions, particularly those relating to ethnicity. It is conceivable that a Shanghainese or Western researcher might be given somewhat different replies by the same set of respondents on the non-factual questions.

I am also an investigator from the university and this has both advantages and disadvantages. Since most of the spinners were highly educated, they appeared to appreciate the value of social research and accept me as a 'disinterested' observer. My assurance of confidentiality possibly encouraged them to speak more frankly. But they might also have been tempted to give what they thought were academically correct answers, especially to attitudinal questions.

These are inherent limitations of the interview method of data collection, which can to some extent be overcome by a comparison of findings with those of other researchers where this is feasible. Precautions were taken to avoid the more obvious pitfalls. For instance, no enquiries were made into the financial and business aspects of their operations as truthful answers were unlikely to be forthcoming. In addition, as far as possible the internal consistencies of the answers were checked and verified against documentary data such as the publications and annual reports of the Hong Kong Cotton Spinners' Association, the mill records in the Company Registry and the Labour Department of the Hong Kong government, as well as newspaper reports. Where verification was not possible, I have made it plain in the analysis so that the relevant pieces of information should be regarded as tentative.

A Shanghainese Enclave

The cotton spinning industry is virtually a Shanghainese enclave. The standard belief among the Shanghainese entrepreneurs I met was that over 90 per cent of the mills were owned by their fellow regionals. In the interests of a more precise assessment, information on the respondents' place of origin was obtained during the interviews. The ethnic backgrounds of the mill owners who were not interviewed were determined by checking the local *Who's Who* and by asking informants. Each mill is required by law to file a company record at the Company Registry stating details of stock ownership. I used the 50 per cent shareholding mark to decide on the ethnic status of a mill. If more than half of the stocks were held by one or more owners from the Lower Yangzi region, then it was classified as a Shanghainese establishment.

Thus classified, the distribution of the spinning mills by ethnic affiliation is tabulated in Table 1.4. It can be seen that the actual share of Shanghainese ownership in the industry was 78 per cent. But the higher percentage given by the Shanghainese spinners themselves was not without foundation. The intrusion of other ethnic groups into the enclave is a recent phenomenon as shown in Table 1.5. In the 1950s the Shanghainese controlled all but one of the mills. Their predominance was maintained in the next decade with 89 per cent of mill ownership. Over half of the non-Shanghainese-owned mills made their entry only in the 1970s. Furthermore, a closer look at these new competitors revealed a characteristic presence of Shanghainese elements. The proprietors of one of the Chaozhou-owned companies were born in Shanghai where their father who founded the enterprise had been a trader. At least four out of seven of these mills relied on Shanghainese directors or mill managers to take charge of production.

Table 1.4. Distribution of Cotton Spinning Mills by Ethnicity of Owners, 1978

Ethnicity	No.	%
Shanghainese	25	78
Chaozhou	3	9
Cantonese*	2	6
Fujianese**	1	3
Sichuanese	1	3
Total	32	100***

Notes: *   Includes one overseas Chinese from Cambodia of Cantonese origin.
      **   With substantial participation by Indonesian Chinese.
      *** Not exactly 100 due to rounding.

Source: Interviews, 1978; and mill records at Company Registry.

Table 1.5. Ethnicity and Year of Establishment of Cotton Spinning Mills

Ethnicity	Year of Establishment			
	1947–59	1960–9	1970–8	Row Total
Shanghainese	20	3	2	25
Non-Shanghainese	1	2	4	7
Column Total	21	5	6	32

$\chi^2 = 11.60$; df $= 2$; significant at 0.05 level.

Source: Interviews, 1978; mill records at Company Registry.

A tiny minority of less than 4 per cent of the population, the Shanghainese had the lion's share of nearly 80 per cent of one of Hong Kong's most modern industries. Without elaborate statistical measurements, it is already clear that their disproportionate representation in the ownership of the cotton spinning industry can hardly be a chance phenomenon. Such a high degree of industrial concentration accomplished by entrepreneurs from the Lower Yangzi region is astounding. How did it come about? In the next chapter the process of their migration will be examined so as to find out the characteristics of these industrialists and the reasons for their relocation to Hong Kong.

2 Migration of an Elite

THE Lower Yangzi region was not traditionally a centre of emigration to Hong Kong. Before the Second World War, a local Shanghainese community was practically non-existent. According to official census reports, in 1872 there were 15 residents originating from the provinces of Jiangsu and Zhejiang. Their ranks grew gradually: 17 in 1876, 12 in 1881, 144 in 1891, 534 in 1897, 512 in 1901, 835 in 1911, 1,698 in 1921, and 3,768 in 1931.[1] By 1940 there were enough of them for a Jiangsu-Zhejiang-Shanghai Merchant (Hong Kong) Association and a Shanghai Motoring Club to be formed.[2] But they did not have a regional association until 1943 when the Jiangsu and Zhejiang Residents' (Hong Kong) Association was established and held its first general meeting three years later in 1946.[3] The latter occasion might be taken to signify the emergence of a Shanghainese community in the colony.

Leaving China

The emigration of the Shanghainese grew with the intensification of the civil war in China. A journalist reported in late 1946 that the 'lounges of the Gloucester, Hong Kong and other hotels are crowded at "tea time" with refugee businessmen from Shanghai [who find] more and more old friends turning up with each boat or plane arrival'.[4] By the end of 1948, the refugee traffic was so heavy that no fewer than eight planes with passengers from Shanghai were reported to have landed in Hong Kong in a single day.[5] These newcomers were said to have filled all the hotels, and caused a dramatic increase in the rents of high-quality flats.[6] The Wu dialect was beginning to be heard on the ferries across the harbour as well as on the streets.[7]

However, the refugees were not a random cross-section of residents of the Shanghai area hoping to better themselves. Instead, they constituted an economic élite in flight. For them to leave the most industrialized metropolis in China where many of them had already acquired a fortune required a push from forces undercutting their élite position.

There is little doubt that the rising power of the Chinese Com-

Table 2.1. Year of Arrival of the Cotton Spinners

Year	No.	%
1946	3	8
1947	2	5
1948	18	49
1949	6	16
1950	3	8
1951	1	3
1952	0	0
1953	0	0
1954	0	0
1955	0	0
1956	1	3
1957	3	8
Total	37	100

Source: Interviews, 1978.

munist Party was one of those forces. When asked their reason for leaving Shanghai, the respondents' stock answer was that it was the coming of the Communists. The timing of their departure reflects their aversion to communism. Table 2.1 shows that nearly 65 per cent of the refugees arrived in Hong Kong between 1948 and 1949, on the eve of the Communist victory.

But for quite a number the move was the result of several years' deliberation. They had started to explore the possibility of a transfer to the British Crown Colony before the outcome of the Chinese Civil War was apparent. In a retrospective account by the general manager of Hong Kong Textiles, Ltd., one such exploration was described:

Early in 1946 my father placed a large order for new spinning machines and power looms with a well-known British manufacturer, with delivery to be made in Shanghai around the middle of 1947. However, political and economic conditions in China failed to improve and it looked as if a civil war between Chiang Kai-shek's Nationalists and Mao Tse-tung's Communists might break out. My father thought it might be wise to transfer our operations to Hong Kong, and he spent six weeks here in the summer of 1946 to look things over. He liked the idea of a free port and the absence of formalities and restrictions, but he couldn't see that Hong Kong offered any market. There were no industrial workers here and no natural resources — not even an adequate water supply. Besides, it was hot and humid here most of the year, and this makes it difficult to spin cotton. My father decided against moving to Hong Kong and returned to Shanghai.[8]

A few Shanghainese had arrived in Hong Kong a decade earlier when the Japanese invaded China. In 1938 Rong Zong-jing, one of the co-founders of the largest Chinese textile conglomerate, sought refuge in Hong Kong where he died. He was accompanied by his eldest son, Rong Hong-yuan, who went back to Shanghai after his father's funeral, only to return again in 1948.[9] These earlier trips to Hong Kong suggest that the Shanghai entrepreneurs were already trying to escape from political instability and government intervention. Chinese communism was, for them, merely the ultimate embodiment of these two evils.

Social and political chaos occurred on a national scale in China with the outbreak of the Anti-Japanese War (1937–45). In terms of their acquiring experience in relocating their enterprises, the war was a rehearsal for the exodus of the Shanghai capitalists to Hong Kong. 'The equipment of 639 primarily defense-oriented factories was removed inland from the lower Yangtze area and 70 per cent of these plants were successfully re-established in Szechwan and elsewhere by the end of 1939.'[10] The Rong family, for instance, was initially reluctant to transfer their plants to the interior provinces as such a move was obviously costly and the prospect for manufacturing in those regions unpromising. But being obliged to comply with the orders of the Nationalist government, they moved two of their companies to Chongqing. In the process, heavy losses of machinery were incurred as expected. But the loss was more than compensated for by the profits to be gained as a result of the scarcity of basic commodities in Chongqing. By the end of the war, the original two companies had spawned eleven enterprises and generated substantial profits.[11] Such an experience must have encouraged the entrepreneurs that another transplant of their enterprises could be attempted if necessary.

The end of the Anti-Japanese War did not bring peace and stability. To make matters worse for the Chinese industrialists, the Nationalist government began to introduce a series of measures to control the economy. A number of state enterprises was created. One of these was the China Textile Industries Inc., established in

1946 to take over direct control of the former Japanese-owned mills in various Chinese cities. This in effect nationalized 38 cotton mills with a total of 1.8 million spindles, or about 40 per cent of the country's spindleage.[12] Then the supply of industrial raw materials, such as cotton, was rationed; the pricing and distribution of basic commodities, such as flour and yarn, were controlled; and private holdings in foreign exchange were prohibited. These measures were instituted in the name of national emergency and post-war rehabilitation. But when government regulation of the economy showed no sign of abating in successive years after the war, and when several prominent industrialists were prosecuted for violating the regulations, the Shanghai capitalists apparently felt that they had been made scapegoats for the Nationalists' economic mis-management.[13] Besides protesting very loudly, they began to look for a safer cover so as to preserve their industrial strength.

The anti-capitalist stance of the Nationalists together with the chaotic state of the Chinese economy were the immediate threats which compelled some of the Shanghai industrialists to transfer their capital out of China.[14] Rong Hong-yuan, for example, visited Hong Kong in 1948 to explore the possibility of setting up a mill there. After the tour, he told reporters why he was contemplating such a move:

During my visit to Hong Kong, it appeared to me that the abnormal prosperity there is a result of the chaotic conditions created by war and the unreasonable controls imposed on commerce and industry [in China]. The industrialists of central and northern China are transferring their enterprises to Hong Kong because there are no other alternatives. They would not lend their talents to another government and contribute to the prosperity of Hong Kong if our government would seize the opportunity to lift foreign exchange controls so that industrial machinery ordered from Britain and the United States could be imported. I regret the erroneous policy of our government...[15]

Soon after making this press statement, Rong Hong-yuan was arrested in Shanghai for an unauthorized purchase of Hong Kong dollars to pay for a supply of cotton. After over two months behind bars and the payment of a bribe said to amount to half a million US dollars, he was given a suspended sentence of six months imprisonment. Upon his release, he left for Hong Kong to set up the Da Yuan Cotton Mill.[16]

The founder of Hong Kong Textiles, Ltd. was similarly compelled to divert his new machinery to Hong Kong in spite of initial reservations about the suitability of the territory for textile production. As his son told us:

In February 1947, my father was informed by representatives of China's Nationalist Government that the importation of his order of textile machinery would not be allowed because of an acute shortage of foreign exchange. My father had sufficient foreign exchange on deposit outside of China, but he couldn't reveal this to the government people. After considerable thought, he cabled the British manufacturer to ship his order to Hong Kong rather than to Shanghai. Late in 1947 his machinery arrived in Hong Kong and was placed in storage in the Hwa Fung Godown, over in Kowloon. My father and two of his submanagers flew here to locate some place and set up the spinning machinery and looms. My father was able to rent an old warehouse and by early 1948 was ready to begin operation. His new enterprise was set up as a separate company, Hong Kong Textiles, Ltd...[17]

Hong Kong as a Refuge

Why did the Shanghai industrialists flock to Hong Kong in the late 1940s rather than to other destinations? One of their major considerations was access. Most countries had strict immigration control. The United States, which had the earliest legislative restriction on Chinese immigration, may serve as an illustration.

A Chinese Exclusion Act was passed in the United States in 1882 to prohibit the entry of Chinese labourers on the grounds that they would create a racial problem. The curb was further tightened with the Immigration Act of 1924 which adopted a narrow definition of student status for the Chinese. In 1943 the Exclusion Act was repealed. An annual quota of 105, the lowest allocation to any nationality, was created in the following year for persons of Chinese ancestry, principally to facilitate family reunion. When the Nationalist government fell in China, special permission was granted to about 5,000 Chinese students, intellectuals, trainees, visitors, and officials stranded in the United States to take up employment and to become permanent residents. The Refugee Relief Act of 1953 provided for the further reception of 2,000 Chinese.

The difficulty experienced by Chinese refugees in obtaining visas to the United States is shown in the low immigration figures. In the 1940s, a total of 8,947 Chinese were allowed entry. From 1951 to 1957, the number was marginally increased to 9,110. According to Rose Hum Lee, nearly 90 per cent of those entering from

1946–50 were women rejoining their families. There were few new immigrants.[18]

In South-east Asia and elsewhere, all gates were closing in anticipation of a tide of Chinese refugees in the wake of the Nationalist collapse in China.[19] The only places Chinese could freely enter were Hong Kong and Taiwan. In 1949 the Hong Kong government introduced in quick succession the Registration of Persons Bill and the Expulsion of Undesirables Bill. But its hands were tied, as the first clause of the 'Objects and Reasons' of the latter Bill made clear:

Hong Kong has traditionally allowed free ingress to Chinese except in times of emergency and the situation of the Colony's land frontier and the ease with which small water-borne crafts can move in and out of the Colony's waters render control of such movement difficult and incomplete.[20]

The then Attorney General, when moving the second reading of the Bill, enlarged on the situation:

In fact, what has happened has been, over the years, that in respect of Chinese who come from China an exception has been extended in practice, though not in law, from the ordinary application of the Immigration Law, which, like the immigration laws of any other country in the world, makes a list of the types and categories of persons to whom entry is refused . . . the consequence of such liberality of practice in the case of Hong Kong is that many persons come to Hong Kong and remain here who would never have been allowed at all had the normal operation of the immigration laws been applied.[21]

Other than ease of entry, the Shanghai entrepreneurs were also concerned about the feasibility of continuing in their chosen vocation. In this respect, Hong Kong, as a Chinese cultural area, was an obvious attraction. There was an adequate supply of Chinese workers whom they knew how to manage with little communication problem. Although such an advantage was also present in other overseas Chinese communities, what distinguished Hong Kong from other regions was that there were fewer obstacles to the immigrant industrialists' setting up of new enterprises. The story of the failure of a Shanghainese venture in Thailand will demonstrate the problems elsewhere.

At the beginning of 1949, Rong Yan-ren, the fifth son of Rong De-sheng who had co-founded the Shen Xin textile conglomerate in Shanghai, went to Bangkok to set up a spinning mill. He had his eyes on a partially completed factory financed by a member of the Thai royal family who did not have the expertise to put it into full operation. But protracted negotiations had to be conducted with the Thai government. Three thorny issues were involved: the Thai authorities insisted on having a majority share in the business; technicians and skilled workers could not be imported because of the annual quota limiting Chinese immigrants to 200 only; and production as well as marketing were subject to government control.[22]

The Rong family enlisted the help of the sons of Wellington V. K. Koo (Gu Wei-jun), the famous Chinese diplomat who was also a native of Jiangsu, to negotiate with the Thai government.[23] A compromise was finally reached which was hardly encouraging to long-term investment. The Rong family was granted a lease of the factory for three years. After two years of operation, it was agreed, a joint partnership with the Thai government would be formed. If, for some reason, such a partnership could not be organized, then the lease might be extended for a further 15 years. Quota restrictions were lifted for 150 Chinese technicians who were permitted temporary residence until such time as indigenous workers had been trained. The Chinese management retained control over production, but the Thai government had the priority right to purchase the products.[24]

These conditions were accepted by the Rong family and the Bangkok Cotton Mill with 23,000 spindles and about 1,100 workers was set up in 1950.[25] But apparently the restrictions were so stifling that the mill went bankrupt after a short period of operation. Rong Yan-ren was reported to be unable to leave Thailand until his elder brothers came to his rescue and settled his business debts.[26]

Similar obstacles existed in Taiwan. Rong Hong-yuan, besides setting up a mill in Hong Kong, also relocated 10,000 spindles and 200 looms from Shanghai to Taiwan in 1948. A site was bought, but the venture was thwarted by the Taiwan administration's refusal to provide it with the needed supply of electricity.[27]

Yet in comparison with South-east Asia, Taiwan was a more congenial haven. Flocks of refugees followed the defeated Nationalists to the island, to which as it was Chinese territory, no entry visa was required. From 1946 to 1950, more than one million mainland Chinese were estimated to have arrived. About half of them landed in the peak period from 1949 to 1950.[28]

Among this mass influx were some textile entrepreneurs. The rapid expansion of Taiwan's cotton yarn production testifies to their presence. The meagre output of 410 metric tons in 1946 leapt to 13,576 metric tons in 1953.[29] By 1966 textile manufacture had become the second largest industry with a spinning capacity of 448,000 spindles.[30] But Taiwan had its own drawbacks for the emigrant mill owners. The Nationalist administration, once installed in Taiwan, exercised direct control over industry. There was a large public sector built on former Japanese-owned factories. In the private domain, official guidance was embodied in an industrial licensing system. To prevent saturation of the domestic market, the government tried to limit industrial growth in textile manufacture to an annual increase of 20,000 spindles and 10,000 looms from 1954. Control was only formally lifted in the early 1960s when inroads were made into foreign markets.[31] Such measures must have been unpopular with many Chinese spinners who bitterly remembered the bureaucratic capriciousness and excessive red tape in post-war Shanghai under the Nationalist administration.

For those who had reservations about Taiwan, Hong Kong was the logical choice. The lack of natural resources, the unfavourable climate, and the slender industrial base were minor disabilities compared with the attractions. It was the only place, other than Taiwan, where a Chinese was free to enter. An estimated 1,285,000 refugees came to the colony between September 1945 and December 1949.[32] Against the 'normal' pre-war population which stood at 1,640,000 in March 1941, this influx represented a doubling of inhabitants within a few years.[33] Such a multitude of refugees turned out to be an industrial asset for Hong Kong. Mostly destitute, they formed a huge pool of cheap labour, who, unlike previous migrants, were not mainly drawn from the rural peasantry. As Table 2.2 shows, the majority of the male immigrants came from urban areas where they had been soldiers and policemen, professionals and intellectuals, clerks and shop assistants. Within a few years of their arrival, many of them managed to find employment in Hong Kong as industrial labourers, unskilled workers in the service sector, or self-employed craftsmen and hawkers. Cut off from home, they were stable resident workers instead of seasonal migrants.[34]

The relative political security of the colony was also attractive to the textile industrialists. Though the then President of the United States, Harry S. Truman, had decided on 21 October 1949 that his government would not 'provide military support to the British for the defense of Hong Kong in the event of a communist military attack',[35] the British government had declared its determination to keep the colony. The British Defence Minister, A. V. Alexander,

Table 2.2. Occupations of Chinese Refugees in Hong Kong

Occupation	% of Immigrant Population	
	In China	In Hong Kong
Housewives	33	25
Army and police	16	0
Professionals and intellectuals	10	3
Clerks and shop assistants	10	5
Farmers	10	2
Businessmen	5	2
Industrial labourers	3	13
Hawkers	2	7
Craftsmen	3	12
Coolies and servants	1	11
Others	5	5
Unemployed	2	15
Total	100	100

Source: Hambro (1955), *The Problem of Chinese Refugees in Hong Kong* (Leyden), Tables 29–31, pp.168–70.

announced in May 1949 in the House of Commons that 'substantial reinforcements' were being sent to the garrisons of Hong Kong.[36] This was reassuring to the Chinese industrialists, especially to those who had sheltered from the Japanese in the International Settlement and the French Concession in Shanghai during the Second World War.[37] They knew from that experience that they would probably enjoy political immunity under the protection of a Western colonial administration. Hong Kong was therefore their best choice.

The Hong Kong government, for its part, tried to be hospitable to the immigrant entrepreneurs. This was in spite of the fact that the colonial officials were not particularly endowed with foresight and were not convinced that an industrial revolution was about to begin. In his address to the Legislative Council in 1949, the then Governor said:

Trade is the life blood of this Colony...I am proud of being Governor
of a Colony of shopkeepers...Industries are now tending to develop
on a larger scale than pre-war and to be housed in proper factory type buildings rather than in tenements. Whilst the spirit of the manufacturers
is encouraging...much has still to be done to modernize equipment. The
future generally in Hong Kong industry, in the long term view, remains
obscure.[38]

Nevertheless, the government adopted a flexible and responsive
attitude to the needs of the incoming industrialists. This was probably due to the administration's preoccupation with making Hong
Kong financially self-supporting so as not to drain the economic
resources of Great Britain. The very survival of Hong Kong as a
colony apparently depended on the government's ability to find
jobs for the multitude of refugees and to tap new sources of
revenue. Therefore administrative measures were quickly introduced to accommodate the newly arrived manufacturers.

Company laws were amended in 1949 'to enable foreign corporations to acquire immovable property in the Colony without the
prior consent of the Governor in Council'.[39] In the same year the
Imports and Exports Department was reorganized to form the
Department of Commerce and Industry and a new post of Assistant Director (Industry) was created. He was to 'devote his full time
to the encouragement of new industries and the expansion of existing ones' as well as 'to advise potential industrialists on factory
sites and allied questions'.[40] Industrial land was often sold by
private treaty instead of public auction. As an inducement to industrial investment the price of an initial lease of about 20 years was
set at a level beneath the market rate. Only when the original lease
expired were the manufacturers required to pay the market value
for their land. The generosity of the original deal can perhaps be
gauged by the industrialists' very strong opposition to the reassessment of industrial land values in 1971. In response, the government
was obliged to abandon the attempt at reassessment.[41]

In the field of labour legislation, the Hong Kong government
also made concessions to the industrialists. In the 1940s under the
Factory and Workshops Ordinance, women and children were not
permitted to work night shifts. Apparently at the request of the textile industrialists, the government relaxed this prohibition in 1948
to permit women and children to work between the hours of 6 a.m.
and 10 p.m.[42]

Characteristics of the Emigrants

In spite of Hong Kong's attractions, it was only a small minority of the Shanghai textile industrialists who settled in the colony in the late 1940s. That minority had special characteristics.

Chinese Communist scholars usually classify Chinese capitalists along two dimensions. One is their relation with 'feudalism' and imperialism, the evil forces oppressing China; the other is the size and financial basis of their operations. Using the former yardstick, the bourgeoisie are divided into the bureaucratic, the compradorial, and the national.[43] According to the latter yardstick, distinctions are made among the upper, middle, and lower capitalist class. According to Fan Bei-chuan, the upper stratum consists of huge conglomerates closely tied to large banks. The middle stratum includes medium enterprises supported by native banks or small-scale modern banks. This stratum can be subdivided into the upper-middle and lower-middle levels. The lower stratum is made up of small industrialists employing fewer than a hundred workers.[44]

However, the criteria for demarcation are often vague, and the use of the above terms has been imprecise. As Marie-Claire Bergère points out:

Many Chinese historians distinguish between a 'national' bourgeoisie, operating with purely Chinese capital and nursing a lively hostility toward foreigners, and a 'compradore' bourgeoisie, completely foreign-dominated in both economic and political matters. The distinction is superficially obvious, but surely rather artificial. In early twentieth-century China with its semicolonial economy dominated by the presence of imperialist powers, there could be no such thing as independent national enterprises.[45]

Furthermore the relationship to banking institutions is not easy to determine as Chinese companies did not usually disclose information about their financial transactions. For the present study, the bureaucratic/private and large/small distinctions will be adopted to differentiate the textile entrepreneurs.

Bureaucratic entrepreneurs are those who derive their income mainly as officials appointed to take charge of industrial enterprises in which the majority share is owned by the government. The prototype is Sheng Zuan-huai who administered the Hua Sheng Spinning and Weaving Mill and other companies under the 'official supervision and merchant management' system in the late Qing period.[46] As mentioned above, state enterprises in the textile sector were greatly increased after the Second World War. The China Textile Industries Inc. was established in January 1946 with Shu Yun-zhang, an industrial banker associated with the Bank of China, as general manager. He supervised 38 cotton mills with 1.8 million spindles or about 40 per cent of the national spindleage.[47] Thus the textile industry was divided into government and private operations with roughly even production capacities.

As the Nationalist government fell, none of the bureaucratic entrepreneurs moved to Hong Kong with their enterprises. Partly responsible was the inherent weakness of state enterprises. Although the China Textile Industries Inc. made an enormous profit of CN$1,000 billion in 1946, about one-fifth of the earnings were channelled to the state treasury. Only about CN$50 billion or 5 per cent of the profit was set aside against depreciation. At a time when private mill owners were ordering new machinery, no move was made to renovate existing equipment.[48] Therefore there were no new spindles to transfer. Furthermore, factional conflict among the Guomindang within its management paralysed long-term planning.[49] It is said that when the Nationalist government collapsed, some of the assets of the China Textile Industries Inc. were taken by the disaffected T. V. Soong [Song Zi-wen] faction to the United States.[50] The rest purportedly followed the main stream of the Guomindang to Taiwan.[51] The Hong Kong government, for its part, was eager to remain neutral in the Chinese Civil War. In order not to antagonize the new Chinese government, Guomindang officials were not made welcome in the colony. Hence, only private Chinese entrepreneurs came to settle in Hong Kong.

It is to be expected that of the private mill owners, only the large and successful ones would have had the incentive and resources to emigrate to the colony. This expectation is borne out by an examination of the characteristics of the Chinese mills owned by entrepreneurs who later continued operations in Hong Kong. A Chinese publication of 1947 recorded the particulars of virtually all spinning mills in Shanghai. From the names of the directors, it is possible to identify 11 mills which were wholly or partly relocated to Hong Kong. It turns out that this group of mills had a longer history of operation and larger capital outlay than the rest (see Tables 2.3 and 2.4). But in terms of workers employed, they did not differ significantly from the others (Table 2.5). Thus it seems

Table 2.3. Year of Establishment of Shanghai Mills

Year of Establishment in Shanghai

Mill	Before 1920	1920–9	1930–9	1940–6	Row Total
Relocated*	1	2	5	3	11
Others	5	9	16	85	115
Column Total	6	11	21	88	126**

χ^2 = 10.8; df = 3; significant at 0.05 level.

Notes: * Mills which were later transferred to Hong Kong.
   ** Only those with relevant data are included, so the grand total is slightly different from those in the next two tables.
Source: Lianhe Zhixin Suo, *A Survey of the Manufacturers of Shanghai* (Shanghai, Lianhe Zhixin Suo, 1947).

reasonable to deduce that it was the cream of the private entrepreneurs, those with experience in managing capital intensive mills, who were siphoned off to Hong Kong.

Chinese mills were normally under family ownership. However, it was not uncommon for the members of one family to go their separate ways. The dispersion of the most eminent textile family, the Rongs, can be taken as an example (see Fig. 2.1). The two brothers, Rong Zong-jing and Rong De-sheng, created the Shen Xin textile empire. The elder, Rong Zong-jing, died in Hong Kong during the Anti-Japanese War. Without him, his branch of the family was rendered leaderless when the Communists approached Shanghai. As Fig. 2.1 shows, all of his sons left China. The eldest, Hong-yuan, was a graduate of the National Jiaotong University. After going to Hong Kong he migrated to Brazil. The second son, Hong-san, was educated at St. John's University, Shanghai. He later moved to the United States. The youngest, Hong-xin, also had a university education. He and Wang Yun-chen, the husband of his third sister, a textile specialist trained at the Lowell Institute in the United States, moved to Hong Kong where they set up a new mill.

In 1949 the younger co-founder, Rong De-sheng, was 74 and had already retired from active business.[52] Old and in poor health, he stayed in China, and part of his branch of the family remained with

Table 2.4. Registered Capital of Shanghai Mills (in CN$ million)

Mills	500	500–2,000	2,001–10,000	10,001+	Row Total
Relocated	1	4	5	1	11
Others	50	26	10	2	88
Column Total	51	30	15	3	99

$\chi^2 = 13.5$; df = 3; significant at 0.05 level.

Source: Lianhe Zhixin Suo, *A Survey of the Manufacturers of Shanghai* (Shanghai, Lianhe Zhixin Suo, 1947).

Table 2.5. Number of Workers Employed in Shanghai Mills

Mills	Under 500	500–999	1,000–1,999	2,000+	Row Total
Relocated	3	1	2	4	10
Others	48	8	15	11	82
Column Total	51	9	17	15	92

$\chi^2 = 5.2$; df = 3; not significant at 0.05 level.

Source: Lianhe Zhixin Suo, *A Survey of the Manufacturers of Shanghai* (Shanghai, Lianhe Zhixin Suo, 1947).

Fig. 2.1 Members of the Rong Family and their Dispersion

Brothers	Children		Post-1949 Abode
	△ Hong-yuan		Brazil
	△ Hong-san		USA
	△ Hong-xing		Hong Kong
Rong Zong-jing	○ Zhuo-qiu	= Ding Li-fang	Not known
(1872–1938)	○ Zhuo-ren	= Xue Shou-xuan	USA
	○ Zhuo-ai	= Wang Yun-cheng	Hong Kong
	○ Zhuo-ru	= George Hardoon	Not known
	△ Wei-ren		Dead
	△ Er-ren		USA
	△ Yi-xin		Dead
	△ Yi-ren		Shanghai
	△ Yan-ren		Not known
	△ Ji-ren		Not known
	△ Hong-ren		Australia
Rong De-sheng	○ Su-rong	= Li Guo-wei	Not known
(1875–1952)	○ Ju-xian	= Jiang Jun-qing	Not known
	○ Min-ren	= Song Mi-yang	Not known
	○ Zhuo-ya	= Li Qi-yao	Hong Kong
	○ Mao-yi	= Tang Hong-yuan	Not known
	○ Shu-ren	= Yang Dao-yi	Shanghai
	○ Ji-fu	= Hua Bai-zhong	USA
	○ Shu-zhen	= Hu Ru-xi	Not known
	○ Mo-zhen		Shanghai

Key: △ Male
○ Female
= Marriage

Source: Wan Lin, 'A History of The Sudden Rise of the Rong Family of Wuxi Which Dominated the Cotton Spinning and Flour Industries of China', *Jingji Daobao* (1947), No. 50, p. 5; *RQS*, Vol. 2; *DGB*, 25 January 1981, 20 January 1982, 22 December 1983, and 17 June 1986; company records of various mills in the Company Registry, Hong Kong.

him. As his eldest son died young, the second son, Er-ren, a graduate of St. John's University, assumed responsibility for the family business which was reorganized into a new company a year after the Communist victory. He became the vice-chairman while his ailing father was given the honorary post of chairman.[53] But soon after the death of his father in 1952, apparently feeling that he had fulfilled his filial duties, he went to Brazil and from there to the United States. The third son, Yi-xin, another Lowell Institute graduate, was killed in 1948 in an air crash on his way to supervise the establishment of a mill in Hong Kong.[54] Subsequently, his job of running the mill there was taken by the fourth son-in-law, Li Qi-yao, who had an American engineering degree. The fourth son, Yi-ren, chose not to emigrate and attained considerable fame in the People's Republic of China. In an interview published in the 1970s, he offered the following explanation for his decision to stay:

During the Anti-Japanese War, I was studying at St. John's University. After graduation, I did not go abroad for further studies. Spending the war period in China greatly influenced my outlook. I was imbued with strong nationalistic feeling...When the war was over, I became disappointed with the political and economic performance of the Guomindang. When the Chinese Liberation Army scored one victory after another in 1948, I determined to stay in Shanghai...Mine was a large family, and people had divergent views. Therefore my children followed some family members to Hong Kong. In 1949, I took them back and waited for liberation...[55]

He became the managing director of the reorganized family enterprise, and in 1959 was appointed Vice-Minister of Textile Industry by the Chinese government. Elected as a representative to consecutive sessions of the Chinese People's Congress and the Chinese Political Consultative Committee, he disappeared from public view during the Cultural Revolution. He re-emerged in the 1970s and attained greater prominence as chairman of the board of directors as well as president of the China International Trust and Investment Corporation, and the vice-chairman of the Standing Committee of the 6th National People's Congress.[56]

Several generalizations about migratory tendencies may be made from this example. First, the propensity to leave China was affected by the entrepreneur's age. The older generation tended to stay while the younger ones went elsewhere to look for a second chance. As shown in Table 2.6, only 8 per cent of my respondents were over 40 when they arrived in the colony. The majority, over

Table 2.6. Spinners' Age at Emigration

Age Group	No.	%	Cumulative %
0–10	6	16	16
11–20	5	14	30
21–30	11	30	60
31–40	12	32	92
41–50	3	8	100
50 and over	0	0	100
Total	37*	100	100

Note: Three of the respondents were born in Hong Kong and were therefore not included.
Source: Interviews, 1978.

60 per cent, were in their twenties or thirties. The few spinners who died in Hong Kong were older than average when they left China: C. Y. Wong was 65, V. J. Song, 53, P. Y. Tang, 50, and Liu Hang-kun, 38.[57] This youthful distribution is in line with that of other immigrant groups. The 1961 Hong Kong census revealed that disproportionate numbers of Chinese immigrants were aged between 15 and 24 when they reached the colony.[58]

Sibling order also exerted its influence in a complicated manner. Since primogeniture has not been practised in China since late imperial times,[59] migration was not related to disinheritance. Nevertheless, a few studies have indicated that first-born sons are less likely to migrate than those born later. G. William Skinner has hypothesized that a son's filial attitude varies according to three factors: the number of siblings, his position in the birth order, and the number of older sisters he has.[60] If the tendency to migrate is assumed to change inversely with the strength of a son's filial attitude, then early-born men in small sibling sets without older sisters are less likely to leave home.

Comparing samples of migrants and non-migrants, Alan Speare Jr. finds this to be the case for the internal rural to urban migration in central Taiwan. He concludes that 'migration is greatest among men with many brothers, men intermediate in birth order, and men with few sisters. Of these relationships, the most important is the increase in migration with the number of brothers.'[61]

Table 2.7. Number of Brothers of Hong Kong Spinners and Taiwan Migrants

No. of Brothers (including self)	Cotton Spinners		Taiwan Migrants	
	No.	%	No.	%
One	2	5	16	5
Two or three	15	39	140	44
Four or more	22	56	165	51
Total	39	100	321	100

Source: Interviews, 1978; Speare, 'Migration', p.326.

I do not have adequate data to examine the older sisters variable among my respondents. In respect of the number of brothers, the cotton spinners resembled the rural migrants in Taiwan. Over half of them had three or more brothers, as shown in Table 2.7. A director of Mill 1 had as many as 15 siblings while the managing director of Mill 24 had nine. Speare interprets this phenomenon in terms of the stress inherent in large families which compels the sons to depart. In the case of my respondents, however, the large sibling set is more likely a reflection of the wealth of these spinning families which coincides with my previous finding on the bigger capital outlay of the Chinese mills that were transferred to Hong Kong.

In terms of birth order, however, my respondents differed considerably from the Taiwan migrants. While there were proportionally fewer eldest sons in Speare's sample, they formed the biggest category of Hong Kong spinners interviewed. A similar predominance of first-borns was also found in the small-scale factory owners of Hong Kong surveyed in 1978 (see Table 2.8). This divergence indicates that the Taiwan migrants and the Hong Kong emigrant entrepreneurs were different in kind. The former were sojourners closely tied to their villages, while the latter consisted of refugees who no longer looked homewards. Thus the relationship of filial attitude to birth order differed. In the refugee situation, filial piety could propel the eldest son to leave in order to continue

Table 2.8. Birth Order of Cotton Spinners and Small Factory Owners in Hong Kong, 1978

	Cotton Spinners		Small Owners	
Birth Order*	No.	%	No.	%
First	14	36	174	42
Second	9	23	96	23
Third	7	18	68	17
Fourth	7	18	31	7
Fifth and below	2	5	44	11
No response	1	—	2	—
Total	40	100	415	100

Note: * Among brothers only.
Source: Interviews, 1978; Sit, Wong and Kiang, *Small Scale Industry*, Table 10.12, p.250.

the family line of business. His departure would depend on who was there to look after the immovable family assets in China.

There were three usual arrangements. The most common one was for the head of the family to take on the task. In the Liu family, for instance, Liu Guo-jun, who was 64 in 1949, dispatched his eldest son, together with an experienced manager, to Hong Kong to set up another mill. He himself continued to operate the Hang Fung Mill in Shanghai for some time, and died in China at the age of 95.[62]

But if the family head was too old or too infirm to work, then the eldest son had to delay his departure until his duty was discharged. The Wu family is an interesting illustration of this trend. Wu Kun-sheng, aged 65 in 1949, ordered his eldest son to come back to Shanghai from Hong Kong. His son resigned from his directorship of the Hong Kong mill in 1951 and returned to look after the parent company. After nearly two decades in China, he managed to give up the business and in 1973 took his dying father to Hong Kong. There he resumed the chairmanship of the Hong Kong company which had been left vacant for him.[63]

The third arrangement was for the family head to emigrate with

Table 2.9. Nationalities Adopted by Cotton Spinners

Nationality	No.	%
British	24	60.0
Stateless Chinese	11	27.5
Hong Kong British	1	2.5
Australian	1	2.5
Pakistani	1	2.5
No response	2	5.0
Total	40	100.0

Source: Interviews, 1978.

his sons. In this case the eldest son was obliged to remain. On 7 June 1950 an advertisement appeared in the Shanghai edition of *Da Gong Bao* in which the eldest son of the Yen family, Yen Xing-xiang, appealed to his father and five brothers to return and not to forsake the family-owned mills in Shanghai and Suzhou. His fourth brother had opened a mill in Hong Kong and the sixth had set up another one in Taiwan.[64]

Whichever of the three arrangements was adopted, the result was the presence of a disproportionate number of first-borns among the refugee textile entrepreneurs. Such a distribution underlined the fact that they were uprooted migrants.

Industrial commitment was yet another factor with a significant impact on the entrepreneur's decision to emigrate. As the example of the Rong family has suggested, those who preferred Hong Kong, such as Rong Yi-xin, Wang Yun-cheng, and Li Qi-yao, tended to be technical experts. Having acquired their skills through prolonged training, they wished to remain in the industry, whereas those with a more general education would be more prepared to leave for the United States or Latin America where they could adapt their less specialized skills to new vocations. Hence the high concentration in Hong Kong of technically equipped spinners (to be substantiated in the next chapter).

Finally, political involvement played a part in determining how the entrepreneurs would move. The nationalistic sentiments expressed by Rong Yi-ren who stayed in the mainland might well be

coloured by retrospective rationalization. But he was also politically active. Before 1949, he was already a member of a minor
political party, the Chinese Democratic National Construction
Society.[65] Probably he represented the politically active bourgeoisie
who believed that they had a role to play in the building of a new
China. Those who fled to Hong Kong were doubtless pragmatists
who tried to avoid politics. None of them, it seems, were members
of minor political parties in the 1940s. Sixty per cent of my
respondents were also sufficiently pragmatic to become naturalized
British subjects. Only about 27 per cent, through choice or circumstances, were stateless Chinese (see Table 2.9). For the majority, expedience and adaptation evidently overrode national identity.

The Mechanism of Migration

All the cotton spinners arranged to come to Hong Kong on their
own. Chain migration was the usual pattern. Cases where company
assets and personnel were transferred will be described in the next
chapter when the financial and managerial resources of these entrepreneurs are discussed. Let me just describe how one individual
arranged for his escape. A director of Mill 3 was an employee of
the Bank of China before he emigrated. A year after the Communist victory, he decided to leave:

> The head office of the Bank of China had to be moved from Shanghai
> to Beijing after the Communist victory. I applied to stay in Shanghai,
> pleading that my mother was old and the climate in the North would
> not suit us. My application was turned down, so I asked for leave and
> came to Hong Kong by myself. My brother was already here, and I stayed
> in his house. He introduced me to the deputy manager of a bank, a
> Sichuanese. This man in turn introduced me to the president of this
> company for a vacancy in accounting. After I got the job, I went back
> to Shanghai and obtained exit permits for my family. We arrived in
> Hong Kong in January 1951.

Few of my respondents had kinsmen or fellow regionals already
in Hong Kong, and many recalled feeling like strangers when they
arrived. The major network utilized for emigration was therefore
neither that of kin nor that of ethnicity, but of business acquaintance. Some had sales offices or representatives in the colony,
others depended on friends in business. A director of Mill 14

replied when asked if he had acquaintances in Hong Kong before his arrival:

Yes, business associates. But they were not in textiles. They were my father's friends in the construction business. When we were in Shanghai, my father served as a director in an enamelware company. One of the other directors had a daughter in Hong Kong managing a branch company. So my father decided to come here with their assistance.

When Rong Zong-jing sought refuge in Hong Kong during the Anti-Japanese War, his passage was arranged by a Mr Saker, manager of a British import and export firm, and Mr Yin Shun-xin, a comprador.[66] A decade later, Li Guo-wei, the son-in-law of Rong De-sheng, redirected a shipment of new spindles to Hong Kong to set up the Kowloon Cotton Mill. He also relied on the assistance of the manager of a British firm and a comprador in making that transfer.[67] From the invoking of this particular network for emigration, it can be inferred that business connections were consequently reinforced. This consolidated mutual assistance and forged a tightly knit industrial circle.

Orientation to the Host Society

The first few years of their settlement in Hong Kong saw a succession of rapid changes in the attitude of the emigrant entrepreneurs to the territory. From being shuttlers commuting between the colony and Shanghai, they took their families out of China on the eve of 1949 and became sojourners. Many still hoped that the Communist victory was temporary and to go back when the political situation changed.[68] It was only when population movement between Hong Kong and the mainland was stopped around 1952 that they became exiles. From then on, they pulled up their roots.

The rupture in home ties is clearly shown in the litigation between the Pao Yuen Tung Hsing Yieh Co. Ltd. and the Pao Hsing Cotton Mill. The former company was owned by the People's Republic of China and in 1981 it brought in a claim that it was the beneficial owner of the latter mill which was ceasing operation in Hong Kong. According to the statement of claim, the Pao Hsing Mill had been set up in 1948 with funds provided by the plaintiff which was then a private textile company in Sichuan.

Three employees, Yang Sen-hui, Chang Jye-an, and Tung Teh-mei, were sent to Hong Kong to take charge of the new mill.

At the beginning they held shares together with 18 other persons as nominees or trustees of the Sichuan company. In 1952 Yang, Chang, and Tung allegedly introduced a resolution in a shareholders' meeting calling for a payment of HK$25 per share before the end of the year. Notices were sent to the other 18 shareholders living in China. When they did not respond, a further resolution was passed by the mill in Hong Kong to forfeit their shares. By that resolution, only Yang, Chang, and Tung remained shareholders; Yang was elected chairman of the board of directors and the other two directors.

From then on, the mill became an independent concern owned by the three directors with apparently no communication with the original shareholders in China. Only when they were all dead and their descendants proposed to sell the mill did the Sichuan company try to intervene. The company attributed its belated action to the political situation in China in the intervening 28 years which allegedly had not permitted effective intervention on its part. The court in Hong Kong rejected the claim of the Sichuan company on the grounds that it had come too late.[69]

Most of the emigrant industralists have apparently relinquished social links with their kin in China. Data on their relatives in China are incomplete. Six of the 26 respondents for whom I have information told me that they had no kinsmen there any more. Of those who had, seven said they had no contact with them; ten were occasionally in touch; and only three maintained that they were in close touch with their relatives.

Their exile mentality also shows in their lack of attachment to the host society. Unsure of the political future of Hong Kong, they obviously regarded their stay as temporary, and were constantly looking for safer shores. During the early phase of their immigration, the political situation was so volatile that many of them tried to hedge their bets. The managing director of Mill 7 recalled those years:

In 1947, we started building a new factory here. I travelled back and forth between Hong Kong and Shanghai. By the end of 1948, my family left China. We settled here permanently in 1949, a few months before the Communists took Shanghai...In March 1948, our factory began production with 15,000 spindles. I also started another mill in Taiwan at about the same time. Then between 1950 and 1951, I went to Argentina to establish a third mill. Everyone in Hong Kong was scared that the Communists would be coming. We had to have a place to go.

During the interviews, I asked the spinners whether they had ever seriously considered leaving Hong Kong and settling elsewhere. The majority of them denied it. Only six of the spinners affirmed a disposition to leave. But the denials should be treated with caution. They may simply mean: 'No, I am too old to bother'. As the managing director of Mill 1 said, 'It is difficult at my age'. Or they may be qualified by 'not now, but I have made preparations'. After the chairman of Mill 3 had answered the question in the negative, I noticed that his home address on his visiting card was in California, USA. The general sentiment was ambivalence, which was well expressed by a director of Mill 33:

No, I have not seriously considered moving elsewhere. But like everybody else, I am prepared for the worst. I cannot bring myself to leave here. For a Chinese, Hong Kong is the best place to live. The next best is Taiwan. Being an overseas Chinese in South-east Asia is no comparison.

In anticipation of a second-step migration, nearly all the mills had diversified their investments. Subsidiary companies in textiles and other lines of business spread to South-east Asia, Canada, Latin America, and parts of Africa. Mill 25, for example, had an associate textile company in Indonesia, a holding company in Panama, and four shipping companies incorporated in Liberia. The conglomerate owning Mill 1 had the largest geographical scope of operation, including five branches in Taiwan, four in Malaysia, one in Singapore, one in Mauritius, one in Thailand, and one trading company in the United Kingdom. Contingency planning is obviously behind such expansion. After maintaining he had no intention of leaving Hong Kong, the managing director of Mill 8 said, 'But subconsciously I must be thinking about it, otherwise we would not have diversified our business elsewhere.'

Diversification is also evident in the place of residence of their children. All except one of those whose children were grown-up had some offspring resident in a foreign country. The following cases are illustrative.

The managing director of Mill 3 has five sons. Two of them are in Hong Kong working with the family enterprise. The others are in the United States working as an architect, a teacher, and studying at the university.

The managing director of Mill 6 has five sons and three

daughters. Three sons are in Hong Kong engaged in the textile trade and the import and export business. The fourth son is a physician in the United States, and the youngest is in the United Kingdom working for the BBC. The daughters are married.

A director of Mill 9 has four children. One is working in mass communications in Canada; two are in Canada studying for their master's degree in business administration; and the youngest is still at a secondary school in Hong Kong.

The chairman of Mill 12 has five sons and three daughters. Two sons are in the family business; one in commerce in Hong Kong; two in industry in the United States. Three daughters are married and living in the United States.

The managing director of Mill 17 has three sons. One is in textiles in Taiwan; one in the garment industry in Hong Kong; and one in banking in the United States.

The burials of deceased spinners also furnish a clue to their shift in orientation. The doyen of the industry, C. Y. Wang, died in 1965. His coffin was temporarily lodged at the cemetery of the Tung Wah organization, indicating that the intention was probably to transport it back to China for burial.[70] The same procedure was followed for Lu Zuo-lin, managing director of one of the mills, who died in the same year.[71] Other entrepreneurs who died later were either buried in local cemeteries or cremated so that their remains could be easily moved. More recently, an interesting trend has appeared. The chairman of the Zhejiang First Bank, Li De-quan, was a director of one of the spinning mills. After his death in San Francisco in 1978, he was buried at Cypress Lawn Memorial Park in California[72] where his body joined that of the chairman of the Paul Y. Construction Company who had died a few days earlier. The latter was also a Shanghainese whose son and daughter were both married to members of the Rong family.[73]

The Shanghai cotton spinners left China in the late 1940s because of political changes in the mainland. They chose Hong Kong as their sanctuary because of its accessibility, stability, and relative absence of government regulation in economic life. They tended to be the younger generations of Lower Yangzi textile families who had considerable experience in operating modern and capital intensive factories in China. Many of them were eldest sons who were apparently charged with the responsibility of continuing the family line in industry. The fact that they sought shelter in a British colony rather than in Communist-ruled China indicated that they were pragmatic men. Their commitment to private enterprise evidently transcended nationalistic considerations.

Through the mechanism of chain migration, they moved to Hong Kong and constituted a distinct regional group in a mostly Cantonese population. As exiles, they displayed orientations towards the host community which were different from those of previous migrants to Hong Kong who were mainly sojourners. They had therefore a tendency to be more cohesive and enterprising, and devoted their energy to the creation of a new cotton spinning industry in the colony. Their subsequent success in building this economic niche for themselves attested to their drive as a special group of migrants. But their achievement also depended to a large extent on their ability to adapt to their advantage in the new environment the industrial skills and resources they possessed.

3   Industrial Skills and Resources

HISTORICALLY Shanghai was quick to adopt innovations; it first encountered trains only seven years after the completion of the first transcontinental railroad in America; its first textile mills were built before any in the American South, and by 1930 it had, according to some methods of calculation, the largest mill in the world; its first cinema opened only five years after San Francisco got its first large movie house; and by the late 1930s its Commercial Press was publishing each year as many titles as the entire American publishing industry — most of which were, of course, pirated.[1]

Before 1949 Shanghai was the leading urban industrial centre in China, and accounted for half of China's foreign trade. Nearly 60 per cent of the country's modern factories were located there, providing employment for the same percentage of the nations' industrial workers.[2] As a metropolis, Hong Kong was clearly overshadowed. In the view of the governor who saw Hong Kong launched into industrialization, 'Shanghai in pre-communist days was a great cosmopolitan centre; a sort of New York-Paris in an oriental setting. Hong Kong, by comparison, was a small village.'[3] It is therefore to be expected that the Shanghai entrepreneurs would be well equipped to compete in the field of manufacture, and would possess useful industrial skills and valuable resources in financial, productive, managerial, and marketing activities.

Financial Resources

It is popularly believed that the Shanghai industrialists, especially those engaged in textile manufacture, brought substantial assets with them when they migrated to the colony, and that this helped them to overcome the first hurdle of capital accumulation. Their industrial success has often been attributed to this strong financial position which gave them an edge over local competitors.

There is no doubt that Hong Kong benefited financially from the Chinese civil war. In the late 1940s a huge amount of flight capital had entered the colony as China's political and economic situation rapidly deteriorated. But we have no reliable data on the exact magnitude of this capital inflow. No official figures were available as the movement of money and other assets were not subject to government regulation in Hong Kong. Since the owners of the capital were in flight, they had every reason to be secretive. However, some idea of the size of that capital inflow can be formed from the information provided by contemporary newspaper reports and from later academic estimates.

Large quantities of money began to pour into the colony in mid-1946. It was believed in Shanghai financial circles that ten to thirty billion Chinese dollars had left that city for Hong Kong between July and October.[4] (In December 1946 the market exchange rate between American and Chinese dollars was 1:6,063. The rate had dropped to 1:8,683,000 by August 1948.) It was 'conservatively estimated' that in 1947 about fifty industrial concerns in China had been transferred to Hong Kong with 'at least HK$50 million in machinery and capital'.[5] The tempo quickened in the following year. In October 1948 twenty million Hong Kong dollars were said to have found their way into one 'major foreign bank' in Hong Kong.[6] (The exchange rate between the pound sterling and the Hong Kong dollar was fixed at that time at the rate of 1:16.)

The total influx up to this stage was a matter of guesswork. The financial agency of the Chinese Nationalist government in Hong Kong alleged that it amounted to sixty billion Hong Kong dollars. Their estimate was supposedly based on the value of deposits in the major local banks.[7] Since banking statistics were not published in Hong Kong before 1964, this figure cannot be verified.[8] Some journalists believed it to be greatly inflated and instead put the figure at four to five billion Hong Kong dollars.[9]

The climax of capital flight came with the Communist victory in late 1949. The total funds entering Hong Kong in the following year were said to be not less than one billion Hong Kong dollars.[10] In the first fortnight of April 1950, it was reported that 'approximately HK$10 million worth of capital escaped from Shanghai and were carried southward to Hong Kong in the form of gold, commodities, and shares'.[11]

The economist Edward Szczepanik has also attempted to estimate the inflow of capital from 1947 to 1955. According to his calculations (see Table 3.1), the annual injection of foreign capital and the net balance of invisible earnings made up on average about 40 per cent of Hong Kong's national income. There were two main deviations. From 1949–50 when the People's Republic of China was established, the inflow had reached 65 per cent or over one

Table 3.1. Estimates of Foreign Investment in Hong Kong 1947–
1955 (in HK$ million, rounded figures)

Period	National Income	Foreign Investment*	Investment as % of Income
1947–8 to 1948–9	1,600	700	44
1948–9 to 1949–50	1,800	1,200	67
1949–50 to 1950–1	2,300	800	35
1950–1 to 1951–2	2,800	200	7
1951–2 to 1952–3	2,800	1,300	46
1952–3 to 1953–4	3,200	1,400	44
1953–4 to 1954–5	3,600	1,500	42

Note: * Including inflow of capital from abroad, net balance of invisible earnings,
    and net balance of government and private transfers.
Source: Szczepanik, *Economic Growth*, Table 46, p.183.

billion Hong Kong dollars. Then at the outbreak of the Korean
War in 1951, this had dropped to around 7 per cent, reflecting a
temporary loss of confidence in the future of the territory. It is difficult to separate the inflow of capital from invisible earnings, but
Szczepanik refers to 'a fairly uniform opinion prevailing in the Colony' to the effect that 'the annual inflow of capital was in the
region of HK$300–600 million in recent years [around 1957] and
was even larger during the period of 1948–50'.[12] From these
figures he concludes that the part played by internal savings at the
start of Hong Kong's industrialization was comparatively small.
'Approximately one-third of investment was financed by internal
savings, the remaining two-thirds by capital from abroad.'[13]

   How much of the capital inflow was channelled into the cotton
spinning industry? The first mill in post-war Hong Kong, the South
China Textile Company, was set up in August 1947. With 5,000
second-hand spindles bought from the United States, the total investment including the costs of land, buildings, and equipment was
estimated at about four million Hong Kong dollars.[14] Five other
mills came into existence in 1948, four of which were established
by members of the Rong family.[15] A report in the *Far Eastern
Economic Review* asserted that the total investments of these six

pioneering mills exceeded HK$100 million. This estimate is too high. The total number of spindles listed as 120,000 was merely a projection as some of the mills were either in the preparatory stage or not yet in full operation. The actual number of spindles installed at the end of 1948 was 22,000.[16] A new American-made spindle cost about HK$400, nearly twice as much as a Japanese-made one.[17] Allowing for some Japanese and second-hand spindles in these pioneering mills, it is reasonable to assume that the average cost of a spindle was HK$300. Thus the installation of all the projected 120,000 spindles would have involved about HK$36 million. If we assume that the spindles made up about half of the fixed investments of a spinning mill,[18] the other half being spent on land, plant construction, air-conditioning, insurance and so forth, then the total capital outlay at the six mills adds up to HK$72 million instead of HK$100 million.

Subsequent reports in the *Far Eastern Economic Review* scaled down their estimates to a more realistic level. In July 1950 it cited the plausible figure of HK$115 million as the amount invested in a total capacity of 173,000 spindles in the nascent spinning industry.[19] In a speech to the annual general meeting of its members on 2 April 1951, the Chairman of the Hong Kong Chamber of Commerce stated that the aggregate investment of the 13 mills with nearly 200,000 spindles totalled HK$105 million, with another HK$100 million tied up in stocks of raw cotton and spun yarn.[20] This is the best available estimate, and it gives a gross capital engagement of about HK$200 million.

Table 3.1 shows that the value of foreign investments in the colony from 1947 to 1951 was about HK$2,700 million. Szczepanik maintains that of these, invisible earnings accounted for some HK$500 million per year.[21] This left the net inflow of capital from abroad in this period at HK$1,200 million. If this estimate is accepted, it means that nearly 17 per cent of the flight capital was committed to the cotton spinning industry up to 1951, a substantial amount at a time when there were only 13 mills in the industry.

How important was the initial capital? Was it crucial in enabling the Shanghainese to establish dominance in the spinning industry? One thing was certain: the injection of flight capital had created some of the most modern spinning factories that Hong Kong, or even the whole of Asia, had ever seen. This was not merely the result of the magnitude of the investment. Of greater importance was the form in which the industrial capital was transferred, most of it being embodied in machinery, cotton yarn, and to some extent in company shares.

The economic and political situation of China made such a form of capital transfer mandatory. In the protracted war with Japan from 1937 to 1945, the cotton mills in China continued to make a profit.[22] But as it was impossible to import machinery, their equipment became seriously run down and in urgent need of renovation and replacement. When the war was over, the pent-up global demand for basic commodities such as cotton yarn made cotton mills singularly prosperous. The managing director of Mill 17 told me that 1945 to 1947 were the 'golden years' when 'those whose factories did not get bombed made a hell of a lot of money'. Although the Nationalist government demanded that the private mills sell half of their products at officially fixed prices, it was unable to enforce this regulation effectively. Reaping a record profit said to be approaching 12,000 billion Chinese dollars in 1946, the private mill owners began to carry out plant repairs without having to rely on government loans or officially supplied foreign exchange.[23] With adequate foreign exchange deposits outside China, they ordered new machinery from Great Britain and the United States. Between 1946 and 1947, it was reported that the purchase amounted to two and a half million spindles.[24]

This buying spree was spurred on by the runaway inflation in China.[25] Within eighteen months from the beginning of 1946, the Chinese currency had reportedly depreciated by around 5,000 per cent against the Hong Kong dollar.[26] In order to preserve the value of economic assets, Chinese industrialists rapidly converted their funds into machinery, commodities, and foreign-quoted shares. When the situation worsened and Shanghai became an increasingly inhospitable place for industry, some of the mill owners diverted these assets to Hong Kong. We were told that 35,000 bales of cotton yarn were imported into the colony in late 1948.[27] After the Communists had captured Shanghai, over 100,000 bales of yarn were estimated to have arrived from China, glutting the Hong Kong market and depressing yarn prices.[28] Shares of the Shanghai-based and British-owned Ewo Cotton Mill had been brought down to Hong Kong and sold for the local currency as an 'expedient capital transfer'.[29]

But it was new machinery which formed the bulk of this flight capital. Little of the existing machinery was dismantled in the

Shanghai cotton mills and shipped to Hong Kong because of its age and the cost of transportation.[30] In 1949 China had a total spindleage of about five million.[31] The 200,000 spindles transplanted to the colony were a mere 4 per cent of China's capacity, but as they were all new and modern, the tiny percentage actually constituted the hope for the future of China's spinning industry. It was as if the new shoots had been picked and grafted to the trunk of Hong Kong. Even before they began to bloom, the sight was quite spectacular. The *Far Eastern Economic Review* described in glowing terms the advanced design of one of these new mills:

The machinery is the newest one-process combination, consisting of nearly 200 different kinds of machines for scuttling, carding, roving, and two stages of spinning...Many aspects of the construction are new to Hong Kong and some are even for the first time introduced in the Far East. The factory building will be windowless, artificially lighted and airconditioned to bring the degree of humidity and temperature inside the factory to the desired level best suited for the production of cotton yarn as well as to the health of the workers.

Working under the latest cold cathode lighting system which has just been perfected in the United States and which is for the first time introduced in the Far East, workers of the factory will enjoy easier working conditions and their eye-sight will be better protected by this system than by natural sun lighting or ordinary lighting system. The cold cathode lighting does not produce as much heat as ordinary lighting system and thus it will be easier to regulate humidity and temperature inside the factory...

Due to the shortage of steel, all structural supports of the roof of the factory building will be made of aluminium which is light and non-rusting and costs considerably less in maintenance. Such installations of aluminium structures have not yet been made more than a dozen times all over the world. Throughout the factory building, copper tubes will be installed as a system — also the first time in Hong Kong — to detect smoke in order to prevent any outbreak of fire...[32]

Textile experts visiting Hong Kong in the early 1950s were all impressed.[33] Arno S. Pearse, an official of the International Federation of the Master Cotton Spinners' and Manufacturers' Association, observed:

The yarn was fairly uniform and the cloth from the automatic looms was faultless. The inspection rooms were well organized and provided with modern machinery; the girls were sharp in noting defects. In the yarn-bundling room, both the girls and the men worked with great speed, quicker than in the Shanghai mills (which I had seen) 25 years ago.

Table 3.2. Capitalization of Mills Established from 1947 to 1957 (in HK$ million)

Mill	Initial Capital	Present Capital	Growth in Capitalization (%)
Soco	0.2	20.0	9,900
Beautex	1.0	1.0	0
Majestic	1.0	10.0	900
Central	1.2	40.0	3,230
Nan Fung	4.0	10.0	150
Pao Hsing	5.0	10.0	100
Lea Tai	5.0	20.0	300
Eastern	5.0	5.0	0
South	5.0	6.0	20
East Sun	5.0	15.0	200
Tai Hing	10.0	20.0	100
Wyler	15.0	30.0	100
Kowloon	15.0	30.0	100
South Sea	20.0	50.0	150
Nan Yang	25.0	30.0	20
Textile Corp.	25.0	20.5	−18

Source: Records of individual mills, Company Registry, Hong Kong.

The machinery used emanates from almost all the textile machinery works of the world...All the machinery in mills is up to date and new. Their mills have air-conditioning and vacuum plants; trolley transport for the warp-beams; Toyoda automatic looms seem to preponderate. There are no ordinary looms — all are automatic...[34]

Thus the transferred capital gave the Shanghai spinners an important competitive advantage, from the start, in the form of highly modernized equipment. But as they were not the only group with capital to invest its importance should not be over-exaggerated. The overseas Chinese from South-east Asia and elsewhere,[35] the powerful Western firms in the colony, the large Cantonese commercial organizations such as the Wing On Company and the Sincere Company were all potential contenders. The initial investment for a spinning mill, though substantial, was not

Table 3.3. Initial Capital and Growth Rate of Capitalization among Mills Established between 1947 and 1957

Initial Capital	Growth Rate (%)			
	Low (100 & less)	Medium (101–500)	High (501 & over)	Row Total
Small (less than 5m)	1	1	3	5
Medium (5–10m)	4	2	0	6
Large (over 10m)	4	1	0	5
Column Total	9	4	3	16

$\chi^2 = 8.7$; df $= 4$; not significant at 0.05 level.

Source: Records of individual mills, Company Registry, Hong Kong.

inhibitory. An examination of the capital outlay of the mills set up during the first decade after 1947 (see Table 3.2) shows that several of the most modestly funded companies expanded rapidly to catch up with the well-endowed ones. Table 3.3 demonstrates further that initial investments did not significantly affect the rate of growth in capitalization. These figures are, of course, open to several interpretations.[36] It is likely that the well-funded mills were already close to the optimal scale for the local economy at their foundation, making it not worth while to increase capitalization. The meagrely funded ones, on the other hand, had to grow fast to attain viability and efficiency. It is also possible that many under-capitalized mills had gone out of operation, and that those remaining were the resilient and successful ones. The scanty information on bankruptcies and changeovers shows that the second interpretation is not likely to be very important. But the main thrust of the two tables remains that a mill can start with little capital and still compete successfully.

One feature of the cotton spinning industry is the slow rate of business turnover. A mill must have at least two months' supply of raw cotton to begin production, and the finished yarn is usually sold on credit. Therefore, besides fixed investments in machinery and the plant, sufficient working capital is essential. As already indicated, the Shanghai spinners brought with them capital mainly in the form of machinery and stock. They had little cash to finance day-to-day operations. Their original plan, it seems, was to rely on profits which could be gained in the favourable post-war market, and also, possibly, on remittances from the parent companies in China. But many of them missed the opportunity for high profit owing to delays in the delivery of machinery. Then the outbreak of the Korean War closed off the Chinese and some other markets. By late 1950 some of the spinners were in serious financial difficulties. They had to borrow money at high rates of interest, sometimes as much as 2 per cent per month.[37] In order to obtain ready cash, they sold yarn at unprofitable prices, said to be 'approximately 10% cheaper than Japanese yarn, and at about the same as Italian prices, though the quality is superior to both'.[38] In January 1953 the scarcity of operational capital led to the collapse of a mill with 13,000 spindles and a debt of over HK$11 million.[39]

Thus the amount of transferred capital only enabled the Shanghai spinners to take the first stride, but did not ensure success. More important than the possession of capital was the ability to raise and utilize outside funds. The editor of a textile journal remarked of the Shanghai industrialists:

They know how to make use of capital. They can do ten million dollars' worth of business with one million capital. Unlike the industrialists in Britain who are very conservative, the Shanghainese are similar to the Japanese who do big business with limited funds. So they are either very successful, or they go bankrupt.[40]

Himself a Shanghainese, the editor was perhaps trying to project an image of his fellow regionals that would justify their industrial predominance. Yet it was a typical comment, for most Hong Kong people believed in the financial prowess of the Shanghai industrialists. Stereotypes often contain some grains of truth so let us examine the factual basis of this belief. How did the Shanghainese do big business with small capital? There are three ways: to make use of bank loans, to reinvest retained profits, and to utilize the stock-market.

Bank Loans

There are grounds for believing that the Shanghai entrepreneurs were conversant with bank financing. Before Western banking institutions were introduced into China, the merchants of the Lower Yangzi region had already developed a vigorous system of native banks known as *qianzhuang* or *yinhao*.[41] Prominent in the business were the financiers from Ningbo.[42] These native bankers accommodated themselves to Western influences and grew into a powerful Jiangsu-Zhejiang financial clique which captured leadership among modern-style Chinese bankers after the 1911 revolution.[43] In the first half of this century, Shanghai emerged as China's financial centre. In the opinion of a European observer, the city seemed 'to support an excessive number of banks'. There were four Chinese central banks, 14 foreign banks, and 388 Chinese-owned financial institutions in 1946.[44]

Most of the Chinese mill owners had borrowed from these institutions and seemed to be adept in making use of modern credit facilities. In the 1930s half of the capital in the Chinese textile industry was reported to be made up of bank loans.[45] As Kang Chao has observed, the Chinese mills showed a general tendency to 'overuse capital'.[46] The Shen Xin Fourth Mill, for example, had bank loans that exceeded twice the amount of its capitalization in 1942 and 1943.[47]

Such a tendency persisted when some of the mill owners moved to Hong Kong. It might even have been reinforced by their feeling of insecurity as immigrants. As a Chinese banker who has close contacts with the Hong Kong spinning industry puts it:

Industrialists 'made do' with minimum investments and borrowed as much as they could from the banks. They took out their profits for deposit or investment outside of Hong Kong. They did not hesitate to grow in order to meet their markets' demand, but they financed as much of their growth as possible through bank credit. In this way, if Hong Kong were suddenly taken over or lost its markets, the banks could have their businesses. On the other hand, if Hong Kong remained stable and prosperous and their businesses did well, they could reap the profits themselves.[48]

By the 1960s according to a prominent Hong Kong banker, the average borrowings of spinning and weaving companies from banks amounted to 75 per cent of the proprietor's funds.[49]

Besides making maximum use of bank credits, a number of the mill owners had banking experience themselves. Rong Zong-jing and Rong De-sheng had both begun their careers as apprentices in Shanghai native banks.[50] Rong Hong-yuan had set up a bank during the Anti-Japanese War in order to finance his textile operations.[51] Among my 40 respondents, the fathers of four of them had once engaged in banking. The managing director of Mill 6 and the director of Mill 17 had formal training and practical experience in the finance business. The chairman of Mill 24 was a director of a local Chinese bank at the time he was interviewed. Many of them had family members involved in the field of finance, 'working in a Hong Kong bank, in a New York investment firm, or developing his own mutual fund'.[52]

Hong Kong had by no means been devoid of financial organizations before the Shanghainese came. It had a reasonably developed monetary and banking system in the pre-war period.[53] A 1947 survey of local Chinese factories showed that quite a number of them had the backing of banks, though probably just in the provision of short-term working capital.[54] It indicated that the local industrialists were not inexperienced in the general handling of bank loans. The advantage of the Shanghai entrepreneurs seemed to rest on three specific resources. The first was a long-term time horizon. Many of my respondents conceded that the local Cantonese were 'sharp' when dealing with money. But they also asserted that the locals were affected by the commercial tradition of Hong Kong as an entrepôt and tended to avoid prolonged financial commitments in industry. As the Shanghainese mill manager of Mill 7 said:

The Cantonese mainly invest in fields such as restaurants. The capital can be huge and sometimes goes up to several tens of millions of dollars. But they want high and quick turnover. They prefer to have cash in hand. They lack vision and stamina. In spinning, one has to wait before the capital will yield profit...The business style of the Shanghainese is to employ large capital to obtain small but steady profit.

The second resource was that they were relatively free of the psychological handicaps imposed by colonialism. For instance, according to a Shanghainese banker, the entrepreneurs from his region were more daring in approaching the British banks in Hong Kong for assistance. He told me:

At that time [in the late 1940s], Hong Kong was still very colonial with the government and foreign firms high on top. Local people were not even welcome in the Hong Kong and Shanghai Bank. The Bank was like a Chinese magistrate's court which locals would avoid. And the Bank was not interested in their deposits. When we first arrived, we were not used to this environment. Although there had been the International Settlement in Shanghai, it was returned to China after the War...Some of the textile people brought part of their capital with them, but most of their investments stayed in China. . .The majority of them needed money to start again, so they went and knocked on the door of the Bank and said, 'We want to see your manager.' The staff of the Bank were surprised. 'Who are these people who dare to demand to see the manager?' They did not know how to handle them.

But at the beginning, before 1949, the Shanghainese had not been very successful in enlisting the help of the large banks which had branches in China at the time. During the early phase of the development of the Chinese cotton spinning industry, these banks had provided the mills with funds. But later they became reluctant to lend because of the heavy borrowing of the Chinese mills.[55] The mill owners then turned to the Chinese banks such as the Bank of China and the Chinese Commercial Bank for loans, and their relationship with the British banks weakened.[56] Therefore, after their arrival in Hong Kong, the Shanghai spinners had to re-establish a business relationship with the British financial institutions. Intermediaries were needed as guarantors, and this led to the mobilization of the third and most significant resource commanded by the Shanghainese — their regional network which will be discussed in detail in Chapter 5.

Reinvestment of Profit

Another way of using capital effectively is by retaining business profits for reinvestment. Since I refrained from probing into financial matters in the interviews, I have no empirical data to assess the magnitude of reinvestment ratio in the spinning mills. But there are various indications that, by the time they arrived in Hong Kong, the Shanghai spinners had already acquired the necessary capitalist spirit to re-harness profit for long term investment.

Prior to 1949, as Kang Chao points out, the financial planning and management of some of the Chinese mills were rather weak. Some mills would distribute virtually all the profits they made as dividends, especially if they had adopted the fixed dividend system when they were incorporated. Adequate provision for depreciation often was not made.[57] But the more successful operations, such as the Shen Xin mills, were able to avoid these pitfalls. The Shen Xin Fourth Mill, for example, began to make a profit at the outbreak of the Anti-Japanese War after a long period of losses. In 1937 about 43 per cent of the profits were designated as dividends for shareholders. But instead of paying out cash, these dividends were distributed in the form of additional shares in spite of protests by the minority shareholders.[58] From 1939 to 1945, nearly half of the dividends were converted into new share subscriptions. Consequently the capitalization of the mill rose from two million to ten million Chinese dollars during that period.[59]

The overriding concern to plough back profit for expansion and renewal was subsequently also manifested in the Hong Kong mills. Minority shareholders of the publicly held textile companies in Hong Kong were often treated in a perfunctory manner when it came to the distribution of dividends. A 'can I have more?' incident occurred during the 1973 annual general meeting of Mill 16 in which a shareholder protested, to no avail, against what he regarded as meagre dividends after successive profitable years for the company.[60]

Reinvestment was apparently spurred on by two main motivations — a sense of vocation and a desire for autonomy. A palpable sense of vocation and industrial commitment could be felt during an internal controversy in the Shen Xin Company in 1938. As mentioned above, the Shen Xin Fourth Mill began to make a profit after being relocated to Hankou in 1937. The directors immediately proceeded to use the profit to order 19,000 new spindles from abroad. But due to the war, the machinery was stranded in Shanghai and could not be transported inland. The import and export firm proposed to cancel the order and refund the deposits. The Rong family declined the offer and kept the spindles. Rong Desheng then suggested to the directors of the Fourth Mill, headed by his son-in-law, that the new machinery be lent to the other Shen Xin mills in Shanghai in exchange for a fixed share of the future profit. This suggestion was strongly resisted by the Fourth Mill, one of whose directors declared that 'our paramount aim is to retain the machinery and the amount of mid-term benefits is secondary...These 19,000 spindles are our future life-blood.'[61] However they later gave in as there was no other alternative. Fifteen thousand of the new spindles were installed in the Ninth Mill while the remaining 4,000 were operated to provide employment for the staff of the Third Mill which had fallen into Japanese hands.[62] In spite of this initial set-back, the directors of the Fourth Mill continued to accumulate funds during the Anti-Japanese War and, when the war was over, managed to place orders for 75,000 new spindles.[63]

Such devotion to the industry has been reaffirmed periodically by the Shanghai spinners in Hong Kong. Even in the 1980s when their industry was sometimes portrayed as a declining sector, they would renew their pledge of commitment. In 1981 in a letter to the editor of the *South China Morning Post*, the managing director of the Central Textiles (Hong Kong) Ltd. wrote:

The Hong Kong textile industry is going through a difficult phase. The surviving members are re-equipping, restructuring and reorganising in order to change industry's traditional direction of direct export of yarn and fabrics to Europe and the U.S. to its new direction of catering for the needs of the Hong Kong garment industry...We are determined industrialists who are committed to the well-being of Hong Kong. We certainly do not need featherbedding or subsidies from the taxpayers. What we need is the moral support of the Government and the public during the process by which we are tranforming the textile industry into one of the industries that Hong Kong can be proud of.[64]

In 1984 the South Sea Cotton Mill invested HK$70 million in the building of a new plant. Its chief executive, Mr Jack Tang, told reporters that 'as industrialists, we have responsibilities towards our enterprise and our employees. We either have to continue to invest or we have to quit. There is no middle road to follow.'[65]

Besides a sense of vocation, the spinners also showed a tendency to make use of retained earnings to maximize financial autonomy. Self-financing systems were often set up within the framework of a conglomerate or an 'economic group' which is 'a multicompany firm which transacts in different product markets but which does so under common entrepreneurial and financial control'.[66] Among other advantages, such an organization facilitates internal transfer of capital so that different units can support one another and reduce the cost of dependence on external loans. This method was quite widely used by the earlier generation of cotton spinners in the Lower Yangzi region. After making a profit from the Da Sheng Cotton Mill which he founded, Zhang Jian diversified his enterprise into the manufacture of iron, oil, silk, matches, electric light bulbs, and flour. He also established a shipping company, a telephone company, and an agricultural land-reclamation and cultivation concern.[67] The Rong family is another example. The central pillars of their enterprise were flour milling and textile manufacture. These were reinforced by a shipping firm and several factories producing machinery, paper, and chemical products.[68]

In contemporary Hong Kong, the success of the Winsor Industrial Corporation, a Shanghainese-owned textile conglomerate, was partly achieved with this technique. Each member company maintained its own account. It had to contribute a fixed percentage of its annual profits to the corporation. This arrangement gave it an incentive to increase its earnings since it could keep the rest of the profits for its own use. If it should make a loss, the corporation would lend it money to be returned when business prospered again. According to one of its directors, subsidiaries would borrow from the corporation and paid twice as much interest as the rates charged by banks. In this way, poor performance was penalized and interest payments were retained within the group. Internal competition was thus instituted with mutual financial sustenance. By 1977 this corporation had a vertical set-up with four cotton spinning mills, four woollen spinning mills, four knitwear companies, four garment companies, and two dyeing and finishing factories. These were supplemented by a godown, four investment companies in addition to four property development and estate management concerns.[69]

This technique of internal financing was not unique to the Shanghai entrepreneurs however. Before the war, the Cantonese-owned Wing On Company which had operated five spinning mills in Shanghai had used this method effectively.[70] In Hong Kong, at least two mills, Mill 8 with Chaozhou capital and Mill 4 with Cantonese capital, have also adopted this financial format.

The Stock-market

Shanghai was the first Chinese city to have its own stock-market. The Shanghai Sharebrokers' Association was formed by Western brokers as early as the late Qing dynasty.[71] In 1920 Chinese financiers started their own Shanghai Chartered Stock and Produce Exchange.[72] At its peak, there were over a hundred exchanges in Shanghai operating day and night, dealing with all kinds of commodities. Excessive speculation led to widespread bankruptcies. By the 1930s only six survived, including the Chinese Cotton Goods Exchange.[73] Although the institutional mechanism was available and some of the mill owners, such as Rong Zong-jing, were active sponsors of these exchanges, very few spinning mills in Shanghai had issued public shares to raise capital.[74] The preference for the private form of company organization among my respondents will be dealt with in the next chapter. It is sufficient to note here that the stock-market was little used either by Shanghainese or non-Shanghainese textile men in Hong Kong.[75]

Productive Resources

There was a long tradition of textile manufacture in the Lower Yangzi region. Since the Yuan dynasty it had been the main productive centre of domestic handmade cloth. Various indigenous spinning and weaving instruments had been invented there, although they had not achieved the breakthrough to mechanization.[76] In the Ming dynasty a vigorous cloth trade was recorded in the Shanghai area. Individual transactions, sometimes reaching several hundred thousand taels of silver, were said to have been conducted, and the products sold all over China.[77] This tradition had enabled the region to maintain its lead even after the introduction of modern textile technology. An official survey of Jiangsu in 1932 showed that 58 per cent of the nation's cotton spinning mills were located in the province, owning 61 per cent of the national spindleage, employing 60 per cent of all textile workers, and producing 64 per cent of China's yarn.[78]

This regional tradition meant that many of the emigrant Shanghai spinners were experienced industrialists. As professional yarn manufacturers, they persisted in what they knew best even in a new environment. 'We know how to make a profit in this industry', one of my respondents said, 'Even when we lose money, we know why.' Some were the third or even fourth generation engaged in the industry. But they represented a limited number because of the relatively recent development of modern industry in China. As Table 3.4 indicates, only three of the respondents' grandfathers were owners of spinning mills. As many as 35 per cent of my respondents claimed to be ignorant of their grandfathers' background, a few of them apparently genuinely so. For instance, the director of Mill 33 said: 'My grandfather was an overseas Chinese. Even my father did not know him.' Others might have been reluctant to tell, and it seems reasonable to assume that they were not impressed by their grandfathers' humble origins. The majority of those who knew had grandfathers who were merchants. This supports the analysis that the merchant group of traditional China was 'best schooled for the modern business role'.[79] But for reasons which are still unclear, the compradors who must have acquired Western commercial and industrial skills by working for

Table 3.4. Occupation of Grandfathers of the Cotton Spinners

Occupation	No.	%
Unknown	14	35.0
Merchant	10	25.0
Farmer	5	12.5
Cotton spinner	3	7.5
Scholar	3	7.5
Government official	2	5.0
Company employee	2	5.0
Comprador	1	2.5
Total	40	100.0

Source: Interviews, 1978.

foreign firms, did not figure prominently in the genealogies of the cotton spinners.[80]

Nearly half of the respondents came from families with industrial experience (see Table 3.5). At least 30 per cent had been engaged in the spinning industry for two generations, and 15 per cent had fathers operating other kinds of factories. Commercial activities remained an important breeding ground for industrial entrepreneurs. Some 12 per cent of the fathers were traders, often, as cotton or cloth merchants, closely involved with textiles. The remaining fathers had usually acquired skills with industrial application, as executives and accountants for instance. Even the fathers of the three respondents who were civil servants were not of the traditional kind. One was employed as an interpreter in the Shanghai Municipal Council dealing with Chinese factories, another worked for the Chinese Maritime Customs, and the third was in the transport department of the Chinese government.

On the whole, there has been a moderate degree of occupational inheritance and accumulation of industrial experience in the last generation or two. By itself, this would not have made the respondents competent operators. One of the main obstacles to China's industrialization, according to some scholars, was the low social status accorded artisans and merchants.[81] The official ideology of traditional China relegated merchants to the bottom of

Table 3.5 Occupation of Fathers of the Cotton Spinners

Occupation	No.	%
Cotton spinner	12	30.0
Other industrialist	6	15.0
Merchant	5	12.5
Executive	3	7.5
Accountant	3	7.5
Civil servant	3	7.5
Comprador	2	5.0
Sailor	2	5.0
Technician	1	2.5
Scholar	1	2.5
Farmer	1	2.5
No response	1	2.5
Total	40	100.0

Source: Interviews, 1978.

the social hierarchy. Commerce was despised as a 'non-essential' and peripheral pursuit in contrast to the 'fundamental' occupation of agriculture. Commercial wealth was said to be ephemeral, unprotected from the encroachments of officialdom. Since the traditional stratification system was theoretically open, there was a strong incentive for merchants to seek upward social mobility. Successful merchants would thus convert their wealth into land holdings and encourage their sons to compete in the civil service examinations. It is thought that the dissipation of capital and talents for commercial enterprises resulted from this tendency.

How far did this alleged obstacle affect the formation of technical expertise among the modern Chinese industrialists? The importance of this social structural factor has probably been exaggerated. In the history of European economic development, there were, according to Gerschenkron, 'sufficient cases where magnificent entrepreneurial activities were conducted in the face of a dominant value system that was violently opposed to such activities'.[82] Gerschenkron believes that it is important to identify the 'substitutions' which the entrepreneurs found to compensate for the absence of social approval.

The merchants' practice of 'substitution' is one way in which the alleged obstacle may have been overcome. Another possibility is that society's attitude towards commerce was weaker and less consistent than some scholars have assumed. Suspicion and hostility towards traders were common in agricultural societies presumably because impersonal exchange tended to violate the sense of sacredness that the peasants often attached to their produce. In traditional China, an additional reason for the official antagonism towards the merchant group was probably fiscal. 'Wealth not invested in land remained "invisible" to the extensive imperial administration and could not be reached by its taxation technique', says Weber.[83] During normal times, therefore, traders were not favoured by the state. But during periods of financial need, the state would devise means to raise revenue outside the regular taxation system. In a dramatic change of official attitude, the merchants then became assets as they had money to buy the official titles and degrees which the state put on sale.[84] There are also plenty of examples of officials entrusting funds to traders for investment, and, indeed, a strong symbiotic relationship existed between the two groups.[85] Therefore, it cannot be said that Chinese merchants were always disdained.[86]

Furthermore, social values could undergo rapid changes. The status of traders and artisans could be kept theoretically low only when the traditional social hierarchy was respected. When the hierarchy began to crumble, as it did in the late Qing period, officialdom rapidly lost its attraction for the ambitious and talented who looked elsewhere for advancement. The biographies of some of the earliest Chinese cotton spinners show the shift in values.[87] A German sinologist who lived in China for more than two decades observed soon after the fall of the Qing dynasty that '[the] former separation between the merchant caste and other estates or classes has completely disappeared, and the great merchant today plays in Chinese society the same important role which he is playing elsewhere.'[88]

Another weakness of the 'lowly merchant' argument is that it neglects regional variations. Different localities in China might vary in their ranking of status and prestige, and it was usually the local systems that exerted a more direct influence on the behaviour of their members than the more remote national value system. The reality of regional divergencies in norms and values can be illustrated by the Chinese intellectuals' contempt for modern

Shanghai. These intellectuals brand Shanghai's life-style as *haipai* — superficial, uncultured, over-zealous for monetary gain. They extol the ethos of Beijing calling it *jingpai* — serious, artistic, appreciative of profundity and perfection. In the latter seat of culture, declared a Chinese educator, 'the only "aristocratic" class were the men of knowledge — painters, calligraphers, poets, philosophers, historians, writers, and modern scientists and engineers'.[89] Commercial Shanghai, he lamented, was completely different where wealth was the only measure of a person's worth.

This intellectuals' stereotype points to different subcultures or value orientations in the environs of the two cities. The theme emerged when I discussed the characteristics of Shanghai industrialists with the owners of Mill 32. The following exchanges among the chairman, the managing director, and their personal secretary were illuminating:

Chairman: In our home town, Wuxi, it was traditional to work in the textile industry. When we were young, people respected industrialists more than the rich...

Secretary : So that means you are more concerned with status than profit.

Chairman: Not status. We are *shiye jia* [the Chinese term for industrialists which means literally those engaged in a 'solid' occupation].

Director   : Yes, it is status in the sense of prestige. In China then, you could have prestige either in politics or in industry. In Hong Kong, you now have JP, OBE, and what not.

Lastly, there are numerous ways of harmonizing new activities with long-cherished values. The textile entrepreneurs apparently felt that they were extending what was treasured in their culture rather than infringing it. They saw their work as 'fundamental' because they were producing primary necessities. Some of them likened the textile industry to farming because they regarded both occupations as aiming at long-term returns. So concerned were they for this collective image that with one voice they condemned speculation. Though privately they might not abstain from making a profit in the buying and selling of cotton, in public they censured the practice. The Chairman of Mill 32 said:

A number of mill owners are too ambitious. When cotton prices are shooting up, they make heavy bookings. This is wrong. As an industrialist, you should only purchase what you need. If you want to speculate, why not close down and be a stock-broker?

Table 3.6. Educational Attainment of Cotton Spinners and the Economically Active Population of Hong Kong

Education	Spinners (%)	Population (%)
No schooling	0	14
Primary	0	45
Secondary	20	35
University	55	6
Postgraduate	25	—
Total	100	100

Source: *Hong Kong By-census, 1976, Basic Tables*, p.27; Interviews, 1978.

In 1975 the spinners as a group were reluctant to support the setting up of a commodity exchange in Hong Kong. They were apparently apprehensive of excessive speculation.[90]

Besides trying to project a respectable image, these industrialists have also tried to reinforce their status by acquiring high educational qualifications, the guarantee for respectability in Chinese society. Eighty per cent of the respondents had an undergraduate or postgraduate university degree while only about 6 per cent of the economically active population in Hong Kong were similarly qualified in as late as 1976 (see Table 3.6). The Shanghainese spinners and the non-Shanghainese ones had comparable levels of educational attainment, as shown in Table 3.7. What distinguished them was the type of education they had had. A quarter of the spinners who had been to university had specialized training in textile manufacture, and nearly 19 per cent of them held degrees in various fields of engineering (see Table 3.8). This meant that over 40 per cent of them were technically equipped and knowledgeable about production processes. This eagerness and ability to acquire technical expertise is quite common among modern Chinese industrialists.[91] The pride in flexibility and innovativeness in the handling of machinery is shown by the managing director of Mill 22 who said:

In Hong Kong, we have a lot of information about new textile machines. We know their merits and drawbacks. So we choose the suitable parts, and assemble them. But in neighbouring countries, they usually order the com-

Table 3.7. Educational Attainment of Cotton Spinners by Regional Origin

| | Education | | | |
Origin	Secondary	University	Postgraduate	Row Total
Shanghainese	5	18	7	30
Others	3	4	3	10
Column Total	8	22	10	40

$\chi^2 = 1.3$; df $= 2$; not significant at 0.05 level.

Source: Interviews, 1978.

Table 3.8 Subjects of Study of the University-educated Cotton Spinners

Subject	First Degree	Master's Degree	Doctoral Degree	Row Total (%)
Textile	4	3	1	8 (25)
Engineering	4	1	1	6 (19)
Economics	3	1	0	4 (13)
Management	2	2	0	4 (13)
Law	3	0	0	3 (9)
Accounting	2	1	0	3 (9)
Commerce	2	0	0	2 (6)
Natural Science	2	0	0	2 (6)
Column Total	22	8	2	32(100)

Source: Interviews, 1978.

plete set from one company, down to the last screw. That's why we are ahead of them.[92]

The success of the chairman of Mill 3 who had little formal education was founded on his technical ability. He was a mill ap-

Table 3.9. Types of University Attended by Cotton Spinners

Type	No.	%	Cumulative %
Chinese government	3	9	9
Chinese private	4	13	22
Chinese missionary	8	25	47
American	11	34	81
British	4	12	94
Canadian	2	6	100
Total	32	100	100

Source: Interviews, 1978.

prentice at the age of 19 and six years later he had become an owner. 'I had only one twisting machine', he recalled, 'and I worked day and night and I was the manager, engineer, salesman, labourer.' At the same time, he was also the researcher and developer. He invented a new kind of ornate yarn for women's wear which led to a financial breakthrough for his enterprise. 'Even at night people knocked at my door wanting to buy it', he said.[93]

In Republican China, there were three main types of universities — those financed by the Chinese government, those set up by private Chinese groups, and those operated by Western missionary bodies. The last were in effect Western colleges on Chinese soil as they used English as the medium of instruction and were staffed mainly by expatriate teachers and administrators.[94] If this type is classified as foreign educational institutions, then Table 3.9 shows that nearly 80 per cent of the university-trained spinners had obtained a Western education. The United States was the most popular destination of the prospective entrepreneurs going abroad to study. Some joined the foremost textile schools, such as the Lowell Institute in Massachusetts; and in the United Kingdom, the Bolton Institute of Technology, Lancashire, and the textile department of the University of Leeds. Others attended élite foreign universities such as the Massachusetts Institute of Technology, Chicago, Wisconsin, the London School of Economics, and Imperial College, London. They must therefore have been abreast of modern technological trends in their field when they began their industrial career.

The exposure to Western education also gave them another asset — the knowledge of foreign languages, especially English. Only four of the respondents, mostly self-made men, did not speak English. The other 90 per cent spoke it fluently. The chairman of the Winsor Industrial Corporation was even a polyglot speaking Japanese, German, Spanish, French, in addition to English and three Chinese dialects. Apart from having other economic worth, this linguistic advantage gave them access to Western technical literature.

Not only were they technically proficient themselves, but these spinners had another productive asset in the experienced technicians and skilled workers in their employ. For most of them had migrated with selected groups of their employees. The senior staff and their dependents arrived in planes chartered by the companies.[95] Others travelled overland. The number of such migrant technical workers from the Lower Yangzi region was quite substantial — Mill 3 brought 300 female workers; Mill 12 had 120 female and 100 male employees recruited from Changzhou in Jiangsu; Mill 17 and Mill 24 had about 300 each; and Mill 32 moved more than 200 of its workers to Hong Kong.[96] A director of Mill 24 had been in charge of a team of these workers on the move. He related that experience to me with obvious enjoyment:

I was leading 140 employees with more than 60 female workers. We travelled via Hankou, and there we were stopped by the local government officials. They thought I must be a 'slave' trader. 'Why do you have so many women with you?' they asked. They suspected that I was going to sell them in Hong Kong.

At a time when experienced textile workers were scarce in the colony, these employees formed the nuclei of the work force in the early mills. They helped to train local operatives and enabled the mills to start production almost immediately. But their significance should be seen in perspective. In the lower echelon, the technique required was quite simple. Workers could be trained as skilled hands within three months.[97] Moreover the core workers were not a stable group. Maladjustment and other problems caused a number of them to return to China. The issue of the return passage to Shanghai for these workers sparked off the first wave of industrial disputes involving cotton mills.[98] Then after a few years, many of the remaining Shanghainese workers left for other jobs or to get married.

Actually, more important than the number of workers they brought with them was the ability of the entrepreneurs to plan for their future need for skilled manpower. Technical training in pre-war China was not very impressive, but the experience of the mill owners made them very aware of the need for it. At least three private textile training institutes had been set up in Shanghai by the 1940s. The Nantong College was sponsored by the Da Sheng Mill; the Shanghai Technical College was opened by the Chinese mill owners' association; and the Cheng Fu Textile School of Shanghai was funded by a private textile company.[99] When the Shanghai spinners arrived in Hong Kong, they became the first group to champion vocational education. At the beginning, each mill organized their own classes to instruct technicians. Some of them, such as Mill 32, held competitive examinations to select candidates. When the Hong Kong Cotton Spinners' Association was establish-ed in 1955, member mills contributed HK$300,000 to build and equip a textile workshop in the Hong Kong Technical College which later became the Hong Kong Polytechnic. The association also formed a 'works advisory committee' at its inception con-sisting of mill representatives who met monthly to discuss technical and administrative problems. Then from 1967 onwards, scholar-ships were given by the association to send students to the Bolton Institute and later to Japanese colleges for textile training. The latest development was the sponsorship by the association of a pre-vocational school opened in April 1976 with about 1,000 places.[100]

Managerial Resources

'When we came', the managing director of Mill 1 said, 'the local people used to have frequent tea breaks. They did not work night shifts. There was no discipline. We put in a lot of effort and chang-ed the system of work.' However, he exaggerated the absence of an industrial culture in Hong Kong. At the turn of the century, there were enough factories of scale for a Western observer to conclude that 'the Colony has given promise of becoming a manufacturing centre of great and increasing importance.'[101] In particular, a Hong Kong Cotton Spinning, Weaving and Dyeing Company managed by Jardine, Matheson and Company was established around 1889. It had 55,000 spindles and quarters for 700 workers.[102] But for various reasons, the industrial promise of early Hong Kong was not realized. The cotton mill was forced into liquidation in 1914 after

15 years of operation. Its machinery was moved to Shanghai to form the Yangtsepoo Cotton Mill Ltd. which was later merged with the Ewo Cotton Spinning and Weaving Co. Ltd.[103] Factories were quite numerous by 1940, probably reaching 7,500 establishments, though most of them were small.[104] Therefore, what was lacking was the managerial experience of handling large manufacturing units comparable to those owned by the Shanghai spinners.

The managerial expertise of the Shanghai entrepreneurs was not, on the whole, built upon formal training.[105] As indicated earlier in Table 3.8, among my respondents technological education tended to take precedence over management studies. Only four of them, about 13 per cent, had obtained degrees in management. This order of priority was also reflected in the specialization among members of the same spinning family. In Mill 14 and Mill 32, two pairs of brothers worked side by side in the family business. Both of the elder brothers had been educated in textile production; one of the younger brothers had taken up textile management and the other one had aspired to business management. I asked the younger brother in Mill 14 why he had opted for textile management. He replied:

They asked me the same question in Leeds University when I applied. I have no interest in the technical aspect of textiles. At first I studied accountancy. But I was fed up after a year. It was all figures, and I am more interested in people and relationships. Then my family said, 'Why don't you take up textiles?' You know, here in Hong Kong, family is important. Since my elder brother has a Ph.D. in textiles from Leeds and he is now in charge of the production side of our mill, I thought I had better study something different. So I chose textile management.

There are exceptions of course. The Tang family owning one of the mills deviates in an interesting way from the pattern. Three successive generations had graduated from the Massachussetts Institute of Technology, alternating in management and technological studies. The late Mr Tang senior obtained a degree in industrial management at MIT in 1923. His son received his bachelor's degree in chemical engineering in 1949. Then his grandson graduated in 1973, again in industrial management.[106]

On the whole, the Shanghai spinners acquired their managerial know-how through direct experience. Since many of the mills are family owned (to be discussed in Chapter 6), these entrepreneurs typically assumed responsible positions in the mills at a young age.

They had a long time to acquire administrative skills before they took over the top positions. Family tradition as well as their early socialization into the managerial role had prepared them for the task of disciplining a large work force. By contrast, several of the Chaozhou spinners complained that running a mill was exasperating. They were annoyed by the constant petty problems created by the workers. The managing director of Mill 8, for example, said that he was more and more drawn into the real estate business because he could make more money by dealing with just a handful of people. Such complaints were rarely heard among the Shanghai spinners.

With their accumulated experience, the Shanghai industrialists brought with them an organizational blueprint which was more or less uniformly adopted by the local spinning mills. A textile company usually had an administrative and sales office situated in central business districts. The production plant itself was separately located in some outlying areas of Hong Kong, mainly in the Tsuen Wan area.[107] The basic organizational format of these textile enterprises is shown in Fig. 3.1.

The Shanghai spinners were also quite effective in instituting authority and exerting control over their workers. They evidently realized the usefulness of bureaucracy and the need to maintain social distance in erecting an authority structure. On this point, the critical comments about his Shanghainese competitors made by the Chaozhou director of the newly-established Mill 9 are revealing:

Many of them are very capable and experienced. They did make a contribution in the past. But they are rigid and stick too closely to convention. They have very strict hierarchies. The director is of course very aloof. It is all right if he seldom goes to the mill. But even the mill manager is supposed to be a big shot. Nowadays you have to mix well with the workers and to be more egalitarian. Times have changed.

Without participant observation, I cannot establish whether this is an accurate description of the style of the Shanghai spinners. If it is, it will obviously entail problems such as the communication of dissatisfaction from the workers to the management. Most of the mills had a dual channel of voicing grievances which tended to reinforce the hierarchy. Under normal circumstances, workers had to complain to their immediate superiors. Should this fail, they could go directly to the managing director. As most of the respondents admitted, the latter recourse was seldom used. But such a centraliz-

Fig. 3.1 Organizational Chart of a Spinning Mill

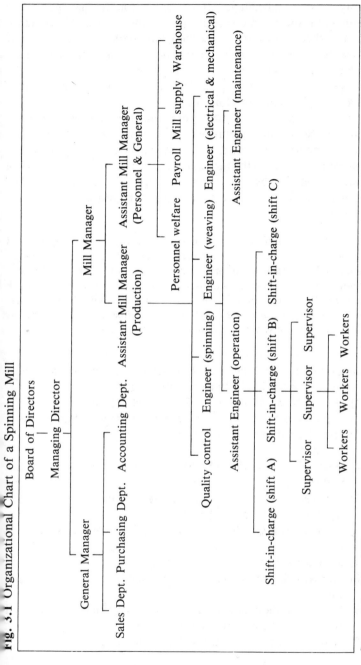

Source: Interviews, 1978.

ed style had its advantages. It was easier for the management to command respect and create obedience among their subordinates. The fact that the directors and senior staff spoke a different dialect probably helped in keeping some social distance from ordinary workers. This might be one of the reasons that most of the Shanghai spinners had not picked up much of the Cantonese dialect after nearly 30 years in Hong Kong.

In order to maintain a stable work force for continuous production, the Shanghai entrepreneurs also employed a paternalistic mode of control embodied in the system of rewards provided in their mills. They were the first group of Chinese employers in Hong Kong to confer substantial fringe benefits on their workers. The Hong Kong Cotton Spinners' Association recorded their achievement with pride:

It was in the days of the [Spinners'] Club that the spinners developed ahead of other industries in terms of industrial wages. The practice was started for all mills to grant a year-end extra payment to workers equal to one month's pay or an amount in proportion to the number of days of work under employment in the calendar year in question. With little modification and to the general satisfaction of the work force, this undertaking has continued to be observed uniformly by all spinning mills to the present day.[108]

Besides the Lunar New Year bonus, the manual workers also received the following welfare benefits in 1977:
  (1) cost of living allowance of HK$2 to HK$4 per day;
  (2) overtime payment at 150 to 200 per cent of ordinary rate;
  (3) attendance bonus of three to six days' pay per month without absence;
  (4) shift allowance of HK$1.10 to HK$8.40 for each rotating night shift;
  (5) long service bonus to those recruited before 1972 after working for more than two years;
  (6) food allowance of 30 cents to HK$5 per day or free/subsidized meals in factory canteens;
  (7) annual paid holidays of ten days;
  (8) annual sick leave of 12 to 36 days paid at two-thirds of daily rate;
  (9) free accommodation in dormitories for single and married workers in most of the mills;
  (10) free transport provided for those not living in dormitories;

(11) workers' compensation and death gratuity;

(12) free medical care, mostly by mill doctors and nurses;

(13) recreational activities, mainly in the form of outings during holidays.[109]

Within this package, only the annual paid holidays were statutory. The remaining benefits were given by the mill owners without government legislation. The motivation underlying this seemingly enlightened practice was two-fold. The first was based on economic calculations. The mill owners seldom gave more than was necessary to achieve their purpose of continuous production. In the late 1940s when labour was plentiful in Hong Kong, they withheld some benefits which they had provided in Shanghai. Instead of a ten-hour work shift normal to Shanghai, they instituted a twelve-hour shift. The Lunar New Year bonus was reduced from the norm of 40 days' pay in Shanghai to a graduated scale ranging from 12 to 29 days' wages.[110]

But in the early 1970s the situation changed. Labour shortages and high turnover led some mills to introduce a long service bonus after negotiating with one of the textile workers' unions. In a move apparently designed to curb inter-mill competition, the Cotton Spinners' Association passed a motion to stop this type of bonus for workers recruited after 1972. Then when business was poor during the depression of 1974, some mills repealed the whole scheme altogether to the dismay of the union concerned.[111]

The careful weighing of costs and benefits can be further illustrated by the provision of free accommodation in dormitories. At the beginning, this provision was created in response to the unstable labour supply in Shanghai during the initial stage of industrialization. In order to attract people, especially young women, from the nearby rural areas to work in the mills, it was essential to guarantee that they would have a place to live in the unfamiliar urban environment. As these new workers were unaccustomed to factory employment, residence in dormitories adjacent to the mills also allowed the management to uphold discipline and to eliminate absenteeism and unpunctuality. Similar economic advantages appealed to these mill owners when they came to Hong Kong. The only difference was that the rural-urban flow of workers was reversed. Owing to the scarcity of land, the mills had to be established in outlying regions. As urban rents were high, free accommodation was a strong inducement to employees from the urban areas.

In addition to economic considerations, cultural factors were involved. The ideal image of the family was often invoked by the respondents when they discussed labour-management relationships. They appeared to feel like family heads who should care for and look after those in their employ. For example, the manager of Mill 26 described his managing director as a stern man who made all the major decisions. Few benefits were laid down in writing. But when the employees had difficulties and approached him for help, he was said to be considerate and generous. This was the way a Chinese father was supposed to behave. To substantiate this point, let us return to the dormitories provided by the mill owners.

Workers living in these dormitories were subject to numerous rules and regulations. Life there was highly regimented, reflecting a moralistic and protective attitude adopted by the management. Single workers were segregated by sex and visitors of the opposite sex were prohibited. Lights were turned off and doors closed at fixed hours at night. Gambling was forbidden. In Shanghai, these regulations had provoked the escape of some female workers while the wardens were asleep; and in Hong Kong, there were conflicts between labour and management over the dismissal of workers for alleged gambling in the dormitory.[112] Just as parents would demand propriety from their children, these entrepreneurs had apparently appointed themselves as the custodians of their employees' morality.

The industrialists dispensed fringe benefits as favours, not as the entitlement of the workers. Such a form of paternalism has the intent of inducing a sense of obligation among the subordinates and inhibiting the growth of class consciousness. The spinners were very careful to prevent the emergence of a strong trade union movement. In most cases of industrial strife involving spinning mills, conflicts were usually sparked off by the dismissal of some workers. In the course of expressing support for their peers who had lost their jobs, other workers would take the opportunity to raise demands over conditions of employment. After brief confrontations, the management normally met some of the demands for higher wages or additional benefits. As an officer in the Labour Department of the Hong Kong government observed, the owners were very concerned about 'face' and their public image. Yet typically, they would not reinstate dismissed workers. They guarded very closely their power to dismiss. Their concern with managerial prerogatives made them unenthusiastic about the idea of joint consultation which was actively promoted by the Labour

Department in the late 1960s. The tenor of their reaction was that they did not wish to nurture labour organizers. The following are some extracts from the reports of labour officials after their promotion visits to the mills:

all along, the employer/employee relationship has been very cordial; the management feared that any change to the status quo might upset such harmony.

Management fears that this would provide chances for workers to group together.

The management had in fact put the idea on trial several years ago but was disappointed to learn that workers [were] reluctant to elect representatives among themselves. Mr Wang (the mill manager) attributed this to the irresponsible behaviour of workers and their high turnover.[113]

A few of the mills which were conscious of the benefits of greater worker participation did introduce regular meetings between labour and management. But the idea of workers' representatives was not encouraged as the report on the 'successful' case of Mill 5 shows. Weekly 'symposia' were held in that mill, chaired by the section head and attended by all the staff as well as 10 per cent of the workers of the section. Minutes were 'kept but not circulated'. Workers were provided with an end of year report on the work of each symposium. The labour officer noted in his visit that workers participated in these meetings by turns and no representatives were elected:

Representatives of workers at the symposia by rotation is assessed by the management as the most suitable form of representation as it overrides factional interests and overcomes the possibility of having the dominant political faction outnumbering the less dominant one in the number of representatives (this may come about if representation is by election). Rotation also helps to educate the workers about the idea of joint consultation by providing actual participation.[114]

Marketing Resources

While the shortage of capital was seldom mentioned by the Shanghai spinners as an initial obstacle to their enterprise in Hong Kong, marketing was considered a hurdle. The managing director of Mill 14 stressed that sales were the main difficulty at the beginning. 'We had not opened up marketing outlets then', he said. 'Now it is secured. We export 60 per cent of our yarn and sell the remaining 40 per cent locally.' A director of Mill 1 emphasized repeatedly the importance of this aspect of the business. 'It requires "touch"', he asserted. 'Either you have it or you haven't. You cannot acquire the technique of sales and marketing through books. That's why you must join a good firm to bring you up.' Buyers were, therefore, carefully cultivated and shielded from competitors. The chief executives usually travelled in person to look for potential markets and to negotiate face to face with their clients.[115] Several managing directors were unavailable for interview because they were away from Hong Kong on business. They seemed to place a high premium on forging personal ties with the buyers. The 'stealing' of buyers was a major problem for some mills. When I asked the director of Mill 10 about the criteria he would use to consider the promotion of an executive, he gave me an unexpected answer:

The most important one is family background. We had two or three bad experiences of people from wealthy families who later became our competitors. It is especially serious with sales. They left after building up contacts with our buyers, so they could become textile traders earning 1 or 2 per cent commission.

Marketing outlets were such closely guarded secrets that I can only infer from fragmentary information how they were established. The educational background of the spinners appeared to have provided them with a valuable social network for making business contacts as well as for gathering marketing information. Graduates of the missionary colleges in China had formed their own alumni association in Hong Kong. The 15 or so alumni associations had jointly organized an overarching body called the Chinese Christian Universities' Alumni Association with rotating chairmanship from the member associations. A Cantonese member of one of these alumni associations said with distaste that his organization had been turned into a very 'commercial' establishment. 'Those Shanghainese who came to Hong Kong', he said, 'found their first footing in the association and began looking for business, especially in insurance, and advertising their ventures.'

Most of the spinners probably did not have to resort to such direct tactics. But it is likely that these alumni communities containing a number of fellow regionals were able to provide a convenient framework for them to reach out to prospective customers. The fact that these missionary colleges had been sponsored by

American religious bodies and were administered by American staff might have facilitated the entry of their graduates into the valuable United States market in the mid-1950s. Those who had attended American or British universities were able to form direct social links with these countries. The 1973 press release by the Massachusetts Institute of Technology on its dedicating a students' hall of residence to the memory of the late Mr P. Y. Tang in recognition of his financial support contained hints of the presence of an old-boy network. Mr Tang was referred to as 'a M.I.T. alumnus in the Class of 1923' and there was a comment that the dedication ceremony was 'coincident with the 50th reunion of Mr Tang's class.'[116] It would be interesting to know how helpful these classmates had been to his business.

It is worth noting that none of the respondents or their children was a graduate of the local Hong Kong universities. Their subsequently high level of educational attainment precludes the possibility that they were unable to gain admission. Most likely they did not apply, one reason being that the potential benefits of friendship made in local universities were probably too small. The children of spinning families were usually sent to the United States and Britain which were principal markets for Hong Kong textiles. The conscious policy of diversifying human capital investment was quite explicit in the family history of Liu Hong-sheng, a Shanghai industrialist popularly known in modern China as the 'king of matches'. After an interview with Liu's son, a reporter wrote:

He understood very well that China was a weak country. Nobody could tell which foreign country would eventually dominate China [in the early part of this century]. Mr Lieu [Liu] Sr. was a smart man. He sent three of his sons and one daughter to England to study, and three other sons and another daughter to the U.S. As for his remaining two sons and one daughter, he assigned them to Japan. He was satisfied that his plan was invulnerable and complete. No matter which foreign power became the overlord in China, the Lieu family would have some relations with it well established beforehand.[117]

Though Liu's explicit aim was to obtain political insurance, his children's connections in foreign countries must also have been useful in marketing.

Another network that the Shanghai spinners could rely on was that of their business contacts with Western, mostly British, firms in Shanghai engaged in the import and export trade. The spinners needed their services in the ordering of textile machinery and raw cotton, and the disposal of yarn and cotton cloths. These firms were not registered under Chinese company law because they enjoyed extraterritorial privileges in the treaty ports. In Hong Kong they were mostly incorporated as 'China companies' or 'Hong Kong China companies', indicating that their operations were mainly conducted in the Republic of China.[118] When American and British extraterritorial rights were abolished in 1943, these companies found themselves in a difficult legal position. Two courses of action were open to them. They could either transfer their businesses to the United Kingdom and the British Dominions, or they could move to Hong Kong. By 1946 about 200 of these China companies had become Hong Kong-registered concerns with headquarters in the colony. They preceded the arrival of the Shanghai entrepreneurs, who, when the latter came, first sought assistance from firms such as China Engineers Ltd. This phenomenon will be discussed further in Chapter 5.

The last marketing asset of the Shanghai industrialists is more elusive. They give an impression of being superior in their 'presentation of self' than their Cantonese counterparts. In their reception areas for visitors, they had usually successfully created a comfortable, cosmopolitan — and yet also Chinese — atmosphere. These areas were either the spacious offices of the managing directors or separate well-furnished rooms. I quote from my field notes on Mill 3:

The reception room is plush. On the wall facing the entrance hangs a black and white portrait photo of the president of the company. Beneath the portrait is a rosewood side-board on the top of which stand four decorative items. On either end is a framed colour photograph. The one to the left shows the president presenting prizes after a tennis match between the members of the Hong Kong Cotton Spinners' Association and the Hong Kong and Shanghai Banking Corporation. The one to the right has the president leading his winning horse at the end of a race in 1972. In between the photographs are a silver plate presented by the staff when the president was made a Justice of the Peace, and a delicately crafted clock. In the centre of the room with wall-to-wall carpet is a medium-sized round table with a green marble top. This is surrounded by six chairs with orange-gold velvet upholstery. One of the walls is decorated with a Chinese landscape painting and several Chinese fan drawings.

Of course, not all of the reception areas are so impressive. But carpets, fine furniture, and Chinese paintings are quite common.

In comparison, those in Chaozhou- or Cantonese-owned companies are normally small and strictly functional. The directors' office of Mill 33, for instance, is on the ground floor of the factory building. In it are crowded three grey steel desks of the same make as those in the general office outside. Apparently the three directors were using the same room. There were also a low coffee table and a simple sofa. The only indications of the status of the occupants were two high-backed directors' chairs and a box of cigars on the coffee table. The walls were devoid of decorations except for a row of twelve framed photographs of ten young men and two young women in academic dress, all members of the directors' families.

In addition, the Shanghainese are also better dressed and groomed. My interviews took place in hot summer weather, but most of the Shanghainese respondents were in suit and tie. The Cantonese and Chaozhou spinners, however, were typically casually dressed in their shirt sleeves and without ties. It may be no coincidence that Shanghai tailors and barbers enjoy a high reputation in Hong Kong, indicating the keen concern for outward appearance among those from Shanghai.

The above examination of the industrial skills and resources of the Shanghai entrepreneurs demonstrates that they were well-equipped as textile industrialists when they arrived in Hong Kong. They brought with them industrial capital in the form of new and modern machinery. Technically, they were highly qualified. As a group, they had considerable experience in the management of large factories, and they had evolved their own approach in handling labour. They were very alert in seizing and protecting marketing opportunities. They diverged most distinctly from their Cantonese and Chaozhou counterparts in three respects. They were able to mobilize the support of Hong Kong British banks by activating social links in their regional network; they had the capacity to plan for future manpower needs by attaching importance to the training of technicians; and they displayed a cultivated style in the presentation of self which probably helped them in promoting sales and securing business.

But their superiority in skills should not be over-emphasized. They were similar to non-Shanghainese industrialists in the reluctance to use the stock-market to raise capital, as well as in the low priority they gave to their own formal managerial training. I have also shown that the relevant techniques in financing, production, management, and marketing were by no means absent in the repertoire of Cantonese, Chaozhou and other Chinese entrepreneurs in Hong Kong. Although these individuals might lag behind the Shanghainese at first, there is nothing inherent in the nature of those skills to prevent their being rapidly acquired. Thus, the Shanghainese could not maintain their dominant position in the cotton spinning industry by relying on skills alone. It is possible, therefore, that the managerial attitudes and norms upheld by the Shanghai spinners might have given them an added advantage over their competitors, and this possibility will be examined in detail in the next chapter.

4 Business Ideology

ETHNIC groups, write Glazer and Moynihan, 'bring different norms to bear on common circumstances with consequent different levels of success — hence *group* differences in status'.[1] Did the Shanghainese have a particular set of norms and attitudes about their occupational activities? How did these differ ideologically, if at all, from those of other Chinese entrepreneurs of dissimilar regional backgrounds? Did their norms and attitudes constitute an asset in industrial competition to help them triumph over competitors?

Since Chinese business ideology is largely an uncharted field, it is very difficult to answer these questions.[2] The dearth of systematic studies undoubtedly reflects the weakness of the Chinese bourgeoisie.[3] The structural supremacy of the polity in Chinese society has obviously drawn scholarly attention mainly to the ideas of political actors.

The neglect of business ideology also exists in other societies in various degrees. As Reinhard Bendix has noted, 'The whole development of industrialization has been accompanied by an intellectual rejection of [managerial] ideologies as unworthy of consideration'.[4] This rejection is apparently based on the assumption that the 'real' motives and orientations of the bourgeoisie are already known. Karl Marx's depiction of the bourgeois mentality has such a finality that it seems superfluous to investigate further:

The bourgeoisie, wherever it has got the upper hand, has put an end to all feudal, patriarchal, idyllic relations. It has pitilessly torn asunder the motley feudal ties that bound man to his 'natural superiors', and left no other nexus between man and man than naked self-interest, than callous 'cash payment'. It has drawn the most heavenly ecstasies of religious fervour, of chivalrous enthusiasm, of philistine sentimentalism, in the icy water of egotistical calculation.[5]

If the quintessence of the bourgeoisie's conduct is 'naked, shameless, direct, brutal exploitation',[6] then it follows that its utterances do not deserve serious attention.

However, this quintessence should not simply be assumed. Whether businessmen are more liable to distort 'reality' so as to camouflage their self-interest than politicians or intellectuals is a matter to be verified empirically. Advances in the sociological study of ideologies, mainly in the political realm, have led to the realization that the relationship between attitude and behaviour is highly complex. Idea and action are seldom completely divorced; neither are they simply translated from one to the other. There is now general agreement that attitudes entail behavioural consequences, and that an ideology can serve diverse functions. 'It is at once a method of self-reassurance, an instrument of persuasion, and a legitimacy of authority.'[7] Therefore, on a macroscopic level, business ideology 'may be considered a symptom of changing class relations and hence as a clue to an understanding of industrial societies'.[8] On a microscopic level, close scrutiny of this kind of ideology may yield a fuller understanding of the social role of industrialists.

In this study, 'forced choice' questionnaire items were used to assess the attitudes of the cotton spinners. Some of the items were developed by Theo Nichols in his study of British businessmen,[9] and have been borrowed for comparative purposes. As Nichols has restricted his attention to one aspect of business ideology, namely the businessmen's conception of social responsibility, other items have been added to cover a broader range of themes.

The forced choice method differs from two other major approaches. The research carried out by Bendix represents the historical cross-cultural approach.[10] It is legitimate for him to eschew the use of questionnaires as he is primarily concerned with what Karl Mannheim calls the 'total conception of ideology'.[11] He wants to assess the ethos of an entire age and society with special reference to the authority relationship between employers and workers. The emphasis is on the ideology *about* industrial activities, not the ideology *of* industrialists. He considers the ideas of theorists who were not businessmen themselves as he is concerned with broad ideological drifts, not individual or group beliefs.

The second approach, which may be called an élitist approach, is closer to the forced choice method in that both are dealing with 'particular conceptions of ideology' or the attitudes of a specific sector in society.[12] Beyond this similarity, however, the élitist approach has its focus on the public statements of prominent businessmen. The contents of the speeches or writings of the 'industrial statesmen' are analysed with varying degrees of rigour. Such a focus has several blind spots. It is not attuned to privately held opinions; it disregards the views of the 'silent majority'; and it tends to neglect unstated assumptions.

The forced choice method, however, is more sensitive to these issues. It is also more specific and representative in its coverage, and the responses can be quantified with less ambiguity. It has, nevertheless, other limitations. The main one is that the themes and 'ideological choices' are imposed on the respondents so that their salience to the businessmen is problematic. With these features of the forced choice method in mind, we will examine the response patterns of the cotton spinners in relation to the following themes — social responsibility; the relationship between government and business; industrial harmony and conflict; competition and co-operation; autonomy and self-employment; and profit-sharing.

Social Responsibility

The emergence of a business doctrine of social responsibility is sometimes thought to be related to the separation of ownership and control in industrial societies.[13] Theorists of this persuasion argue that such a separation has given birth to a new class of professional manager-directors. Just as their relationship to industrial capital is said to differ from that of the traditional owner-directors, so their business outlook tends to be dissimilar. They are presumed to be less concerned with maximizing profits for their companies and are more prepared to adopt the broader interests of the public good and collective welfare.

If the theory is sound, we should expect to find fewer adherents to the ideology of social responsibility among Hong Kong Chinese industrialists than among their Western counterparts because of a much lower degree of dissociation between ownership and control in the colony. As they were mostly owner-directors, the Hong Kong cotton spinners might have adopted the classical *laissez-faire* position. After all, they were living in an environment which was regarded as conducive to this classical ideology. One observer describes Hong Kong as 'John Stuart Mill's Other Island', while another maintains that '[free] competition provides local industries with a Darwinian test of their ability to survive.'[14] The economic jungle once existed in Chinese coastal cities, where, in Fei Xiao-tong's view, the 'morally unstable' elements in Chinese society congregated to become the early Chinese bourgeoisie:

to such ports a special type of Chinese was attracted. They are known as *compradors*...They are unscrupulous, pecuniary, individualistic, and agnostic, not only in religion but in cultural values. Treaty ports are ultra-urban. They are a land where the acquisition of wealth is the sole motive, devoid of tradition and culture...As their children grow up, they give them modern education and send them abroad to attend Western universities. From this group a new class is formed...But, being reared in a cosmopolitan community, they are fundamentally hybrids. In them are [sic] manifest the comprador characteristic of social irresponsibility.[15]

As we have seen in the last two chapters, some of the offspring of this bourgeoisie had migrated to Hong Kong. Their moral rectitude had apparently not been strengthened.[16]

Two hypotheses about the social ethics of the Shanghai industrialists have thus emerged. First, proportionally fewer of them would subscribe to the doctrine of social responsibility than their Western counterparts. Second, they were mostly economic men of the classical *laissez-faire* mould. In order to test these hypotheses, I used a modified version of the forced choice questionnaire developed by Nichols.[17] Nichols assumes the existence of three ideological positions with reference to the social ethics of business. Other than the social responsibility and *laissez-faire* positions, he posits a third orientation that justifies business decisions in terms of the long range interests of the company. He chooses four areas of concern — redundancy provision for workers; the social purpose of business; community participation for the businessmen; and the workers' right to company information. In each area, three statements are formulated to represent the various ideological standpoints. The respondent is asked to select one statement among the three which is closest to his own beliefs. His choice is then taken to indicate whether he is predisposed to a *laissez-faire*, long-term company interest, or social responsibility stance.[18]

I have retained Nichols' areas of concern, except for the group of statements on the workers' right to company information on the grounds that it is too narrowly confined to internal company policy which is not a salient issue in Hong Kong industry. In its place, I substituted a group of statements on political participation for businessmen which provides a clearer ideological contrast. The statements representing the three ideological positions are then as follows:

1. Laissez-faire

(a) Protecting workers against unemployment is not part of management's responsibility. A firm has little control over market fluctuations. During recessions, it is necessary to lay off workers to ensure economic viability of the company.

(b) A firm exists for one purpose only: to make a profit. Managers should not, and cannot, be concerned with social and moral consequences. If they were, the firm's economic position could suffer which would be bad for the economy as well.

(c) An industrialist has enough work to do without becoming a leading figure in the community. If he wishes to do so, that is his affair. But as a manager his place is in the firm.

(d) Politics is politics and business is business. Industrialists should not get involved in political affairs.

2. Long-range Interests

(a) An employee will work better if he has job security. It is therefore in the long-term interest of the company to avoid laying off workers during economic recessions.

(b) Profit is the one absolute in business and it is to the community's benefit that this be so. But in the interest of long-term survival, every firm must gain the sympathetic understanding and co-operation of other members of society.

(c) For the good of the enterprise, industrialists should convince the public that they are concerned citizens contributing actively to the welfare of the society. Community service and public speeches are powerful forms of public relations, and directors should accept invitations to write and speak on public platforms, and to serve on voluntary bodies in the community.

(d) Political decisions inevitably affect industry. Industrialists should have their own representatives to deal with the government and to protect their interests.

3. Social Responsibility

(a) Unemployment will create a lot of social problems. It is not socially or morally responsible for management to use

Table 4.1. Attitude to Social Responsibility among Hong Kong Spinners and British Industrialists

	Cotton Spinners		British Industrialists	
Ideological Set	Choices	%	Choices	%
Laissez-faire	22	16	27	10
Long-range interest	78	57	149	57
Social responsibility	37	27	84	32
No response	3			
Total	140*	100	260	100**

Notes: *   Five of the respondents had not answered this section. Thus the total number of choices are those of 35 respondents only.
   ** Not exactly 100 due to rounding.
Source: Nichols, *Ownership*, Table 14.1, p.169; interviews, 1978.

the laying off of workers as a means of coping with economic recessions.

(b) A business conducted solely for monetary gain is not ethical. A firm is part of society and should further the well-being of the whole community. The management has a responsibility for the welfare of its shareholders, employees, customers, as well as the society at large.

(c) Every industry has a social responsibility to the community. It is the duty of senior executives to fulfil this by contributing their skills and knowledge to public life.

(d) Politics is the concern of every member of society, and industrialists should participate actively in political discussions.

The general ideological orientation of the respondents can be measured by the total distribution of their choices among the three ideological clusters. As Table 4.1 shows, most of the cotton spinners did not regard themselves as pure economic men. They did not advocate unrestrained competition or the single-minded pursuit of profit. As in Nichols' sample of British industrialists,[19] their preoccupation was the long-term benefits of their enterprises. This tendency emerges more clearly if we consider the pattern of non-

Table 4.2. Ideological Preferences of Cotton Spinners by Areas of Concern (%)

Ideological Set	Redundancy	Purpose	Community	Politics
Laissez-faire	9	6	35	9
Interest	77	60	15	75
Responsibility	14	34	50	16
Total	100	100	100	100

Source: Interviews, 1978.

selection. Only one respondent out of 35 failed to choose any of the statements representing long-range interest, while the corresponding numbers for social responsibility and *laissez-faire* statements were ten and 16 respectively.

But these are only gross distributions of ideological choices. It is possible that the attitudinal responses were made haphazardly and without individual consistencies. In other words, ideological positions in the sense of organized patterns of attitudes might not exist. To settle this point, the data can be rearranged in two ways. We can assess the consistency of choice across the four areas of concern. In Table 4.2, it is shown that there are no significant variations across these areas except on the topic of community participation. The same deviation occurs in Nichol's findings. Only 22 per cent of his sample chose the long-term interest item on community participation.[20] One of my respondents, the managing director of Mill 17, provided the explanation for this anomaly. He considered the item in question and said, 'Some people are eloquent and can give a powerful speech without much preparation. I am not. Not that I am unwilling to do it; I can't do it.' He was referring to the particular activity of speech-making, and not to the necessity of promoting public relations for the interests of his company. The 'double barrel' or even 'multiple barrel' nature of the items is an inherent technical difficulty of the forced choice method, so that it is essential to ask the respondents to explain their choices. In future replications, the group of statements on community participation should be changed so that the respondents' attention is not diverted to the making of speeches.

Table 4.3. Individual Consistencies in the Ideological Preferences of the Spinners

Ideological Set	4 Choices in One Set	3 Choices in One Set
Laissez-faire	0	0
Interest	2	13
Responsibility	1	2
Actual no. of consistencies	3	15
Possible no. of consistencies	33*	34*

Notes: * One of the 35 respondents only reacted to two groups of statements, while another reacted to three groups.

Source: Interviews, 1978.

The second way to rearrange the data is to look at consistencies in individual sets of responses. As expected, consistencies in the form of all four choices falling in one ideological set were rare. Nevertheless, nearly half of the respondents made three choices in one set, showing that the attitudinal items were regarded as related by the respondents (see Table 4.3).

It is thus clear that the second hypothesis that Hong Kong industrialists are profit-seeking entrepreneurs unfettered by social ethical considerations is not the self-image of the spinners. But how about the first hypothesis that Hong Kong industrialists are less likely to uphold the idea of social responsibility than Western businessmen? Again, a comparison with Nichols' findings is instructive. For the sake of comparability, I shall follow his classification scheme in placing businessmen into ideological categories. In view of the highly skewed distribution of choices, he decided to adopt less stringent criteria to include respondents in the social responsibility and *laissez-faire* categories. To qualify for the long-range interest category, an individual must choose either all four interest items or three interest items with one from the social responsibility set. For the social responsibility category, individuals who chose either three responsibility items with one interest item, or two responsibility and two interest items are included. Even more lax is the *laissez-faire* category which includes all those who chose one or more of the *laissez-faire* items.[21] Therefore Table 4.4 should be in-

Table 4.4. Hong Kong Spinners and British Industrialists by Ideological Categories

Ideological Category	Cotton Spinners		British Industrialists	
	No.	%	No.	%
Laissez-faire	19	56	16	25
Interest	9	26	23	35
Responsibility	6	18	26	60
Total	34*	100	65	100

Note: * One respondent responded to only two groups of statements and cannot be placed in any of these categories.

Source: Nichols, *Ownership*, Table 16.1, p.191; interviews, 1978.

terpreted with an awareness that the categories do not constitute 'pure' types.

The contrast revealed in Table 4.4 is striking. While businessmen advocating social responsibility formed the largest contingent in Nichols' sample, they were the smallest group among the Hong Kong spinners. Since Nichols has found that 'the "professional manager" is more inclined to find statements about business social responsibility attractive',[22] the relative lack of enthusiasm for the social responsibility stance among the cotton spinners is probably an indication of the low degree of managerial professionalism in Hong Kong's textile industry.

It is worth noting that many of the industrialists did not see a clear distinction between long-range interests and social responsibility items.[23] This is most apparent on the topic of the social purpose of business. Five of my respondents commented that the statement 'A business conducted solely for monetary gain is not ethical' and the statement 'Profit is the one absolute in business and it is to the community's benefit that this be so' were 'more or less the same'. There is little doubt that this perceived similarity between the two positions is a reflection of the spinners' effort to reduce 'cognitive dissonance'. In order to be effective businessmen, they had to convince themselves at least that their work activities were compatible with social ethics. But there seems to be more to this perceived similarity. I believe it also sheds light on the normative framework of the entrepreneurs. Their remarks made it clear that their behavioural decisions were not derived from abstract moral principles. The director of Mill 8 was the most forthright in his reaction to the statements on the social purpose of business:

We cannot afford such talk of morality and ethics. When we lose money, will the government refund us? Everybody wants to make a profit. There is no such thing as mutual benefit. If you advocate that and lose money, you will only be laughed at as a fool.

Pragmatism could, however, lead them to choose the social responsibility items. The managing director of Mill 19 did so on the subject of the social purpose of business with a practical justification: 'The shareholders must be cared for. Otherwise they would not continue to invest'. Similarly, on the question of redundancy, the chairman of Mill 17 said:

There is no unemployment in Hong Kong's textile industry, so these statements do not really apply. But in principle, I try not to lay off workers. 'Because of social and moral reasons', yes, we all say that in public. But more importantly, for practical economic reasons it is also better not to lay them off. Since spinning is cyclical, if you lay off your workers during a depression, they will leave you. They are skilful workers, and you should never lose them. Otherwise during an upturn, you will have to train your workers again. In garment-making, if you don't have work tomorrow, you can tell your workers, 'You don't have to come tomorrow'. In spinning, if we do not work tomorrow, we do not fire them. We would pay them perhaps half of their salaries and tell them not to come. It would also be fair to them as they do not do any work.

This concern for long-term economic interests was rooted in a strong sense of vocation. The same respondent declared in a different context, 'my whole career is in textiles. I don't want to lose my mill'. It is this commitment that led to industrial policies that appeared akin to the social responsibility orientation. The reason that the spinners provided dormitories for the workers, protected them against redundancy, took heed of public opinion was not because these measures were intrinsically right, but because these would be to their advantage in the long run.

It would be naïve to assume that long-range business interest and social responsibility can always be reconciled. There is obviously a limit to the feasibility of synchronizing the two. The degree of incompatibility will vary according to how social responsibility is collectively defined. In other words, the nature of the political system in which industry has to operate is relevant.

Ideal Political Environment

Because of the political set-up and the co-existence of Chinese Communist and Nationalist organizations in Hong Kong, political issues concerning colonialism and communism were regarded as sensitive matters by many inhabitants. Sometimes, discussions of these topics were avoided in public. One of my respondents glanced at the group of statements on the relation between politics and business and simply refused to make a choice. 'Politics — no, I won't even look at them. No politics.'

In order not to risk a massive lack of response, I asked an open-ended question on their conception of the ideal political environment for industry. Their replies reaffirmed the findings on their attitude towards social responsibility. A number of them championed the classical capitalist vision of free enterprise. The answer of the director of Mill 1 was illustrative. 'No social welfare for able-bodied persons', he said. 'Welfare for the handicapped and the old only. Lower the tax. We don't want government help or government intervention. No government interference — that would be utopia.'

But he was in the minority. Most spinners entertained an impossible dream — government support without concomitant control. They criticized the Hong Kong government on three policy areas which threatened their operations, namely the rise in land values, the 'hurried' introduction of labour legislation, and the administration's refusal to impose import control on foreign textile products. The Korean and Taiwanese governments were often mentioned as examples of political systems supportive to industry. But simultaneously, the spinners were aware of the twin evils of red tape and corruption which often accompanied government subsidies. Their real desire appeared to be for the government to provide the 'infrastructure' and leave them a free hand to run their business.[24] As the managing director of Mill 12 said:

The more government assistance the better. But this is difficult to realize. When I say help, it is not necessarily with money. To control inflation is a form of assistance. To regulate finance and prices. Now the government does not know what changes will be introduced tomorrow. If there was a definite policy, then we would know what to expect.

The tone and omissions were as important as the actual content of their answers. Their opinions were strongly seasoned with resignation and cynicism. The director of Mill 33 said, 'I don't want to be dyed red or white [meaning to side with either the political left or right]. There is nothing I can do about these political matters'. This view was amplified by the director of Mill 32 who told me:

Mr Wong, all these statements are against the government. No comment. You see, there is no use participating. It is only superficial democracy. All are yes men. The more 'yes' you say, the more honours you get. So all these statements are theoretical; they cannot be done in practice. For example, take the setting up of the Cotton Commodity Exchange. We are all in opposition, but the government wants to have it. Just another gambling house!

Their professed powerlessness did not, of course, reflect the reality. The spinners had strong political muscles as they provided employment on a large scale. When conflicts of interests did occur, they could force the government to yield. The dispute over the re-evaluation of the value of industrial land on 'Crown lease' in the early 1970s illustrates this well. Immediately after the Second World War (see Chapter 2), the Hong Kong government provided land to industry at cheap prices for a period of about 20 years as an inducement to investors. When the original lease expired, the industrialists had to pay the market price for their land. But when the renewal became imminent in 1971, the cotton spinners joined force with 26 industrial bodies to oppose the reassessment of industrial land value. They also obtained the support of all the unofficial members in the Legislative Council. Even though the government maintained that the legality and validity of the re-evaluation was incontestable, it finally agreed to modify the statutes in June 1973 after a protracted confrontation.[25]

Yet in spite of their substantial political power, the spinners expressed a passive attitude to politics. Their views were couched in a common format: 'It would be good if the government would do this and that. But we know it will not happen.' Even the most prominent public figure among them, the chairman of Mill 22, said that he took up unofficial positions in the government because he was invited to do so and he 'hated to say no'. They were hardly Marx's revolutionary bourgeoisie who 'creates a world after its own image'.[26] They lacked the confidence and self-righteousness of the American businessmen at the turn of the century who could pronounce that '[the] rights and interests of the laboring men will be protected and cared for...by Christian men to whom God in his infinite wisdom has given the control of the property interests of the country'.[27]

Because of the defensive posture of the spinners, political vocabularies were conspicuous by their absence. Terms such as democracy, private property, equality, elections and so on were never mentioned. The recurrent phrase was 'peace and stability'. The theme of nationalism, so dominant among American, African, and pre-war South-east Asian Chinese businessmen, was raised by just two spinners.[28] The director of Mill 1 mentioned this to dismiss the idea. 'In Hong Kong, it is money', he replied when asked the reasons for executive turnover. 'In South Korea, you can say you are working for your country. But here?' The director of Mill 4, the only locally born spinner among my respondents, admitted to some nationalistic sentiment. He said:

I want a sense of belonging and would like Hong Kong to develop. I wish to try to create a society of my own identity, a 'country' or whatever. But we know that's impossible. I think the only realistic attitude is that as long as I am in this place, I contribute as much as possible.

The spinners managed to neutralize controversial subjects such as the Cold War and colonialism by discussing them on an instrumental level. They presented themselves as above politics. As the director of Mill 26 asserted:

Politics have little influence on the textile industry. Mainland China produces cotton, but there is no export. Taiwan is our competitor, and it has nothing to sell us. We buy cotton from the United States as well as from the USSR.[29]

On the dark side, the managing director of Mill 30 said:

Not so good [being in a colony], because in textile negotiations Hong Kong cannot participate as an independent country. Furthermore, Britain is on the other side.

The cotton spinners' political vision, therefore, was mundane, and devoid of larger designs. It was as if they were content to build castles around an oasis, weather permitting. When the storm came, they would move on to look for yet another spring. It never oc-

Table 4.5. Cotton Spinners' Attitude to Organizational Conflict

Choice	No.	%
Similar interest, no conflict	14	42
Dissent healthy and normal	19	58
Conflict harmful but unavoidable	0	0
No response	2	—
Total	35	100

Source: Interviews, 1978.

curred to them that they could perhaps harness the desert. They had not outgrown Marie-Claire Bergère's description of the outlook of the early Chinese businessmen:

The bourgeoisie, combining an atavistic distrust of politics with a philanthropic utopianism, seemed to think that it could change its own way of life without making any change in the lives of the rest of the Chinese people, and furthermore that one province could be modernized without entailing the modernization of China as a whole. In short, the bourgeoisie believed that China's revival could be achieved by non-political means, that is, by practical action which had no need of an accompanying ideology.[30]

Harmony and Conflict

How did the cotton spinners regard politics internal to their enterprises? Did they regard the company as a big family where management and labour have essentially similar interests? Or did they believe organizational conflict to be healthy and normal? Were they convinced that disruptive conflicts of interests are unavoidable in an organization?[31] Their responses to these questions are presented in Table 4.5. The most significant feature in the distribution of choices is that none of them regard disruptive conflicts as inherent in an industrial organization. Although 58 per cent of them agreed that differences of opinion and conflict were good for the company, they made a clear distinction between dissent expressed in words and in deeds. Their attitude was summed up by the managing director of Mill 19. 'Conflicts of opinion, yes,' he said, 'but conflicts of action, no.' Thus in effect, their position was not very different from those who maintained that the company was like a family and there should be no conflict, except that they did not view organizational harmony in terms of homogeneity and complete conformity. They allowed for divergences of opinion. Some of them even insisted on disagreements because they were wary of compliance among employees. The 'yes man' was a target of criticism. The managing director of Mill 19 said, 'When the entire company is made up of yes men, it will decline. It is not desirable to have complete tranquillity.' A non-owner director of Mill 24 emphasized that it was the duty of an executive to speak his mind:

If the managing director said we should go south and I thought north was the right direction, then I would explain the reasons for my belief. If ultimately he said let us go east, I should follow him eastward. The most important thing is not to be a yes man. Do not support going south just because he says so.

The fact that the 'yes man' was singled out for criticism seems to indicate that compliance among subordinates constituted a problem in their companies.

Differences of opinion, according to the spinners, must be contained and resolved before they deteriorate into actual conflict. They followed several rules to prevent dissent from getting out of hand. Steps were taken to ensure that the interests of the key decision-makers were homogeneous. As the managing director of Mill 22 told me, 'All of our executive directors are Chinese, friends. We can argue things out.' Besides ethnic and friendship ties, kinship bonds were also used to guard against irreconcilable conflicts. In Mill 17, a young director said that differences of opinion were settled by those at the top who would take the ultimate responsibility. 'I follow the advice of my uncle and my father', he said. 'My uncle has a son on the Board of Directors as well. So the four of us are of the same family. Only two other board members are outsiders.' Within this framework, the weight of an individual's opinion was graded according to his hierarchical standing. The director of Mill 24 put this best: 'If they are under me, I make the final decision. If they are senior to me, I explain my views to them. If they do not accept them, I do it their way.'

But among peers, the resolution of differences could not be so straightforward. When these occurred, most spinners did not

Table 4.6. Spinners' Attitude to Trade Unions

Choice	No.	%
Unions not needed	3	9
Workers' right to organize	5	16
Joint consultation desirable	24	75
No response	3	—
Total	35	100

Source: Interviews, 1978.

favour settlement by majority vote. The managing director of Mill 27 explained his position:

There will be hard negotiations, but we do not believe in voting. It is not a good way as it would create a split among directors. If you and I are in the minority, it is human nature for us to find faults with the majority. If we cannot compromise, we will leave it to next week. Within three or four months, we are bound to have a solution. Not everybody will be happy at the end, but at least there is no bitterness.

The specific method of reaching a compromise might vary from mill to mill, but the direct confrontation integral to the voting process was generally avoided. The emphasis was on persuasion, or as the chairman of Mill 22 expressed it, 'It is always one party educating the other.'

At this stage of the interviews, the spinners were only reacting to the general idea of dissent and conflict. To make the discussion more concrete, I raised the issue of trade unionism. They were given the following alternatives to show their preferences:
(1) there is no need for employees to form unions when management implements fair policies;
(2) it is the workers' right to organize themselves;
(3) joint consultation between management and labour is necessary for workers' opinion to be heard.
Table 4.6 indicates that two-thirds of them preferred some form of joint consultation. They gave two reasons for their preference. The first was that 'pure, independent, innocent labour unions' were not to be found in Hong Kong. This view has some factual basis. Many unions in the Colony are politically motivated and owe allegiance

either to the People's Republic of China or the government of Taiwan. In the textile industry, there are the left-wing Spinning, Weaving and Dyeing Trade Workers' General Union and the right-wing Cotton Industry Workers' General Union. Between them, in 1971, they had unionized a mere 18 per cent of the textile workers.[32] The numerical weakness and political affiliations of the unions permitted the spinners to dismiss them as a nuisance. The managing director of Mill 12 did not hide his annoyance when he told me:

> Unions are not bad. There should be real unions so that workers' opinions can be expressed. But they should be separated from politics. In Hong Kong, it is difficult. Unions are not fighting for the welfare of their members. Some years ago several union representatives came to talk to me. They were not making any demands, just stating principles. They made several suggestions about welfare provisions. I told them these were already instituted in the mill. They said this was not proper and that the suggestions should come from the unions. At present, there are two unions in our mill, and I absolutely refuse to talk to them.

The second reason was that the workers were uneducated, which implied that they could not look after their own interests. Thus the managing director of Mill 19 asserted, 'There are unions in Hong Kong, but workers' educational levels are not high enough. There should be consultations, but the workers cannot come before management, because they do not have sufficient education.' The spinners were thus bringing to bear the age-old Chinese assumption that their authority was legitimized by their superior knowledge and culture.

From the actual practice of joint consultation in the mills described in the last chapter, it is clear that there is a more fundamental albeit unstated reason for their resistance to the idea of trade unionism, which is that they did not welcome the idea of workers' representatives. This might provide a clue to understanding their rejection of organizational conflict in favour of harmony. It appears that the spinners' views on organizational dissent in general and on trade unionism in particular were derived from the belief that power structures should be unitary, and not pluralistic.[33] Since they did not accept the notion of multiple power centres and divided loyalty in an organization, they could say in the confident voice of the director of Mill 3 that 'you must be fair and without bias. If your actions are reasonable, there will be no conflict'. The chairman of Mill 17 elaborated: 'There should be no conflict. It is

Table 4.7. Spinners' Attitude to Competition and Co-operation

Choice	No.	%
Competition needed for prosperity	18	53
Competition unnecessary	2	6
Co-operation instead of competition	14	41
No response	1	—
Total	35	100

Source: Interviews, 1978.

not good for the company. In turn that means it is not good for them [the workers], and they should know it'.

Competition and Co-operation

Outside the firm, conflict assumes the form of competition. How did the spinners view the central process of capitalism? Olsen, in his opinion survey on Taiwanese school children, finds that competition is negatively valued. He concludes that the 'major connotations of competition in Taipei business culture seem to be those of excess and harm rather than those of vitality and progress'.[34] This does not reflect the attitudes of the Hong Kong cotton spinners. Over half of them (see Table 4.7) believed that competition among mills is needed to encourage people to do their best. Only two respondents considered competition unnecessary.[35] The discrepancy between Olsen's findings and my own could reflect the differences between our samples as well as the respective economic milieux. It is also possible that Olsen might have prejudiced the results with his leading statements such as 'Business firms should get together to stop "cut-throat" competition'.[36] Whatever the reasons for the difference, it is fairly certain that the Hong Kong textile industrialists had little aversion to economic competition. However, their reaction to the statement: 'Local textile mills should join together to overcome external difficulties instead of competing among themselves' is extremely interesting. Most of the respondents, irrespective of their actual choices, said that this was theoretically desirable. They saw clearly the tangible benefits o-combining their medium-sized mills to form integrated industrial organizations. It had been a long-cherished hope, said the director of Mill 32, but it was impossible to attain. He elaborated:

We have the Association, and there are thirty-three spinners averaging 20,000 spindles per mill. Each mill produces over ten varieties of products. This is very uneconomical. If we can specialize, each producing a particular type, then the cost can be lowered — sharing the same office, buying cotton together etc. During recessions, we have discussed this possibility. But once business picked up. . . [he made a scrambling gesture with his hands]

What was the main obstacle to co-operation? The managing director of Mill 25 provided the following answer:

We mill owners are all good friends even though we are competitors at the same time. We talk about technical things, comparing machines and suggesting others try out new equipment. But everybody wants to be their own boss, and all of us [our companies] are almost the same size. It is not as though there were large companies and very small ones. In Hong Kong, all the spinners founded their companies by themselves in the 1940s. We are not professional managers. If we were professionals, we could argue and come to an agreement even if our opinions differ. But as owners, if I am the founder, then my idea is *the* idea.

This view was supplemented by others' remarks such as 'there are large companies and small companies. The small ones do not want to be under others' control'; and 'thirty-three mills have thirty-three managing directors, and who will give way?' The adamant insistence on entrepreneurial independence and autonomy contributes to the stark contrast between Chinese industry and its Japanese and Western equivalents — oligopolistic groupings such as the *zaibatsu*, the cartels, and the trusts are rarely found in Chinese industry.[37]

Autonomy and Self-employment

David C. McClelland has extended his studies on achievement motivation to include the Chinese.[38] But apart from the general question of whether or not the Chinese are keen to achieve, it is important to ask specifically what goals they are striving for with what kind of cost-and-benefit calculations. Various studies on Chinese economic values and conduct point to a common feature:

Table 4.8. Spinners' Preferences for Employment Status

Choice	No.	%
Owner-manager	21	62
Senior executive	11	32
No preference	2	6
No response	6	—
Total	40	100

Source: Interviews, 1978.

self-employment is at a premium. A small factory-owner in Hong Kong expressed this attitude vividly when he reportedly said that 'a Shanghainese at forty who has not yet made himself owner of a firm is a failure, a good-for-nothing'.[39]

Since most of these studies are concerned with Chinese businessmen operating firms of limited scale, it is possible that such a preference for autonomy is engendered by the structure of small industry. Therefore the attitude towards self-employment of the spinners who were large employers will help decide whether the value of autonomy is prevalent throughout Chinese industry. In my interviews, I suggested the following hypothetical situation to elicit my respondents' views:

Let's assume that during the earlier part of your career, you had the option of becoming either the senior executive of a large corporation or the owner-manager of a smaller firm. The immediate financial rewards of both were more or less the same. Which option would you have chosen?

As Table 4.8 indicates, nearly two thirds of those who indicated a preference would have chosen to become owners.

This pattern of choice might be considered normal if all the respondents were themselves owners. It is logical to assume that a process of selective recruitment to the entrepreneurial role is at work so that individuals who have the early ambition to be their own boss will have a greater chance of attaining that goal.

Fortunately for this study, there were in my sample persons who derived their income mainly from salary rather than profit. I shall call these non-proprietary directors as distinct from owner-

Table 4.9. Spinners' Preferred and Actual Employment Status

Choice	Proprietary Director	Non-proprietary Director	Row Total
Owner	16	5	21
Senior executive	6	5	11
Column total	22	10	32

$\chi^2 = 1.6$; adjusted for continuity as df $= 1$; not significant at 0.05 level.

Source: Interviews, 1978.

directors. 'Non-proprietary' means that these directors had been appointed to their present positions before they held any company shares in their name, and that any shares they might possess subsequently were less than the average holding of individual shareholders. Eleven of the respondents, or a quarter of the sample, fell within this category. With such a distinction, we can pursue the question of selective recruitment. Did non-proprietary directors tend to favour salaried employment while owner-directors would choose to be self-employed? Table 4.9 shows that this was not the case. There is no significant correlation between the employment status of the respondent and his preference for independent ownership.

The owner-directors who opted for independent enterprises early in their career were very conscious of the peculiar opportunity structure of Hong Kong. As they saw it, the economy was not yet dominated by huge corporations so that small entrepreneurs could still prosper through hard work. Only two respondents mentioned monetary benefits as the main attraction. The chief motives that emerged from their answers were the lure of self-advancement and the abhorrence of self-subjugation. The director of Mill 22 said, 'Even if it is a small firm at the beginning, you can distinguish yourself and move ahead. But salaried employment is a blind alley.' There was a strong implication that the life of a subordinate was stifling and humiliating. 'It depends on your personality', the managing director of Mill 18 said, 'many people are content with their lot, so they become employees. But if you have high expectations for yourself, you want to do things on your own. You have to take risks.'

Given the dislike of subjugating oneself, why did a handful of the owner-directors express a wish to be executives? It was not because they valued this role for its own sake. When pressed to give their reasons they explained that they regarded it either as a stepping stone to later ownership, or as an escape route from the crushing responsibilities of handling an unwieldy workforce. The former view was typified by the response of the director-cum-mill-manager of Mill 12:

I am an engineer by training, and I have done every type of job in the mill. It is essential for a boss to understand each process of production first. Otherwise he will not be a good owner, especially now that operations are large-scale and very complex.

The complaint of the son of the managing director of Mill 33 who had recently taken on the day-to-day running of the family enterprise illustrated the latter view:

I have my fill as an owner. Controlling the workers is a real headache — there are quick turnovers, sudden shortages of manpower and so on. On top of that, many workers belong to secret societies and would create lots of trouble over severance pay, etc.

Among the non-proprietary directors who were ambitious to be independent owners, the rationale was simple. The terse remark of the manager of Mill 24 summed it up: 'You can have something of your own.' Their desire had been thwarted so far because, as they said unanimously, they did not have the initial capital. But it is likely that the real significance does not lie in their professed reasons but in the act of openly expressing their wish to become self-employed. That they did not find it necessary to disguise this sentiment, even as a gesture of deference to their employers, shows that their ambition is socially valued. Even the owners themselves acknowledged the prevalence of this motivation among their executives. They accepted that it could not be condemned as disloyalty or insubordination. As the managing director of Mill 32 said, 'It is a difficult situation. Many senior staff want to be their own boss. If they can stand on their own feet, they can get more, much more money. In Hong Kong, money is important.'

Although five of the non-proprietary directors would not have chosen to be their own boss, they were in fact upholding the same value as those who would have. The only difference was that they did not perceive the option as feasible in their case. The capital outlay for a cotton spinning mill was enormous, they said, or there were too many fluctuations in the trade of cotton yarn for a small firm to bear the risk. Nowhere did they exhibit any sense of pride in being an employee, no matter how senior their position. The self-deprecation was evident in their answers. A director of Mill 24, who had spent his entire working life in the company, was apologetic about his immobility when interviewed:

Q: Have you ever worked outside China?
A: No. Not even out of this company. It is very foolish of me, isn't it?
Q: Would you prefer to be a small owner or a senior executive?
A: Executive. Everybody's background is different. As I am the eldest son, I cannot afford to take too many risks, or the whole family would starve [he laughed]. In a large company, there is wider exposure and one can learn more. Then one can be an owner.

The high premium placed on individual autonomy by the spinners possibly originates in the cultural world view of the Chinese. Various schools of Chinese philosophy since the Warring States period (403–221 BC) shared the basic premise that men are 'naturally equal'.[40] This means that men are born with common attributes and that social inequality appears because some persons can realize their potential through their own efforts, and especially through education. This conception of man was embodied in an apparently contradictory system of social stratification in traditional China. A strictly hierarchical structure co-existed with an ideology exhorting individual social mobility.[41] No status, no matter how high, was regarded as intrinsically beyond the reach of an individual. In order to maximize one's chances of upward mobility, one should not let one's ambition be suppressed. Thus many Chinese businessmen were fond of the proverb 'better be the beak of a cock than the rump of an ox'.[42]

This outlook affects Chinese economic behaviour and creates problems for the owners, who must devise means to cope with the centrifugal tendency of their executives. This tendency does not necessarily hamper the overall vitality of the industry, but can create its own kind of dynamism. The director of Mill 22 attributed the success of Hong Kong's textile industry to the prevalent desire for self-employment that had created a host of small scale factories:

Japanese and South Korean workers are very obedient. But Hong Kong workers are dextrous and hard-working. They are willing to work over-time. Our recent success in denim manufacture is an example. In the United States, large factories usually carry out the entire process of pro-duction. They cannot take on sudden increases in orders or special requests because everybody is an employee, and workers are not enthusiastic about overtime pay. In Hong Kong, there are numerous small owners. Therefore Hong Kong can take on special production. It is beneficial to existing spin-ners. We can make goods of uncommon specifications even for relatively small orders. Only Hong Kong can do this. After the yarn is spun, there are specialized factories to do the dyeing. Afterwards, we can take the dyed yarn to yet another factory to be knitted. The whole is divided into parts, and this increases our flexibility.

The nub of his observation was that people in Hong Kong were prepared to do their best and make an extra effort when they were working for themselves or when it gave them the chance to accumu-late future business capital. But where individual firms are con-cerned, this urge to strike out on one's own undermines team work. In Hong Kong businesses, according to a Shanghainese manage-ment specialist, the number two is impatient to be number one and number one is impatient to get out and start his own business, no matter how small. 'The result is the atrocious down-grading of standard and quality.' Local employees, he says, 'curse the jobs they are paid for'.[43] During a management seminar, a Chinese executive reportedly said, 'I am on salary...I don't want to take the responsibility'.[44] Employers therefore have to find ways of cop-ing with this low motivation among their subordinates and the threat of desertion.

Most spinners appeared to adopt a defensive strategy based on a distrust of their staff. Areas of executive initiative and responsi-bility were deliberately curtailed. The low degree of delegation of authority was unwittingly shown by the general manager of Hong Kong Textiles Ltd. In an interview, he said,

Since my father and I handle all the negotiations with our buyers, we don't need any sales or marketing departments. Our Export Manager handles all routine correspondence with our buyers and supervises the clerks who make arrangements for shipping and insurance. He is also responsible for the clerks who take care of all export documentation.[45]

The existence of tight supervision emerged during conversations with executives. A sales representative of the parent company of Mill 18 told me:

You are seldom given real responsibility, especially in the signing of documents. All documents and letters in our factory have to be signed and approved by the Manager, though you may have drafted them. You cannot sign them for the company. [Q: Would that over-burden the manager?] Well, for internal production decisions, one has some say. When you are in the factory, you get to know how to get things done. But it is important to get approval from the manager first.

Such a strategy has obvious drawbacks. It can lead to a vicious cycle of low morale on the part of the employees and mediocre performance by the company. A few of the more enlightened spinners used patronage to foster loyalty among their subordinates. This method can be illustrated in the case of Mill 24, founded by the late Mr Zhao.[46] I interviewed the manager who had worked in the company since 1946, just one year after his graduation from St. John's University in Shanghai. The following was the reason for his long service:

Q: Looking back on your career, what would you say is the most significant event or personality that had influenced you greatly?
A: The late owner of our company, Mr Zhao. He was the one who invited me to work for him. We knew each other in 1942 when he gave me a scholarship to study in the university. While I was studying, we met about once a month to discuss my progress.

Later in the interview, the manager said that he would have chosen to be a small owner if given the chance. The same mill adopted the unprecedented policy in the 1950s of opening a secondary school of its own. Part of its aim was, of course, the training of manpower. But it might also reflect Mr Zhao's attempt to make himself the benefactor of his future employees. Yet the effectiveness of this approach is limited. The relationship between patron and client can serve its purpose in the lifetime of the entrepreneur. But since the subordinate's loyalty is to the person and not to the company, managerial succession is made more difficult. Patronage cannot easily be transferred to ensure the perpetuation of the enterprise.

The ideal of self-employment is not, of course, uniquely Chinese. It is also an 'essential part of the American dream' in a land where social ascent is similarly treasured.[47] How is this dream reconciled with the need for stable and dedicated corporate executives? The chairman of Mill 22 was aware of one of the Western solutions to this problem, but he did not think it was practicable in Hong Kong. He said:

Table 4.10. Spinners' Attitude to Private and Public Forms of Company Organization

Choice	No.	%
Private company	16	46
Public company	15	43
No preference	4	11
No response	5	—
Total	40	100

Source: Interviews, 1978.

In the West, there is a contract system to control the subordinates. Contracts are made for, say, two years and then renewed. This will check the managers, and they will watch their step because of the uncertainty. I am sure you have read the news recently about the dismissal of the chief executive of Ford. I saw it work in the West. In the Brussels Fair in the 1950s, I was struck by the maxim written on the banner of a display counter: 'If Heaven should fall tomorrow, I would still plan today'. But the Chinese don't act like that. If you don't know whether you will be fired next year, why should you work like hell? This is a difficult management problem.

The Western system of contracts for senior executives is often accompanied by the incentive of a profit-sharing scheme. This tends to reduce the attraction of self-employment and enable the firms to recruit and keep ambitious and capable employees. How did the spinners regard the admission of senior executives to the circle of owners in their companies?

Profit-sharing

The desire to confine ownership rights to a chosen few emerged when the spinners were questioned on their preferences for the public and private form of company organization. They were evenly divided in their opinions on the relative merits of these two forms, as shown in Table 4.10. Their reasons indicated that the notion of a diffused 'public' as owners, and the related idea of a 'corporation' as an independent and enduring entity have not taken hold among them. Those favouring the private mode believed that it was best to raise industrial capital from their own resources so that profits would return to them. They were suspicious of the motives of the companies that have gone public. The younger brother of the major owner of Mill 32 told me:

Whenever the question of going public is mentioned, tears fill my brother's eyes. 'Why should we give away our hard-earned money?', he says. The ambitious should have their shares floated. But most of them just want to take advantage of the public. We don't want to do that.

Some directors of public spinning companies would rather revert to private ownership. As the director of Mill 17 said, 'In Hong Kong's environment, the private form is better. The stock-market is very abnormal with too much speculation. We try to avoid people who are after a quick buck.' His underlying concern was obviously the risk of take-over by other companies and the lack of protection for the original owners' assets.

Spinning mills usually went public as an expedient. The advantage of the public form most cited by the respondents was that bank loans were more forthcoming. Banks were eager to keep a close eye on the operations of their clients, and the published accounts of public companies were a useful means of control. Partnership and joint ventures also frequently adopted the public form for greater legal protection and mutual supervision with the help of independent accountants. For firms with little capital but big plans for development, raising capital through the stock-market was almost the only way to move ahead. Yet irrespective of whether their mills were in public or private ownership, none of the spinners interviewed mentioned the existence of a profit-sharing scheme for their executives as a form of incentive.[48]

Regional Differences

The above analysis only provides a general picture of the ideological orientation of the spinners. There are numerous ways of exploring possible internal variations, such as along the dimensions of age, educational background and employment status. However, the most relevant cleavage for the present study is that of regional differences. Did the Shanghai spinners profess attitudes differentiating them from their non-Shanghainese competitors? The following tables show that no appreciable difference existed on any of the themes about which they were asked to make a choice.

Table 4.11. Spinners' Attitude to Social Responsibility by Ethnicity

Choice	Shanghainese	Non-Shanghainese	Row Total
Laissez-faire	14	5	19
Interest	8	1	9
Responsibility	4	2	6
Column Total	26	8	34

χ^2 = 1.2; df = 2; not significant at 0.05 level.

Source: Interviews, 1978.

Table 4.12. Spinners' Attitude to Conflict by Ethnicity

Choice	Shanghainese	Non-Shanghainese	Row Total
No conflict	12	2	14
Disagreement healthy	13	6	19
Disagreement disruptive	0	0	0
Column Total	25	8	33

χ^2 = 1.3; df = 2; not significant at 0.05 level.

Source: Interviews, 1978.

Table 4.13. Spinners' Attitude to Unions by Ethnicity

Choice	Shanghainese	Non-Shanghainese	Row Total
Unions not needed	2	1	3
Workers' right	4	1	5
Joint consultation	18	6	24
Column Total	24	8	32

χ^2 = 0.2; df = 2; not significant at 0.05 level.

Source: Interviews, 1978.

Table 4.14. Spinners' Attitude to Competition by Ethnicity

Choice	Shanghainese	Non-Shanghainese	Row Total
Necessary	15	3	18
No need	2	0	2
Co-operation	9	5	14
Column Total	26	8	34

χ^2 = 2.2; df = 2; not significant at 0.05 level.

Source: Interviews, 1978.

Table 4.15. Spinners' Attitude to Self-employment by Ethnicity

Choice	Shanghainese	Non-Shanghainese	Row Total
Owner	17	4	21
Executive	7	4	11
Column Total	24	8	33

χ^2 = 1.2, corrected for continuity as df = 1; not significant at 0.05 level.

Source: Interviews, 1978.

Table 4.16. Spinners' Attitude to Public and Private Companies by Ethnicity

Choice	Shanghainese	Non-Shanghainese	Row Total
Private	14	2	16
Public	10	5	15
Column Total	24	7	31

χ^2 = 2.1, corrected for continuity as df = 1; not significant at 0.05 level.

Source: Interviews, 1978.

The absence of an ideological divergence between Shanghainese and non-Shanghainese spinners is open to at least two interpretations. It may mean that the economic norms and attitudes held by the Shanghai entrepreneurs are similar to those of industrialists from other regions such as Guangdong or Chaozhou, whose business ideology, however, has not yet been studied. The alternative, and more likely, interpretation is that the Shanghai spinners have set the norms and standards in the industry and established 'ideological hegemony'. The minority of non-Shanghainese competitors have thus been obliged to adopt the industry's prevailing business attitudes in order to survive.

Up to now, the predominance of the Shanghainese in cotton spinning has been explained in terms of an examination of their collective attributes. Their social and educational peculiarities shaped by a selective process of migration, their industrial skills, and their ideological stance, are important, among other traits, in explaining how the Shanghainese as a category of individuals succeeded in initially capturing an industrial sector. But collective attributes cannot adequately account for the persistence of the Shanghainese concentration in the spinning industry, since these can, through diffusion, be imitated by outsiders. In order to consolidate their economic power and avoid being dislodged from an occupational niche, the Shanghainese have to organize themselves into a solidarity group with the capacity to achieve economic closure. I shall argue in the next two chapters that ethnicity and kinship are the two major principles upon which the Shanghainese erected their group boundaries to exclude outsiders.

5 Regionalism and Competitive Strategies

SELECTED through migration, endowed with industrial skills, and spurred on by a particular set of managerial attitudes, the Shanghai cotton spinners have created a new economic sphere in Hong Kong. This accomplishment clearly qualifies them to be called entrepreneurs whose distinctive feature, according to Joseph A. Schumpeter, is the ability to innovate.[1] But innovation, when carried out in the context of perfect competition, is not an economically rewarding pursuit. As Schumpeter observes, '[the entrepreneur] draws other producers in his branch after him. But as they are his competitors, who first reduce and then annihilate his profits, this is, as it were, leadership against one's own will.'[2]

In this situation, only short-term profits accrue to the pioneers. Such temporary benefits can hardly be sufficient to motivate the Shanghai spinners who do not regard themselves as romantic dreamers or glamorous adventurers. Like most industrial entrepreneurs in the real world, they can be expected to seek ways to maintain their predominance and to ward off imitators. In other words, a significant part of their entrepreneurial skill is the ability to create conditions of imperfect competition, or to attain closure.

Closure, the process by which a group establishes 'monopolization of specific, usually economic opportunities',[3] can be achieved in a variety of ways. There are economic methods to curb competition such as by product differentiation through advertising, the creation of an absolute cost advantage, or the establishment of an economy of scale. But equally important are the 'extra-market' means such as violence, price-cutting and boycotts, deception and fraud, or collusion in restricting recruitment, wages, and output. These techniques are often not institutionalized, nor strictly legal, nor respectable. This is why particularistic ties and multiplex relationships are likely to figure prominently in situations of imperfect competition.

Such ties can be used to fulfil two crucial functions. First, they provide a firmer basis for trust within the group. Members can have more information with which to evaluate each other by relying on particularistic networks. They can also exert greater control over those who do not conform by invoking communal sanctions.

Second, they furnish a justification for discrimination. It can be claimed that people with common particularistic ties belong to a moral community with shared rights and obligations, so that it is legitimate to keep economic benefits within the group. As outsiders have no such moral claims, their exclusion can be justified.[4] This practice tends to create ill-feeling on the part of the outsiders who feel unfairly treated. Thus it is not simply competition for scarce resources,[5] but *restrictive* competition essential to entrepreneurship that makes communal hostility so emotive and intractable in most multi-ethnic societies.

To achieve closure, an individual can activate numerous particularistic ties, some of which are more effective than others. Among Chinese entrepreneurs, one of the most important type of relationship used in economic competition is the regional tie forged with reference to a common native place.

The native place is not necessarily an individual's place of birth. A person born in Hong Kong might regard that locality as his place of 'abode' which is temporary and not his *jiguan* or place of 'residence' which defines his origin.[6] The importance of *jiguan* to an individual in traditional China was reinforced by social custom as well as official policy. It was common in late imperial China for lineages and other rural organizations to provide some form of assistance to members venturing into the outside world. These members, even though physically absent, generally retained their social positions in their native place. In times of adversity, they could return to this sanctuary for sustenance and protection. When they prospered, it was where their newly won status would be celebrated and recognized.

Regional identity was basically an ascriptive characteristic. Nevertheless, migrants could try to change their *jiguan* through a difficult and protracted process. In order to sink roots in an area of abode, the migrants must gain acceptance into the local status system. The key was usually the right to own landed property. It would often take several generations before this right could be obtained.[7] Only after land was purchased to endow an ancestral home, or an ancestral hall in the case of a new lineage segment, was the metamorphosis from an outsider to a local resident accomplished.

The Chinese state, for its part, used to rely on local rural organizations to exercise social control. This is shown in the etymology of the term *jiguan*. *Ji* was the register recording the names of persons and households, and *guan* referred to the place where one was permitted to enter one's name into the register after residing there for a legally specified period of time.[8] Before permission was granted, a resident could, at best, only claim affiliation status. He and his offspring were not allowed to sit for the Civil Service Examination in their place of affiliation. If a resident committed an offence, a severe punishment was to send him back to his native place, presumably to be shamed and discredited among kinsmen and neighbours. This administrative practice has such a long history that even in contemporary Hong Kong, Chinese residents are still routinely asked to list their *jiguan* in official forms as part of their personal data.

Regional ties as used by the Chinese have two major characteristics. The first is that they are pervasive, permeating social interaction in various spheres of activities, geographical settings, and hierarchical levels. In her study of the Ningbo community in Shanghai from 1800 to the 1920s, Susan Mann Jones concludes that '[native-place] ties provided the primary channels through which family, class and business interests were articulated in Chinese cities'.[9] In an analysis of urban Chinese settlements in South-east Asia and North America, Lawrence W. Crissman locates the basic division of these communities in 'speech' groups which are linked to territorial origin.[10] J. Bruce Jacobs, attempting to construct a model of the relevance of particularistic ties in Chinese political behaviour based on his field study of a township in Taiwan, also assigns the greatest weight to '[the] importance of the locality *kuan-hsi*...at all levels of the various Chinese polities'.[11]

The second characteristic of regional ties is their flexibility. According to the situation, a Shanghainese can activate regional ties of various scope. His potential membership ranges from that of his native village, for instance, Xia Che village, his native county of Wuxi, his native province of Jiangsu, to the broader categories of Shanghainese, southern Chinese, Asian or Oriental, and even a member of the Third World. Like insects with a protective colouration, his identity can undergo subtle, and if need be, rapid changes to suit the context of interaction. In international forums such as textile negotiations, the cotton spinners usually present themselves as industrialists from Hong Kong, a vulnerable free port of the developing region of Asia. *Vis-à-vis* their foreign buyers or the senior British officials of the colony, they are Chinese. Meeting in regional associations, they are people from Ningbo or Shanghai city who enjoy their local cuisine and theatrical entertainment. When they participate in the activities of their trade association, they are modern, Westernized businessmen.

The same flexibility can be found in their linguistic pattern. English is used in external dealings, whereas within the company and factory, Chinese (the written form and also various spoken dialects) is the main medium of communication. Managing directors and senior executives converse in the Shanghai dialect, and give instructions to local subordinates in accented Cantonese. Oksenberg's description of the furnishing inside one of the textile companies gives us an interesting glimpse of how ethnic tones are adjusted in different functional areas of the enterprise:

The décor of the president's suite was quite plush — thick carpets, elegant furniture, all in a French Renaissance style. I then went to the mill and was greeted in the main sales room. This too was elegantly furnished, this time in a Danish style. I went on to a meeting room where Westerners are sometimes taken but where members of the mill also sometimes assemble. The décor here was also basically Western, but I began to note Chinese touches. Finally, I was ushered into the inner-sanctum of the mill — the place where the mill supervisors meet almost daily to plan production teams. This is a place where Westerners rarely stray. The décor is fully Chinese: the monk chairs with circular marble inlays are pushed against the wall, the tablet with the picture of the founder of the firm stared down from one end of the room, the table with flowers placed beneath it create the atmosphere of a shrine. The atmosphere is elegant but stark.[12]

With the characteristics of the regional ties in mind, let us examine how the spinners make use of such ties in running their enterprises, in dealing with other firms, and in pursuing status and power in the community.

Internal Organization

Within a productive unit, there is normally a hierarchical structure. Manpower requirement at each level varies, and this influences the relevance of regional ties. In a spinning mill, we can distinguish among the manual workers, the executives, and the owners. The viability of a mill in Hong Kong depends on continuous operation and the ability to fulfil orders on time. This requires a large number of low-skilled operatives, preferably employed at a cheap rate. Thus to the Shanghai entrepreneurs, the ethnicity of the workers was of little significance as long as there was an adequate supply of labour so that production would not be disrupted. What concerned them was the stability of their mill hands, and not whether they were Shanghainese or Cantonese.

As mentioned in Chapter 3, the cotton spinners brought with them some skilled workers from Shanghai in the late 1940s. Once they discovered that wages were lower in Hong Kong, they reduced the workers' pay and benefits, provoking an outburst of industrial disputes. Instead of clashing with Cantonese workers, the Shanghai spinners had their first confrontation with employees from their own region. The common ethnic background, instead of reducing incompatibility in economic interests, actually heightened conflict. Shanghainese workers, who remembered the more favourable terms of employment back home, felt betrayed. Industrial stoppages occurred in eight of the cotton spinning mills. The disputes were finally settled with an increase in benefits such as the New Year Bonus. But the improved benefits still fell short of the Shanghai norm.[13] When the disputes were over, the mill owners began actively training local Cantonese workers. By 1951 it was reported that the Nanyang Cotton Mill which had started operation with two thirds of its work force imported from Shanghai had reduced that ratio to one third.[14]

At the time of my interview, the major complaint of the spinners was directed at labour shortages and the erosion of the 'virtue' of loyalty among workers. The young people of Hong Kong, according to my respondents, were too materialistic. They would leave their posts as soon as higher wages, however slight, were offered elsewhere. In order to cope with rapid labour turnover and rising wages, some companies such as Mill 16 were employing a number of Pakistani workers while other mills made plans to import Filipino workers until they were thwarted by the Immigration Department.

The particular manpower requirement of cotton spinning and the shortage of local industrial labour compelled them to act as impersonal employers in the labour market.[15] But this does not mean that the Shanghai spinners treated all manual workers alike. In their personnel policies, they did take regional variations into account. For instance, usually both Shanghainese and Cantonese food were provided, sometimes in separate canteens in the factories. In Mill 16, Pakistani workers were housed in their own dormitory away from local employees.[16] But such measures were no more significant than adjusting maintenance routines to different makes of machinery. Thus, at this organizational level, it was the workers who were much more concerned to maintain ethnic boundaries because their livelihood was directly threatened by the hiring of members of other ethnic groups.[17] From time to time tension would surface, as in Mill 16 in 1977, when Chinese workers protested against what they regarded as housing privileges accorded to the Pakistanis.

The employment of executives is a different matter. Since the demand for executive services is obviously much smaller than that for manual workers, the management has fewer worries about the supply of personnel. On the other hand, the executives play a more critical role in the organization by having access to business information and experience. They can damage the company by joining other mills or setting up on their own. Thus in deciding on the promotion of this grade of staff, mill owners emphasize the importance of loyalty alongside ability. Loyalty can be fostered in several ways, and shared regional origin is one of the bases on which to build mutual trust. But ethnic discrimination in the promotion of executives is not explicit. I do not have hard evidence to establish the extent of discrimination, though the prevalence of the Shanghainese dialect among senior management is an indication of such a tendency. In any case, many local Cantonese executives believe that regional favouritism exists, and that their prospects are hampered as a result. Such grievances emerged during my conversation with an executive of a dyeing company that owned Mill 18 as a subsidiary:

Q: How is your company organized?
A: The top ranks are nearly all occupied by the Shanghainese. They used to employ their own people, their relatives and people they trust, in responsible posts. Now as the younger generation is taking over, they place more emphasis on qualifications and more Cantonese and university graduates are employed. Anyway there are not that many Shanghainese in Hong Kong. When the factory has to expand, they have to take in local people.
Q: How is promotion decided?
A: There is no fixed rule. It depends on the boss, whether he likes you or not. I have been working there for six to seven years now, and I am not advancing smoothly. Partly it is because of my personality, and partly because of the system. I don't like to curry favour...Another characteristic of my company is that very few of us can get a title, even

though you may have worked there for a long time. My supervisor, for example, has been working for some twenty years now. He is already in his late forties. While I am just called sales representative, he is called senior sales representative.

Q: Is he a Cantonese?

A: Yes, he is. There are very few senior positions in our factory...

Q: Who gets the fastest promotion?

A: A man originally from another textile mill.

Q: Is he a Shanghainese?

A: Yes.

Q: How old is he?

A: Fifty something...

Q: Besides being a Shanghainese, are there other criteria for promotion?

A: Seniority. The longer you work in the firm, the more loyal you are thought to be. That helps promotion...

Then the Chaozhou director of the newly established Mill 9 also told me:

There are regular luncheons held by the Cotton Spinners' Association. But I am too busy so I let the mill manager go instead...I wish to be friends with them [the Shanghainese mill owners], but it is not easy. I have talked to their senior executives, and discovered that they have not been promoted for a long time. I asked them where they were from, and invariably I found that they were not Shanghainese. One of them said to me, 'If I were a Shanghainese, I would not be here talking to you.' He meant that he would have been promoted so high that he did not have to deal with public relations work...

At the apex of the organization, among the owners, mutual trust is even more important. Yet at the same time, it is more problematic and precarious. As cotton spinning involves considerable capital investment, mills can rarely be established through sole proprietorship. Partners are usually sought to pool resources. An examination of the company records revealed that half of the 32 mills were originally partnerships, which means that there was no majority shareholding by an individual or a family. But this mode of ownership is very unstable. By 1978, only four mills remained in this form. The strain inherent in the relationship among partners was underscored by the managing director of Mill 19:

It is very difficult to find a business partner. For instance, you can form a joint venture with foreign companies. But I am not interested in that. Co-operation in business requires thorough understanding, otherwise conflict will easily occur. You can easily find partners to start a business. Trouble begins when you want to break up. It is not something you can do with strangers, because everyone wants to get the controlling share. You don't necessarily want to take advantage of others. But you must protect yourself, to prevent others from stabbing you in the back.

In such a situation, particularistic ties such as ethnicity are essential cementing forces. Without a common particularistic bond among the owners, a partnership is very brittle. In the small Hong Kong glass factory studied by Barbara E. Ward, the two directors 'were refugees, one from Central and one from North China'.[18] The partnership broke up after three years. There is also the example of a Fujianese entrepreneur who migrated to Hong Kong in 1950 and formed an enamelware factory together with a 'village friend' and a Shanghainese acquaintance. After two years of vigorous growth of the firm, the other two owners were locked in irreconcilable conflict and the partnership had to be dissolved. The entrepreneur was given an offer by the Shanghainese to stay on, but he felt he had to decline:

I was sure the business would flourish because my Shanghainese friend was very dedicated to the venture. But I had to turn down the offer so as to avoid causing misunderstanding with my village friend. I tried to observe propriety and to preserve friendship on both sides.[19]

Therefore, most enduring partnerships in cotton spinning consisted of directors who were fellow regionals. Co-operation between Shanghainese and Cantonese at directorial level only existed in Mill 4, and this partnership was unequal as the Cantonese family held the major share. There were a few joint ventures between Chinese and foreign investors. In these ventures, additional institutional safeguards had to be devised in lieu of common ethnic ties. Strict division of labour was common, with Chinese directors in charge of production and foreign owners supervising finance or administration.

The most elaborate arrangement was in Mill 10. The mill had been established by two companies, one Chinese-owned holding A-type shares and the other Japanese-owned holding an equal number of B-type shares. By company regulation, the shares could only be increased at the same rate. Holders of either A-type or B-type shares could appoint and remove no more than three 'A' and 'B' directors respectively. In turn, the 'A' directors were vested with the authority to appoint the general manager and the assistant mill manager. The 'B' directors, for their part, were empowered to select the mill manager and the assistant general manager. This arrangement persisted for 11 years before the company went public. The absence of trust among the partners could not have been made more obvious.[20]

External Economic Dealings

Externally, a spinning mill engages in two major types of inter-firm relationships. One is symbiotic, involving interactions with suppliers, subcontractors, and buyers. The other is competitive, concerning how to cope with fellow producers.

In the symbiotic dealings, regional ties are often activated to help initiate a business relationship. It is customary, when dealing with strangers, for Chinese businessmen to enlist the assistance of intermediaries with whom they have some common particularistic bonds. When the Shanghainese spinners arrived in Hong Kong, they also followed this practice in seeking bank loans. As the large banks were initially reluctant to lend them money an intermediary was needed as a guarantor.

The first go-between was the China Engineers Ltd, whose head was a Eurasian of Anglo-Chinese parentage. The firm had branches in Shanghai involved in the import and export aspect of the textile trade, where at one time it had also managed a spinning mill. As a result, it had previously had dealings with the Chinese spinners as well as the Hongkong and Shanghai Bank in Shanghai. When the spinners needed bank loans after their arrival in Hong Kong, the China Engineers Ltd. acted as a broker. It obtained loans from the Hongkong and Shanghai Bank at an interest rate of 7 per cent per annum, and re-lent the money to the cotton spinners at the rate of 9 per cent.[21] A loan estimated to exceed HK$50 million in 1951 was transacted in this manner.[22] In return, the spinners had to purchase their machinery and raw cotton and also to sell their yarn through a central marketing organization called the Cotton Mill Pool formed by the China Engineers Ltd. The Pool consisted of 13 spinning and weaving mills, and charged commission of 2.5 per cent.[23]

The spinners were unhappy with this arrangement and complained about what they felt to be unreasonable expenses attached to the loans.[24] They sought the help of a Shanghainese banker who arrived in the early 1950s. A graduate of Qinghua University in Beijing, with a master's degree in commerce and business from the

University of New York, this banker had first been employed by the General Electric Company in China. Later he worked for the Bank of China, promoting industrial lending.[25] He was a man with extensive financial experience and contacts, a one-time manager of the Hunan–Guizhou Railway, member of the committees on export control and the foreign exchange stabilization fund in 1947, as well as member of the committee on cotton supply jointly established by the Chinese and American governments in 1948.[26] He told me how he had made new financial arrangements for his fellow regionals in cotton spinning:

When I arrived, I told them that they did not have to do this [to go through the China Engineers Ltd]. I knew these spinners personally, so I approached the Hongkong and Shanghai Bank on their behalf. We had to persuade the colonial officials and the Bank that textiles were good for Hong Kong. It was not too difficult when they saw the financial side of it. This was the period just after the war, and there was a big demand for textiles. Because of the demand, textiles were very profitable. The factories could recoup their capital investment within three years. When the Bank saw the profit, they said, 'Here's the money. Lend it to them.' So I functioned as an informal adviser for the Bank. I held a dinner on its behalf every week. Later I became very busy. But the Bank said, 'We need you'. So I stayed, first for three years, then six years, until now. There has never been any contract.

By 1954 it was estimated that the two largest banks in Hong Kong had lent a total of between HK$80 million and HK$100 million to the cotton spinning industry.[27]

A similar case of an industrial go-between is recorded by Oksenberg. An American petroleum company attempting to supply petroleum products to Hong Kong textile firms in the early 1970s hired 'on a retainer plus commissioned fee basis a lower Yangtze businessman with good ties in the textile community and who, as a young man, worked for this corporation's current major rival in Shanghai before 1949'.[28]

There are indications that ethnic considerations also influence the choice of subcontractors and brokers. The director of Mill 33, who came from Chaozhou, recounted an incident which showed how the relevance of personal relationship altered with changing contexts of production:

Several years ago we had an employee who organized a Chinese New Year party for other workers. He intended to build up a power base for himself.

This threatened my position [the director was then in charge of technical operations]. I had no other choice but to move first and fire him. So he went around attacking me behind my back. Some years later we had to dispose of some old machines. By then he had become a dealer in second-hand textile equipment. We had the choice between him and another Shanghainese dealer. I gave the business to him. He brought some chickens to thank me. I said to him, 'It is not necessary to thank me. You are my former employee. Of course I would take care of you. At that time, you did not understand my situation.'

He did not make clear whether his former employee was from Chaozhou or not, but he implied that he preferred not to use the services of a Shanghainese dealer.

There is, however, a limit to the usefulness of regional bonds in facilitating symbiotic transactions. Normally the spinners cannot afford to pick and choose suppliers and buyers on the basis of non-economic considerations. Over-reliance on ethnic ties can hurt business. For instance, the Cantonese-owned Nanyang Brothers Tobacco Company which recruited mainly fellow Cantonese as distributors had great difficulty in penetrating the Chinese market beyond south China during the first decade of this century.[29] Usually it is only when serious market imperfections occur that the utility of ethnic and other particularistic ties is heightened. In the post-war sellers' market in China, for example, the directors of the Shen Xin Fourth Mill entrusted for storage some of their products to a yarn dealer with whom they had strong personal ties in order to evade government controls on stock-piling.[30]

When it comes to inter-firm relations that are competitive rather than symbiotic, the key problem the spinners have is how to erect entry barriers to discourage potential rivals.[31] When the entry barriers of an industry are low, it is more difficult for established entrepreneurs to maintain closure. Therefore it can be hypothesized that the lower the entry barriers of an industry, the more energetic will be the use of particularistic criteria by the incumbents to form solidarity groups in order to fend off intruders.

In a comparison of thirteen industries, an economist has found that textile manufacture has one of the lowest entry barriers because economies of scale are quite unimportant, because there is little opportunity for product differentiation, and because neither technological patents nor tight control over raw materials exist.[32] Yet the Shanghai cotton spinners are quite reticent in expressing their ethnicity as will be demonstrated later in this chapter. This phenomenon does not disprove the above hypothesis because the textile quota system instituted in Hong Kong has greatly reduced the accessibility of the spinning sector and has raised the entry barriers substantially.

The quota system cannot be described in detail here and only the essential features will be noted.[33] As a result of the Lancashire Pact (1959–65), the Cotton Textile Arrangement (1962–73), and the Multi-Fibre Arrangement (since 1974), Hong Kong has agreed to limit textile exports to Western industrialized countries. Annual ceiling figures of export to these countries are negotiated periodically, but the Hong Kong government manages to retain the autonomy to allocate quotas internally to individual manufacturers. The basic principle of allocation was originally one of productive capacity, but this was later modified to rest on the past export performance of the companies in the preceding twelve months. The more yarn a company had sold overseas in the previous year, the larger the quota. Quotas can be withdrawn or reduced if the companies fail to make full use of them. But this is unlikely to happen because the firms are allowed to sell their unused quotas to other producers. Thus, in effect, the export restrictions confer enormous advantages to textile mills which were in operation before 1960, the year when the quota system came into being. The imposition of the quotas has more or less frozen the relative competitive positions of the mills. Each has been given a fixed share of the export market, creating a *de facto* oligopoly. New competitors are greatly handicapped by the lack of quotas, and have to bear a higher production cost by buying quotas from existing firms.

At the outset, the industrial incumbents were apparently fully aware of the potential benefit of the quota system in curbing competition. One of them emphasized this in an article published in 1962:

This state of affairs [referring to the impostion of export quotas] obviously means that the days are over for expansion and new investment in the local textile industry. In future, our emphasis should be laid on making better use of the existing production resources through improved efficient management, instead of stressing further investment, additional machinery and increased productivity...In view of this situation, new investment in the industry will prove detrimental rather than profitable.[34]

This benefit was apparently given to the established Hong Kong mills by the importing countries in exchange for an acceptance of trade restrictions. During the critical stage of the initial negotiations on restrictions, strenuous efforts were made by the textile entrepreneurs to protect their own interests. The growth in power of the Hong Kong Cotton Spinners' Association was based on the need to present a common front in the negotiations.

In anticipation of the negotiations, alliances were formed between the cotton spinning and weaving sectors. This led to an incident that highlighted the ethnic aspect of industrial competition. Unlike the Shanghainese-dominated spinning sector, the weavers were divided between Shanghainese and Cantonese mills. The Shanghainese weavers founded the Federation of Hong Kong Cotton Weavers, while the Cantonese ones controlled the Hong Kong Weaving Mills' Association. In the early part of 1959 the three industrial associations held round-table talks to co-ordinate their tactics. Their aim was to oppose an extension of a three-year 'voluntary undertaking' to limit exports to the United Kingdom so as to give Lancashire mill owners a 'breathing space'. An inter-association agreement was made in June 1960, binding the associations to refrain from participating in the 'cotton industry's inter-sectional discussion on quota problems with respect to the U.K. and the U.S., asking that a satisfactory clarification of certain basic issues be reached in advance'.[35] In the meantime, the Hong Kong government was under pressure from Britain to intervene and to set up a Cotton Advisory Board to find solutions to the quota proposals from the United Kingdom and the United States.

Then on 11 July 1960 the inter-sector alliance suddenly collapsed. The Cotton Spinners' Association informed their members in a confidential memorandum that '[one] of the weavers' associations had expressed willingness to the Government to name nominees to the proposed Cotton Advisory Board. The other association closely followed this step.'[36] The culprit was not named, but it is most likely that it was the Cantonese weavers' association that first broke the pledge. Since many Shanghainese weavers were also spinners, they could not have broken it without incurring the wrath of their peers in the Cotton Spinners' Association.

Once it was no longer possible to uphold the agreement, economic self-interest triumphed. The weavers quickly secured an assurance from government that export quotas would be allocated according to existing loomage of the mills, leaving the spinners in the lurch. The spinners maintained that they could not fight a lost cause and reluctantly agreed to send representatives to the Cotton Advisory Board.

The quota system erected a formidable barrier to new entrants and stabilized internal competition in the textile industry. But one route remained open for potential competitors to gain access. They could take over existing mills with quotas that were not doing well. In order to maintain closure, the established spinners had to find ways to regulate the transfer of productive assets to outsiders. Ethnicity played an important part in this. An examination of several cases of company transfer is illuminating.

The Shanghainese-owned Mill 6 had been in chronic trouble since its foundation in 1949. It sought funds from a Cantonese financial consortium in 1955. In exchange, four Cantonese directors with the power of veto were appointed to its board. After three years, the owners switched to borrow from Shanghainese financiers, and two Shanghainese were consequently appointed to replace all the Cantonese directors. This move was apparently taken to forestall a take-over bid by the Cantonese who still retained 20 per cent of the company shares after their resignation. The plan of the Cantonese consortium was finally destroyed in 1972 when the mill was sold to the prosperous Shanghainese-controlled Winsor Corporation.[37]

The Shanghainese mill owners were able to keep the circulation of productive assets among themselves because of their information network. As my respondents had reiterated, the spinning industry was like a 'club' where everybody knew each other. 'Most members in the medium and high strata of the local spinning, weaving, and dyeing industries', one of them observed, 'are generally of the same geographical origin and have much in common in their living and working habits.'[38] Not only did they meet during functions of their association, they also communicated by phone to discuss the credit standing of their clients or technical matters such as export regulations. They met after work, and directors of competing mills might attend horse-racing, or play tennis and *mahjong* together. They would be the first to learn about fellow spinners in financial trouble, and would be able to make an early bid to buy their equipment.

In July 1978 Mill 11 closed operations and sold the factory site for a huge profit. The work-force of over 1,000 workers was disbanded. Commenting on the sudden closure, the Shanghainese managing director of Mill 19 told me:

We are very good friends [referring to the owners of Mill 11 and himself]. But this time they did not discuss their problem with us. It is perhaps a question of face. Otherwise we would have offered to buy their spindles, because we believe spinning will continue to be important in Hong Kong. Their closure does not mean there is no future for spinning. They cannot do it, very well, let us take over. It is the same with Mill 29. Over the past year, we have been in touch with them. But they want to sell their land. We tell them, 'Land is too expensive. After you have sold your land, we would like to buy your plant and machinery.'

Sometimes better offers were available outside the ethnic group. But monetary gain could involve substantial dangers, for the sellers would lose control over what the outsiders might do with the mill. This happened to the Shanghainese-held Overseas Textiles Company which was making an annual profit of HK$2 million in 1976. A Cantonese land development corporation, the Hopewell conglomerate, proposed to buy the mill for HK$25 million, nearly nine times its capital value. The temptation was so great that the directors decided to sell to the developer in spite of an earlier offer by the Winsor textile group. As soon as the Cantonese developer owned the company, he suspended production and discharged without notice all the workers, provoking their angry protests. A locally published textile journal condemned the mill owners in a strongly worded editorial:

In Hong Kong's economic circumstances, it might well be unsound to suggest that an industrialist does not have a full right to do as he likes with his own property, but then those who profit from this situation have a particular duty to see that their actions do not have socially damaging consequences. Even in a developed country a cotton mill has a very considerable social value, and much more in a developing one. Nor is it just a matter of ethics. Anywhere else the manner of the closure of the Overseas Textiles mill would have raised a riot, and in 1966 an industrial dispute touched off three days of disturbance in Hong Kong itself.[39]

It should be noted that the editor was a Shanghainese, and his indignation was aroused at least partly because the reputation of his ethnic community in the textile field was tarnished. A director of Mill 32 recalled how they were held collectively responsible for the incident by the colonial administration. He complained that the Hong Kong government was prejudiced against them:

When the Overseas Textiles Company changed hands several years ago and was sold to Hopewell, Hopewell shut down the factory. The Governor was very angry with us Shanghainese. But look at CTV [a Cantonese-owned television station closed in 1978], what happened?

This bitter lesson did not entirely stop the spinners transferring mills to outsiders. But those who did so had to proceed with care. In 1977 another Shanghainese mill went out of business, and the plant was bought by a Chaozhou weaving company to become Mill 33. This was the first time a Shanghainese spinning mill had been taken over by non-Shanghainese textile manufacturers. It was a blow to regional pride, because the directors of Mill 33 seized every opportunity to boast about their acquisition. During the interview, a director of Mill 33 diverted the conversation to this topic:

As we are both Cantonese, I will tell you this. Our company has gained much face for the Cantonese. Formerly, there were only Shanghainese spinners, such as Mr A of Mill 15, swallowing Cantonese weaving mills. As for Cantonese weavers swallowing Shanghainese spinning factories, we are the first.

In spite of the loss of regional pride, the Shanghainese owners still made the deal for two main reasons. First, the Chaozhou weavers had made enormous profits during a denim boom in the late 1970s. They had the surplus capital to give a good price. Second, the spinning mill had been the major supplier of yarn to this particular weaving factory. A long-standing business relationship existed, and the Shanghainese could be sure that the factory would not be closed in a repetition of the fiasco of the closure of the Overseas Textiles Mill. As it turned out, the entire work-force in the spinning mill was retained by Mill 33 and no stoppage occurred.

The Shanghainese spinners were thus quite successful in restricting entry to their industry. However, when they sought to diversify their investments in the local economy, it was their turn to come against entry barriers. As noted in Chapter 3, these spinners regarded themselves as 'determined industrialists'. Few of them strayed into commerce. Some of the reasons for their industrial commitment have been touched on — their technical training and the machinery they already owned. But this commitment was also shaped by their status as immigrants. Well-established occupations and lines of business were relatively inaccessible to them. The situation can be highlighted by examining the entrepreneurial decisions of the Cantonese-owned Wing On Group.

Wing On had the second largest private spinning operation in Shanghai before the war. When it evacuated to Hong Kong in the late 1940s, it was in the same position as other Shanghainese spinners. But there was one crucial difference. The headquarters of Wing On's retailing business had been in Hong Kong for a long time, and, in that sense it was also an indigenous company. Probably because it had readily available commercial opportunities in the colony, it did not revive its spinning operation there, much to the regret of one of its founders later on.[40]

The vehement objection of the spinners to the establishment of the Hong Kong Cotton Commodity Exchange for its purportedly speculative nature can also be seen in a similar light. There is a hint of a 'sour grapes' reaction since after all, there had been a Chinese Cotton Goods Exchange in Shanghai before 1949 with the eminent spinner Rong Zong-jing as one of its active sponsors.

Another instance of blocked opportunity can be found in the real estate business. Comparing the traits of Shanghainese and Cantonese industrialists, the director of Mill 1 said to me:

It is mostly the Cantonese who are involved in real estate while very few Shanghainese are. If we had used our investments in cotton spinning to buy land, we would be getting gigantic profits by now. We might have been as big as Hong Kong Land [the largest real estate company in Hong Kong]. But we had burnt our fingers in Shanghai. We learnt that when the political situation changed, we could not bring the land with us.

The managing director of Mill 30, himself a Shanghainese, elaborated:

The Cantonese, such as the owner of Mill 33, made money in the denim boom. They then invest in land. Good idea. The Shanghainese just expand their textile companies into foreign countries, such as South-east Asia and Africa. Fundamentally, the Cantonese consider Hong Kong as their native place; not so the Shanghainese.

The Shanghainese refugee mentality obviously affected their investment behaviour, but there were other reasons for their letting the lucrative opportunity of real estate development pass them by. For some time, Cantonese developers seemed to be able to keep the business largely to themselves. But in the property boom of the early 1980s, entry barriers were crashed by newcomers scrambling for a share of the profit. The Shanghainese spinners were not above such temptations. Nan Fung Textiles, which owned the largest cotton mill in Hong Kong, started a large housing estate project called Nam Fung Sun Tsun and also acquired several other sites on which to build luxury resort houses.[41] The Winsor Industrial Corporation, run by Shanghainese spinners, set up a joint venture company with the Far East Consortium to redevelop the site of another cotton mill that it had just bought. The plan was to construct a multi-purpose industrial building complex for sale.[42] It is perhaps no accident that the owner of the Far East Consortium also came from Shanghai.[43]

Status and Power

'*Rational* operation of industrial enterprises which are introduced into a racially ordered society', Herbert Blumer writes, 'may call for a deferential respect for the canons and sensitivities of that racial order.'[44] As a colony, Hong Kong has a clearly defined ethnic hierarchy. The key cleavage is the ethnic boundary separating the 'European' minority (including Americans) from the Chinese majority. Among the Chinese, the Cantonese group is by far the largest. Such a pattern sets Hong Kong apart from the highly segmented Chinese communities in South-east Asia which are made up of regional groups of more or less equal numerical strength.[45]

By the time the Shanghainese spinners entered the scene in Hong Kong, the division between Europeans and Chinese was narrowing as a result of the Japanese occupation.[46] The more blatant practices of racial discrimination were beginning to be abolished, but the basic ethnic pattern remained unaltered. Adapting themselves to the local status and power structure, the Shanghainese directed most of their social energy in an attempt to gain the endorsement and support of the European élite.

In order to ensure protection for their investments in the colony, some of them engaged in the well-tried method of disguising the ethnic origin of their enterprises.[47] Several of their companies were registered in the name of prominent local British businessmen to make them appear British. The Kowloon Cotton Mill, established in 1948 with capital from the Shen Xin Fourth Mill, had adopted this approach. The chief executive of the British-owned China Engineers Company, who had made no investment in the new mill, was listed as a major shareholder. He was also given the post of managing director in the mill's early years. Documents specifying the true owners of the shares held in the name of the China

Engineers were exchanged between the parties concerned. China Engineers was willing to do this apparently because it had benefited as a supplier of equipment and loans to the mill. Simultaneously, the Shanghainese owners succeeded in obtaining a certificate from the British Consulate at Hankou stating that the parent company of the Kowloon Cotton Mill had major British interests and was therefore entitled to the protection of the British government.[48]

The Nanyang Cotton Mill, another enterprise set up by members of the Rong family in Hong Kong, also tried to acquire a Western appearance. It enlisted the help of Lawrence Kadoorie who has served as the chairman of its board of directors since its inception although he is not a major shareholder. Kadoorie, a British citizen born in Hong Kong, was brought up in Shanghai where his Jewish father had established himself as a notable businessman. In the early 1950s Kadoorie was a member of both the Legislative and Executive Councils of the Hong Kong government while running his major business of the China Light and Power Company.[49]

The Shanghainese spinners had one important skill at their disposal when dealing with the expatriate community — their fluent English acquired through Western education at some of the most prestigious universities in Shanghai or abroad. For at least two decades after the war English was the language of government in Hong Kong and consequently the key to upward social mobility.[50] The ensuing cosmopolitan aura of the spinners, coupled with their economic prowess as big employers of labour, meant that they commanded more respect from government officials than did most local Cantonese. They took obvious pride in their mastery of English which they used as their business language and as the main medium of their external social intercourse. The publications of their industrial association were mostly in English,[51] as were the minutes of the meetings of the general committee of their association.[52] Since 1960 they had been publishing technical journals in English for their employees. Not until 1970 did they come to realize that '[a] large number of those engaged in mill production operations could find it easier to absorb fully the substance of the technical articles written in Chinese'.[53] During my interviews, most of them opted to use English. Rong Yi-ren's wife, who has been living in Shanghai since 1949, also spoke English in a recent interview given to a Chinese reporter.[54]

Besides their command of English which facilitated access to the colonial administration, regional ties also helped them to establish rapport with government officials. Most of the senior Chinese civil servants in Hong Kong were indigenous Cantonese with a local university education. Even though only a few of them came from Shanghai, one of the Shanghainese civil servants has succeeded in reaching the top of the government hierarchy against all apparent odds.

Peter K. Y. Tsao (Cao Guang-rong) was an immigrant, not born to wealth. Without a university degree, he joined the Hong Kong government first as a scientific assistant in the Royal Observatory and then as a public health inspector. In 1966 he managed to get a transfer to the Department of Commerce and Industry. It was there that he flourished. He rose from the rank of assistant trade officer to become one of the directors of the department in charge of international trade negotiations. In that capacity, he led delegations from Hong Kong of members of the Textile Advisory Board, some of whom were spinners. It is said that he won the praise of the industrialists represented on the Board.

In 1983 he was promoted to the position of Director of Information Services and then Secretary for Home Affairs, later retitled Secretary for Administration. To celebrate his promotion to one of the most senior government posts, a group of directors of the Po Leung Kuk, a prominent charitable organization in Hong Kong, held a banquet in his honour at the Shanghai Fraternity Club. Mrs Sally Leung (Liang Wang Peifang), daughter of the chairman of Hong Kong Spinners Ltd. and herself the director of the Leighton Textile Company, represented the group in presenting a memento to Mr Tsao.[55]

The Shanghainese spinners, active in cultivating relationships with expatriates in business and government, were far less enthusiastic about dealing with the local Cantonese entrepreneurs. When they arrived, there existed in Hong Kong three major business associations. They were the Hong Kong General Chamber of Commerce dominated by British merchants and informally known as the Westerners' Chamber of Commerce; the Chinese General Chamber of Commerce of Hong Kong; and the Hong Kong Chinese Manufacturers' Union. Many of the spinners soon joined the Hong Kong General Chamber of Commerce.[56] But few of them became members of the Chinese General Chamber of Commerce of Hong Kong.[57]

In 1947 a bitter election dispute erupted in the Chinese Chamber of Commerce between the so-called Shanghainese faction and the local faction. The controversy, which had to be arbitrated in court, was resolved in favour of the locals, although it is not clear whether the spinners were involved in that dispute.[58] In the 1950s none of the spinners participated in the Chinese Manufacturers' Union, which organized the annual exhibition of products made by local Chinese factories.[59]

Hailing from the most prosperous metropolis of China, the Shanghai industrialists tried to project an image of themselves as members of the national élite, rather than a parochial minority in the Hong Kong Chinese community. In spite of their high concentration in the spinning industry, the Shanghai entrepreneurs did not emphasize their regional identity as did the Chaozhou, the second largest Chinese regional group in Hong Kong, who had organized a separate Chaozhou Chamber of Commerce and a score of other Chaozhou associations.[60] During the early years when the spinning industry was informally organized as a club, its meetings were chaired by the only non-Shanghainese mill owner, S. H. Yang of Pao Hsing Cotton Mill.[61] The spinners persistently played down their identity as Shanghainese. When asked to describe the differences between Shanghainese and Cantonese entrepreneurs, one of them said to me:

When I first came here about twenty-five years ago, I was very sensitive to the differences. But now they have become blurred. . . Some people are talking about forming a Shanghai club. I tell them Shanghai crabs may be better. The crabs from Shanghai do look different.

The gradual growth in the number of Shanghainese associations should not automatically be taken to mean a heightening of regional awareness. It might indicate the opposite trend. One of the founders of the Shanghai Fraternity Club revealed that their main aim was to raise funds to establish a hospital. Unless they went ahead quickly, he told me, Shanghainese of the old generation would pass away and their children would not be so generous and forthcoming in their financial contributions. The first fund-raising event of the association was a Chinese opera performance. They chose to put on a Mandarin opera instead of a Shanghainese one.[62]

A similar linguistic preference was shown in the educational institutions sponsored by the well-established Jiangsu and Zhejiang Residents' Association. During the inauguration ceremony of the Jiangsu and Zhejiang Secondary School, the president of the association emphasized in particular that people from his part of China had 'a good tradition' of 'not being restricted to the narrow view of regionalism'.[63] Not only were pupils recruited irrespective of regional background, but these were the only schools in Hong Kong using Mandarin, the national language, as the medium of instruction. Invited to address the graduation ceremony of the schools, a Shanghainese director of the association felt obliged to apologize for his poor command of the national language.[64]

Their aloof and élitist attitude did not endear the Shanghainese entrepreneurs to the local Cantonese leaders. 'The feeling of the Cantonese towards the Shanghai-Chinese who had come to live and set up business in Hong Kong was one of resentment', observed Alexander Grantham, a former governor of Hong Kong. 'They regarded them as altogether too smart and slick.'[65]

In the local status and power hierarchy, there were already established avenues of ascent for the Chinese by the late 1940s. English education was a crucial prerequisite for competition. Thus equipped, the ambitious could then climb the social ladder made up of rungs of Chinese associations. Starting with Kaifong associations, they could move up to the Po Leung Kuk, the Tung Wah Hospital Board, government consultative committees, and ultimately the Legislative and Executive Councils.

Few of the Shanghainese spinners joined the climbing of this conventional ladder, although this does not mean that they spurned the system. Seats on the Legislative and Executive Councils were apparently the same crowning social glory for them as for other Chinese residents. To some extent, the Shanghainese may have been excluded by the local élite, as shown in incidents connected with some of the associations. One illustration is the experience of the Shanghainese founder of Kader Company in the North Point Kaifong Association which was said to be so unpleasant that he withdrew his donations for the building of a school.[66]

But if they were indeed being excluded, they did not try very hard to push their way in. On the whole, the Shanghai industrialists by-passed the existing routes of social advancement for locals and opened up their own avenues of ascent. They founded their community associations by sponsoring a hospital (the Yan Chai Hospital) mostly by themselves, and by supporting New Asia College and Chung Chi College, two post-secondary institutions which later came to form part of the Chinese University of Hong Kong. Then on the basis of their industrial strength, they were invited by the Hong Kong government to join the Cotton Advisory Board and the Federation of Hong Kong Industries which were set up in 1960.

Once they had reached the springboard of the consultative committees and statutory bodies, it did not take long for the first Shanghainese entrepreneur to reach the apex of the local power structure. P. Y. Tang was appointed to the Legislative Council in 1964 and then to the Executive Council in 1969.

His appointment indicated official recognition of the fact that the composition of Chinese community leadership had changed. The established Cantonese families no longer had the field to themselves. Previously, Cantonese unofficial members in the two Councils acted as representatives of the Chinese inhabitants. In the budget debate of 1948, for instance, Chau Tsun-nin closed his speech by saying:

Finally, I would like, *on behalf of the Chinese community*, to endorse your excellency's remarks at our last meeting on the question of the recent customs agreement recently concluded with China.[67]

By the mid-1960s, scarcely two decades after their immigration, the Shanghainese had their own legislative councillor who spoke for the industrialists. P. Y. Tang devoted his entire maiden speech in the 1965 budget debate to the subject of 'the inadequacy and costliness of industrial land'. He concluded with the following remark:

I should feel there is not the slightest doubt that the demonstration by Government of an earnest wish to probe a matter vital to the future growth of industry will be received with satisfaction on all sides. *Industry in particular* will then be reassured that the possible reorientation of the land policy will now be given full and urgent consideration.[68]

The political rhetoric employed by the bifurcating Chinese leaders had changed. The idiom of ethnic politics employed by the Cantonese was superseded by the idiom of economic interests championed by the Shanghainese. With P. Y. Tang in the two Councils, the Shanghai industrialists had re-established themselves as an economic élite in their adopted community.

6 Familism and Industrial Enterprise

KINSHIP and ethnicity, as organizing principles for collective action, have much in common. Both involve social relations formed on the basis of an individual's origin. Biological descent is the essence of kinship, while territorial background constitutes the core of ethnicity. In most cases, an individual will have either his agnatic or maternal kinsmen as his fellow regionals as well. But at least some of his consanguineous relatives will have a territorial affiliation different from his own. Besides genealogical descent, kinship also includes social ties forged by marriages. The affinal relations thus formed are of a more voluntaristic nature, and an individual's affines will generally come from a different ancestry or locality except in instances of kinship endogamy. Therefore kin and ethnic categories do overlap, but are seldom identical.

Kinship confers some of the most cohesive social bonds to an individual. For this reason, Neil J. Smelser identifies it as a major form of solidarity grouping in the economy.[1] But its economic importance varies in different societies, depending on the degree to which the family and kinship system is the dominant institution in the social structure. It is widely recognized that family and kinship are the nuts and bolts of Chinese society and that they were the centres of loyalty for every Chinese at least in the late traditional period. It is therefore not surprising that many observers believe '[that] in Chinese economic life "family" is all; that the strength of Chinese business lies in the solidarity of relatives; that Chinese success rests on a firm foundation of unrenounceable kinship obligation'.[2] On the basis of his field experience, Maurice Freedman casts doubt on such conventional wisdom and tentatively suggests that 'much of the economic organization to be seen in Singapore Chinese society rests on solidarities constructed on a non-kinship basis'.[3] He maintains that the crucial distinction between Chinese and Western economic behaviour is not that of kin and non-kin, but personal and impersonal. Chinese individuals tend to personalize their economic relations, and kinship is just one of the possible bases for solidarity.

If this general formulation is accepted, it is still worthwhile asking further: what is the relative significance of kinship in different areas of economic activity? It is likely that kinship plays a more important role in cementing the internal organization of Chinese industrial firms than in regulating their external relations. The reasons for this will become clear when the characteristics of ethnic and kinship ties are compared.

In the last chapter, it was indicated that one of the strengths of ethnicity for group formation is its flexible boundary. Kinship ties, by contrast, are more restrictive and less amenable to extension. An individual is born with a limited number of agnatic relatives. With marriage links established through female members of the family, his affinal kinsmen will tend to be more numerous and geographically dispersed. But they are still quite narrow in scope. As a result, kinship ties are most effective in confined arenas. In the political realm, Jacobs has demonstrated that Chinese kinship relations are important on a village level. But he goes on to say that '[biological] limits on the number of one's kin require that other *kuan-hsi* also be utilized at higher levels in the political system where a successful political career cannot be based solely on the insufficiently extensive affinal and agnatic kinship *kuan-hsi*'.[4]

The same principle applies in economic competition. Besides flexibility, the kinship bond differs from the ethnic one in its greater intensity. Rights and obligations are more specific and binding. This gives cause for individuals to avoid economic dealings with their kinsmen under certain circumstances, thus reducing the economic range and utility of kinship. One possible exception to this rule is clan relations which I shall examine later in connection with economic transactions among Chinese firms. Meanwhile, let us turn to the role of kinship in the internal organization of Chinese industrial enterprises.

Internal Organization of Enterprises

It is interesting to note that most of the small number of sociological investigations on the internal set-up of Chinese companies are conducted among the overseas Chinese. This may be no coincidence as Chinese entrepreneurship tends to thrive on alien soil. Donald Willmott sets the theme for these studies when he states that the 'most striking feature of Chinese business organization in Semarang [in Indonesia] is the familism which, in the great majority of cases, forms its core'.[5]

M. I. Barnett, an anthropologist, finds a similar pattern among the Cantonese in the United States. He observes: '[Personnel] practices in Chinatown are based, in large measure, upon familial and personal relations. Priority is given to relatives and fellow villagers when a proprietor engages a staff of employees'.[6] He concludes that '[in so far] as North American urban situations are concerned, Chinese economic adaptation has been accompanied by a persistent adherence to many Kwangtung behavioral norms, especially those related to kinship'.[7]

As for the Shanghai textile industrialists in Hong Kong, Oksenberg thinks that 'all the spinning and weaving companies might loosely be labeled "family firms"'. He notes that 'The ownership and management of the firm tends to be by a single extended family', and that 'those who hold major positions of responsibility in the company, if not members of the family, have long been associated with it'.[8]

From these statements, it is clear that the concept of 'familism' carries several layers of meaning which must be separated before fruitful analysis can proceed. In one sense, the concept refers to managerial practices. The management may extol the ideal of the family as a model for personnel administration. For this wider usage, *paternalism* would be an appropriate term. Or it may mean specifically the preferential recruitment and promotion of kinsmen inside an organization. This mode of behaviour is generally called *nepotism*. In yet another sense, the concept is concerned with the ownership of a company. I shall reserve the term *family enterprise* for firms in which the majority of the assets are held by a single family. Paternalism, nepotism, and family enterprises may coexist in some Chinese firms, but theoretically they are not inherently related. Family enterprises can adopt an impersonal approach to management, and paternalism and nepotism can occur in companies that are not family-owned.

Paternalism

In the chapters on industrial skills and business ideology, paternalism has already been dealt with at some length. Suffice it to call two more witnesses to demonstrate the prevalence of the paternalistic outlook among the mill owners. Responding to my query as to whether he has relatives employed in his company, the governing director of the privately owned Mill 12 answered in the affirmative. When I probed further for the number of relatives involved, he replied: 'It is very difficult to say. We Chinese have a wide definition of relatives. Who is a relative? For example, an employee in the company, after a long service, is like a relative.'

Such sentiment can be found within publicly held textile firms as well. A director of Mill 1 offered the following comments when I asked him about the other benefits his executives had besides their regular wages:

We are as close as a family [he had said earlier that he preferred not to employ relatives]. There are annual bonuses for employees. The amounts vary according to the performance of each division. Our staff are more interested in cash, and we will advise them on how to invest...

Paternalism entails two main consequences. In the first place, it demands formal obedience from subordinates. The emphasis is on outward deference to one's superiors in the organization. Employees, for example, avoid eye contact with their chief executive during board meetings.[9] Dissenting views and personal opinions may be advanced by executives, and are sometimes even demanded of them, but they must be made at the appropriate moment so as not publicly to contradict the superiors.[10] In the second place, it can inhibit the growth of class consciousness among the workers. This does not mean the absence of friction in Chinese firms. Rather, conflicts tend to be manifested in individual actions such as absenteeism and resignations and not in collective bargaining that arises from a polarization of interests between management and labour. A prominent Cantonese entrepreneur is well aware of this when he writes:

In a western industrial society, paternalism is frowned upon; in Hong Kong it has been an instrument for industrial success and social equilibrium in a period of great social upheaval. Here again it is worth noting that in 1968, out of a total of about 170 million industrial man-days, only 8,432 man-days were lost through disputes.[11]

Barnett makes a similar observation about the Chinese in the United States in the early 1960s:

the existence of a highly developed American trade union movement notwithstanding, the traditional Chinese guild, comprised of employers and employees, still plays a decisive role with respect to wages, hours and conditions of work. The social bonds of genealogical relationship and locality ties, rather than class identification, provide the framework for the *hua ch'iao* (overseas Chinese) economy.[12]

However there are signs that the objective foundation for this paternalistic approach is being undermined. 'Studies of large Chinese firms', writes Frederic C. Deyo, 'have noted a marked transformation of informal paternalism into impersonal and highly formalized systems of personnel and supervisory control.'[13] With their Westernized form of education and training, young Chinese executives are familiar with the norms and role expectations of impersonal bureaucracies. They are less willing to accept benefits as patriarchal favours from their employers, and they are readier to demand benefits as their right. A classmate of mine resigned some time ago from a Shanghainese shipping firm which has welfare provisions for its staff. He expressed his dissatisfaction over the weight of paternalism:

The company has housing loans for its staff, but nobody wants to take them. Everything is very personal. To get a loan, you have to plead for it, and it is granted as a favour. It will make you feel morally obliged. There is no system. But in the University of Hong Kong, you get it as a rule, without personal debts.

A more important factor in the decline of a paternalistic approach in industry is perhaps Hong Kong's transition from a labour-surplus to a labour-scarce economy. Since more work opportunities are available, higher staff turnover is inevitable, which reduces the possibility of a sense of dependence and gratitude in the workforce. As the value of loyal and long service fades among the employees, it is becoming more difficult for owners to maintain a patriarchal stance.

Nepotism

Nepotism, the preferential employment of one's relatives, is the standard whipping boy for Chinese and Western scholars alike when China's modernization or industrial organization is discussed. Marion J. Levy Jr. develops a forceful theoretical critique of its harmful effects. Upholding the particularistic-traditional and universalistic-modern dichotomy, he argues that contemporary industry and the traditional Chinese family are mutually incompatible because the latter was more or less the particularistic structure *par excellence*. 'The introduction of modern industry is the first genuine threat to the stability of the "traditional" Chinese family', and 'the nepotism fostered by the "traditional" family is one of the greatest obstacles to an efficient industrial system.'[14] Kinship obligation is so strong, he asserts, that few Chinese entrepreneurs can refuse to find positions in their firms for their relatives without risking social ostracism. So businessmen are faced with two equally unattractive options. 'The attempt to use these people in ordinary roles endangers the efficiency of the operation, and their sinecures are a great financial burden to the venture. In either case, the modern business role is hindered.'[15]

Chinese commentators also feel that the appointment of relatives is one of the gravest handicaps to the administration of large industrial plants such as cotton spinning mills. In his study of the development of China's cotton industry, Kang Chao compares the organizational characteristics of Japanese, British, and Chinese-owned mills in modern China. He finds that the Chinese-owned mills cannot match the performance of the Japanese-owned ones, which he attributes partly to widespread nepotism. 'It seems unlikely that mill owners were unaware of the undesirable nature of nepotism', he observes, 'yet it nevertheless continued to prevail.'[16]

One particular feature of the Chinese kinship structure seems to lend credibility to this line of argument. The Chinese have an unusually large vocabulary of kinship terms, reflecting a recognition of a wide web of mutual responsibility with one's kinsmen which probably has significant economic consequences.[17] Contrasting it with its Japanese equivalent, John C. Pelzel throws this aspect of Chinese kinship into relief:

Chinese kinship terminology allows explicit recognition of many attributes of the relation with ego, such as sex, generation, lineality, relative age, and collaterality for a circle of kinsmen that includes even quite distant relatives. Japanese terminology, on the other hand, is even more niggardly than American English in its description of their attributes...Insofar as kin terms are signs that guide behaviour, ...Japanese usage alerts ego only to those closest kinsmen with whom he might, for household reasons, be expected to interact intensively, leaving behaviour toward others to be prompted by other kinds of cues. Chinese terminology, on the other hand, guides ego to recognize a large number of particular relationships and a wide range of behavioural duties, from the intense to the relatively weak, and in a set of categories...[18]

It can therefore be inferred that the dead weight of nepotism is much heavier on a Chinese businessman than a Japanese one because more people can make claims on him on kinship grounds.

It is interesting to look at how widespread the phenomenon of

Table 6.1. Employment of Relatives in Hong Kong Spinning Mills

Relatives Employed	No.	Adjusted %*
Yes	20	59
No	14	41
No response	6	—
Total	40	100

Note: * Only those who gave an answer were included.

Source: Interviews, 1978.

nepotism is in actual practice. Levy has little doubt that it is all pervasive. On the strength of the opinions of Chinese social scientists and informants, he puts forth the view that

[if a man] fails to help close relatives...[he] may be said to be unfilial or to demonstrate *pei-te*, that is, not loving those to whom one is bound by natural ties, both of which are extremes of inhumanity...The pressure brought can be extreme, and all Chinese involved in the new industries are subjected to it. The owners, engineers, executives and foremen are all more or less vulnerable to such pressure.[19]

When my respondents were questioned, nearly 60 per cent said they had relatives employed in their mills (Table 6.1). Yet this percentage reveals at once too little and too much. Too little as it is what the cotton spinners chose to tell me. Without a comprehensive survey of the mill employees, I have no independent means of verification. Sometimes under-reporting was not deliberate. A number of respondents did not count immediate family members as relatives, and I have corrected these errors if I know for certain that they had fathers, brothers or sons working with them. It tells too much in that all the respondents who answered in the affirmative emphasized that only 'one or two' or 'a few' relatives were engaged. Keeping in mind that the companies had at least 200 employees each, the percentage of kinsmen in the entire work-force is negligible.

Other studies in the colony have produced similar findings. Espy interviewed the chief executives of 27 large Chinese industrial firms in 1969 (11 of which were Shanghainese-owned). Among the 23 from whom information was obtained, 14 of them or 61 per cent, had 'family members' employed in their companies. But nine of these cases involved only the sons of the chief executives.[20] In a survey in 1978 of 415 small scale factories in Hong Kong, it emerged that about 47 per cent of the factory owners had relatives in their work-force.[21] Ward's case study of the glass factory with just over 20 workers reveals that none of the employees was related to the two managing directors and that the criterion of recruitment was universalistic.[22]

These findings suggest that nepotism exists in probably about half of the Chinese firms in Hong Kong, but that, unless the company is very small, relatives as employees apparently make up a tiny fraction of the personnel in the companies practising nepotism. If this is indeed the situation, then it is likely that Levy and others have over-estimated the extent of favouritism towards relatives among Chinese entrepreneurs, while at the same time it is possible that Chinese kinship values have been rapidly changing under the impact of industrialization in Hong Kong.

When nepotism is practised, what types of kinsmen tend to be appointed? Are they assigned to important posts, or are they relegated to sinecures? To answer these questions, it is necessary first to differentiate the following kinship categories: *jia*, kin network, lineage, and clan. The *jia* is the smallest kinship unit in Chinese society which has generally been identified by social scientists as the family. It is a property-holding unit, and the *jia* group 'is made up of those persons who have rights of some sort or another to the *chia* [*jia*] estate at the time of *fen-chia* (family division)'.[23] Beyond the *jia*, there is the so-called 'greater family'. According to D. K. Lieu, this is a 'large, shifting organization, including all kinds of relatives, both by blood and by marriage, centering around some particular individuals as the nucleus, and differing in composition with different individuals'.[24] As an ego-centred web of traceable kinship relations devoid of an organizational structure, it is roughly equivalent to the meaning of the Chinese term for relatives. I shall call this the kin network. Both lineage and clan are agnatic units, but the proper demarcation of these two concepts for Chinese society is controversial. Freedman makes the distinction that the former is an enduring grouping which has established some focus for its unity, typically in the form of an ancestral hall, ancestral estate, or endowed tomb. When such a focus is absent and collective action is only transitory, then the agnatic unit is a clan.[25]

Table 6.2. Types of Kinsmen Employed and their Positions in the Spinning Mills

Respondent*	Type of Relative	Position
B6	'a few relatives'	not known
A8	2 brothers	directors
	'cousin'	mill manager
B8	2 brothers	directors
	'cousin'	mill manager
A9	'a few relatives'	not known
B9	father	chairman
	brother	director
	'a few relatives'	'low positions'
B10	father	director
	'cousin'	director
A12	brother	director/manager
	2 sons	executives
B12	brother	director
	2 'nephews'	executives
A13	brother	director/manager
	son	director/manager
B13	father	director
	'uncle'	director
A14	father	chairman
	wife	director
	2 'nephews'	mill manager and executive
B14	grandfather	chairman
	'uncle'	director
	'aunt'	director
	brother	executive
B16	'a few relatives'	not known
B17	father	director
	'uncle'	director
A19	brother	director
A30	wife	director
	brother-in-law	director
A32	brother	director/manager
	'a few relatives'	'junior staff'

Table 6.2. (*cont.*)

Respondent*	Type of Relative	Position
A33	father	director
	'uncle'	director
	brother	executive
B33	brother	director
	2 'nephews'	executives

Note: * 'A' stands for the senior director and 'B' stands for the other director interviewed. The number stands for the mill.

Source: Interviews, 1978.

If the kinship statuses of the relatives employed by my respondents are listed as far as the information permits, it is clear that the overwhelming majority of them are *jia* members (see Table 6.2). The remaining few cases are members of the entrepreneurs' kinship networks: cousins (since they did not have the same surname as the respondents, they were obviously not father's brother's sons), brothers-in-law or distant relatives. Lineage members or clansmen were not mentioned. There is a tendency for *jia* members to be placed in key decision-making positions, and for other relatives in the kin networks to be engaged at junior levels. The dominance of *jia* members among all the kinsmen employed is confirmed by other studies. Espy has no concrete data on this point, but he is of the impression that '[a] Chinese industrial firm in Hong Kong is more likely not to employ relatives of the chief executive (other than especially chosen sons or nephews) than to employ them'.[26] The 1978 sample survey of small industrialists shows that nearly 83 per cent of the owners who had relatives as employees, were employing only family members.[27] The Hong Kong Chinese entrepreneurs are nepotistic mainly with respect to persons of their own *jia*, and much less so regarding kin network, lineage, or clan members.

The hiring of relatives is generally regarded as incompatible with bureaucratic efficiency. However an objective assessment of the economic consequences of nepotism is very difficult. One possible approach is to explore the reasons that Chinese entrepreneurs employ kinsmen. For various reasons, they may positively prefer to

Table 6.3. Spinners' Preference for Relative or Non-relative as Employee

Preference	No.	Adjusted %*
Relative	9	26
Non-relative	18	51
No preference	8	23
No response	5	—
Total	40	100

Note: * Only those who gave an answer were included.
Source: Interviews, 1978.

employ relatives, thus practising *active* nepotism. Or they may feel an obligation to appoint them against their business judgement. In this case, nepotism is *passive*.

Only a minority of the cotton spinners subscribed to active nepotism. They were asked a hypothetical question: 'If you have two applicants with similar qualifications and abilities for a post, and one is related to you but the other is not, which one would you employ?' As Table 6.3 shows, only one-quarter of the respondents said they would appoint the relative. Over half of them preferred to hire a stranger. The main objection to relatives as employees was that they would interfere with the impersonal operation of the enterprise and weaken the entrepreneur's authority. Kinsmen as employees were usually seen as a source of trouble. As the chairman of Mill 3 said, 'If I am good to him, he will not be grateful; but if I am a bit harsh, he will say that I treat him badly'. Most of the spinners wished to appear to be fair to their employees so as to encourage them to work hard. Therefore several mill owners made it a rule not to employ relatives. The directors of a publicly held textile corporation took the more radical step of excluding their own children from participating in the company. One of the directors told me:

I will not appoint relatives. It creates administrative problems. No one can control them. Our top management has decided that no children of the directors are to be employed in the company. They have to set up on their own. Otherwise the staff would not be dedicated because promotion prospects are dim. Now we always keep an eye open as to who can succeed.

For instance, we have an employee from the Social Welfare Department. Our wages are lower than those of the government. But he still joined us because of the prospects.

The chairman of the corporation went further to stress that they tried to eliminate nepotism throughout the organization:

We don't like staff introducing relatives either. Because then you can't exercise your judgment. If you fire them, you make your staff unhappy; but if you tolerate them, you have dead wood.

The awareness of the liability of employing kinsmen is by no means a new trend or unique to the spinners. At least one major Chinese company in Indonesia placed qualifications above particularistic ties. As Willmott tells us, '[long] before his death in 1924, Oei Tiong Ham laid down the concern's strict personnel policy. It was considered revolutionary because it rated brains, ability, and training above family connections'.[28] In Singapore during the late 1940s, Freedman heard 'Chinese businessmen say that a growing acquaintance with western standards of efficiency is causing many heads of firms to bid for the best qualified man in the market rather than place, say, a *chhin-lang* [relative] in an executive or technical position'.[29] During his research on a Chinese community in Java, Ryan found that 'an informant, in the presence of his mother, expressed an unwillingness to give a job to a young kinsman, [and] the old lady reacted with indignation: "You must help Tjoing", she said, "He is your kinsman"'.[30] The significant point is that the first impulse of the young businessman was to avoid recruiting the relative.

To ask whether Chinese business practice is hampered by nepotism would only produce generalizations; much more revealing is to determine conditions under which kinsmen will be actively sought to fill positions in a profit-making organization. It is often too readily assumed in discussions of nepotism that relatives are *ipso facto* substandard employees. As the director of Mill 6 said in response to my hypothetical question, 'I prefer the relative. I know him better'. Therefore hiring kinsmen can be a rational economic decision in a small enterprise with limited capital. Family members, and to some extent other kinsmen, can provide cheap labour to reduce operational costs. Only 67 per cent of the small Hong Kong factories gave as much pay to their kinsmen-employees as to ordinary workers.[31] Kang Chao, in his study of the Chinese handicraft weaving industry, points out that the resilience of these domestic enterprises in the face of mass-produced Western imports was founded on the low opportunity costs of family labour.[32] In Singapore, Lee Sheng Yi finds that during the recession of 1975–6, '[small] industries and trading companies claim that they can survive because of the family members working in the firm (who are) not so demanding in wages and salaries and are more willing to work harder with less pay'.[33]

But, obviously, such economies will not be of much benefit to large scale operations such as cotton spinning mills. As the predominance of *jia* members among the relatives employed by our respondents indicates, preferential recruitment of kinsmen in Hong Kong cotton mills was very much a derivative phenomenon of the family mode of ownership. In order to prevent the dissipation of family property and business profits to outsiders, entrepreneurs would put their sons or other *jia* members in responsible positions. Espy's data on large Chinese industrial firms suggest that the inclusion of family members in management probably has little adverse effect on the performance of the company. Growth rate of the enterprise and the employment of family members are not correlated in his sample.[34]

The reasons for this are not hard to find. Entrepreneurs usually take meticulous care to equip their family members for the top positions. As the data on the educational background of the spinners show, most were qualified and technically trained. The case of the general manager of Hong Kong Textiles, Ltd. is illustrative. He obtained a master's degree in mechanical engineering from the California Institute of Technology in 1961. He worked for two years as a design engineer for General Pump and Corporation in the United States. In 1963, he was recalled by his father who began grooming him for succession. He recounted:

I tried to get my father to let me work on some technical problem, but he said these were not important. Instead, he made me sit in on his negotiations with foreign buyers. After each production contract had been signed and the buyer had left, my father went over his calculations with me. He would show me the basis of his price quotations and how much gross profit he expected to make. He soon had me preparing all price quotations. After I had been doing this for about three months, my father made a three-week business trip to the United States and I met the buyers by myself.[35]

Dwight H. Perkins, weighing the pros and cons of Chinese nepotism, maintains that it is necessary to distinguish between public and private employment. In public bureaucracies, he says, 'Chinese officials could appoint relatives to government positions at no cost and conceivably with some financial benefits to themselves'.[36] In private companies, however, relatives were hired because there existed a greater basis for trust and possibly they were more highly motivated than other employees. However, the important distinction is not between public and private organizations, but between security or insecurity as perceived by the employers. One good reason for Chinese officials to appoint relatives was that, as a rule, they were assigned to regions where they had few particularistic ties. In a hostile and strange environment, it was reassuring to have kinsmen as assistants. Similarly, in profit-making organizations where entrepreneurs feel that their interests or positions are threatened, kinsmen or others who can be relied on will be rallied.[37] The mill manager of the newly established Mill 9 explained why he needed relatives in the factory: 'The workers are very violent, and fights are frequent. Relatives help me and give me security when I try to maintain discipline'. The director of Mill 10 was in his late thirties with an American doctoral degree in chemical engineering. In spite of his youth and Western education, he was emphatic that he preferred employing relatives because 'trust and loyalty are primary'. There were signs that his company was fraught with factionalism. It was a joint venture between his family and two Japanese firms, and had been losing money for several years. An informant told me that 'directors would put the profitable orders to their own factories and leave the group to lose money'. Nepotism, in these instances, probably intensifies organizational problems. But it is obviously the symptom and not the cause of the malfunctioning of the business enterprise.

So much for active nepotism. The discrepancy between the expressed attitude and actual practice of employing kinsmen among the cotton spinners implies that quite a number of them were accepting relatives into their companies against their will. Of the small factory owners surveyed in Hong Kong in 1978, about 46 per cent of those who employed relatives said they did so out of a sense of kinship obligation.[38] Yet there is little evidence that passive nepotism will overburden the enterprises. Several factors tend to ensure that few people will invoke the kinship tie to secure a job. The managing director of Mill 14 set out clearly the conditions for giving employment to relatives. 'I may make an exception for relatives of a senior generation so as to give them face. As for relatives junior to me, the only situation in which I would help is when they are in economic difficulty.' The director of Mill 12 said: 'But if they [the relatives] had no work to do, I would have to give them some.' The corollary of this is that a kinsman can make claims on the entrepreneur only at a cost. He has to admit that he is in dire need, thus risking humiliation for his family in the kin network. In addition, he would have to accept whatever is offered with little choice over pay or position. Thus, he would most probably approach his entrepreneur-kinsman only as a last resort. Even then, when the entrepreneur acknowledges the obligation to help, he might find a job for his relative through his connections in other firms and avoid causing administrative complications for himself. Lastly, since Chinese entrepreneurs ordinarily leave their native region to conduct business in the urban area, in a different province or a foreign country, relatives will not, anyway, be abundant in the communities where they work.

In this connection, it is interesting to record that several Shanghainese respondents attributed the practice of nepotism to Cantonese businessmen. The director of Mill 22 said, 'Many people are like that [showing preference to relatives], especially the Cantonese. This is their greatest problem so that they can't grow. People of other provinces are less like that.' This opinion was echoed by the managing director of Mill 1 and a director of Mill 4. Such an assertion can hardly be supported empirically on the grounds of regional variations in kinship sentiment among the Chinese. It is most likely an expression of regional condescension which reflects the rejection of nepotism as a social value. These respondents may be led to this belief because most of the local small family enterprises are Cantonese-owned since the Cantonese constitute the majority of the population. The comment also reveals an objective difference between indigenous and migrant entrepreneurs. The former will inevitably have more kinsmen in the community to look after than the latter.

Family Enterprise

After assessing the role of kinship in managerial practices, let us look at its significance in the possession and transmission of industrial assets. The most systematic and reliable information on mill ownership can be found in the files on individual firms kept at the Hong Kong government's Company Registry. Each company

is required by law to register with the government at its incorpora-
tion and to provide the Company Registry with an article of
association and a list of directors and shareholders. Any changes
in these respects have to be reported in an annual return to the
Registry. Thus the date as well as the amount of share transfer is
clearly shown in the files. We can assume that the records are fairly
accurate because it would be in the interest of individual
shareholders to protect their own possessions in case of dispute. In
most cases, shareholders are identified by individual names. But
there are two exceptions. It is permissible for shareholders to take
the form of an unlimited liability company, usually called *ji*, such
as Zhang San Ji or Li Si Ji. As unlimited liability companies, they
are only obliged to file sketchy records, and it is very difficult to
discover the personal identities of their owners. Fortunately, the
ownership by *ji* only happens in a few cases. In the case of public
companies, many stocks are held anonymously by bank nominees.
This practice, which provides confidentiality to the stock owners,
makes detailed analysis of the ownership in public companies quite
impossible.

Using these records, I tried to determine the relative proportion
of different forms of mill ownership. I divided forms of ownership
into four main categories: sole proprietorship, family enterprises,
partnership, and public companies. By sole proprietorship, I refer
to a firm in which one individual holds over half of the total assets.
If it is a family rather than an individual that owns the majority
share, then it is called a family enterprise. The kinship ties among
the shareholders are not immediately apparent from the company
records. But since most of the mills have been established for over
twenty years, there is a likelihood that at least one death in the
family has occurred. It is customary for wealthy Chinese to publish
a funeral notice in the major Chinese newspapers listing the names
and kinship statuses of family members of the deceased. I have
noted all the deaths recorded in the company files, and these were
checked against the two major Hong Kong Chinese newspapers,
namely *Xingdao Ribao* and *Huaqiao Ribao*. Funeral notices are
available in the majority of cases. When this type of precise data
could not be found, I relied on deduction based on home addresses
and personal names. If several individuals shared the same address,
and if most of them had their surname and one character of their
personal name in common, then I assumed they were siblings. The
individual with the same address and surname but different per-

Table 6.4. Distribution of Mills by Form of Ownership

Form of Ownership	No. of Mills	%
Family enterprise	16	50
Public company	11	34
Partnership	4	13
Sole proprietorship	1	3
Total	32	100

Source: Mill records in Company Registry, Hong Kong.

sonal name was taken to be the head of the family, and the woman with a different surname was assumed to be the wife of the head. In some cases, I managed to obtain confirmation from the brief biographies of prominent Chinese published in *Huaqiao Ribao*'s annual report on Hong Kong. The third form is partnership in which neither an individual nor a family has a controlling share of 50 per cent. Public company is the last form which has shares floated in the local stock-market. In this category, are included mills that were subsidiaries of other public companies as well as mills which had gone public in their own right.

Table 6.4 shows the distribution of mills among the four types of ownership. Half of the mills were family enterprises. But even this proportion does not adequately convey the importance of the family in the possession of industrial assets. Although the identities of owners of the public companies are partly shrouded in secrecy, there are strong hints that the pattern of ownership among public textile companies does not differ significantly from that of the family enterprises. Such resemblance was made possible by the local commercial legislation which only required public corporations to offer a quarter of their shares to the public. As the managing director of Mill 22, himself the chairman of a public concern, said, 'Nearly all of the textile companies are family-owned. Even the floated ones. They only have to offer 25 per cent of the shares to the public. The rest are held by a few families. The operators are usually owners.'

The family also figures prominently in firms owned by partners. Although there were only four mills belonging to this category at the time of investigation, it was found that 16 mills or 50 per cent of the total were actually partnerships when they were first established. Besides underscoring the instability of this mode of ownership, it indicated a tendency for partnership to be turned into family enterprises after disintegration.

The single case of sole proprietorship was actually an artefact of my definition. The managing director of the mill owned 84 per cent of the shares. But his wife was a co-owner with 16 per cent. It was probably because his children were still young that he did not assign some shares to them, thus making his company a family enterprise in my sense of the term. The process of development of Mill 21 was illuminating in this regard. The mill was incorporated in 1948 with a capital of HK$5 million jointly subscribed by 21 partners. Among these was Mr Huang who had 4 per cent of the total shares.[39] In December 1952 the partly-paid shares of 18 of the partners which made up 90 per cent of the total capital were forfeited by the company. Seven years later, Mr Huang purchased a large number of shares from the company and became the sole proprietor with 56 per cent of the shares. His possession increased steadily to 75 per cent in 1975. It appears that at about this time he learnt that he had cancer. In April the following year, he transferred most of his shares to a newly created company completely owned by his wife and children. When he died in 1977 the company had become a family firm. The case indicates that in some sense, the proprietor was holding the assets as a trustee for his offspring, not for himself. Schumpeter's statement that 'the family, not the physical person, is the true unit of class and class theory' applies, therefore, to the Hong Kong Chinese entrepreneurs.[40]

When industrial capital is held by the family as a unit, what effect does this have on the enterprise? Does this tend to keep the firm small and impermanent? Restriction on the scale of a firm and ownership by the family might go hand in hand, as David S. Landes implies in his study of the French industrial scene. 'It is widely known', he writes, 'that the typical French business is small. What is less often realized is that most businesses are family-structured.'[41] He argues that in a system of family firms, the 'compulsive urge toward growth...is either diluted or absent'. This is because:

the main objective is to avoid use of credit and to make the highest rate of profit possible on a given turnover; to amortize expenses rapidly and build up huge reserves; and to finance expansion out of such reserves, or by what the French called *auto-financement.*

The retardative effect of this emphasis on conservation and consolidation is reinforced by an all-overriding concern for family independence. The French entrepreneur is inclined, if anything, to postpone possibilities of development, simply because expansion might sooner or later compel recourse to outside capital and seriously, if not definitely, compromise the exclusive character of the entrepreneur...[42]

Willmott paints a similar picture of the Indonesian Chinese economy. He says that the 'great majority of Chinese enterprises are small enough for one family to handle without employing outsiders above the level of workers or clerks'.[43] He adds one more factor which shortens the life span of Chinese firms. 'The constant dividing of fortunes among many inheritors means that Chinese business enterprise must operate with a minimum of ready capital. In many families the sons do not care to take on their father's business, and the enterprise dies with the father.'[44] Besides the system of equal inheritance among heirs, the dissipation of commercial or industrial capital by spendthrift sons is an often-cited cause of the decline of family economic endeavours. Ping-ti Ho takes the case of the Chinese salt merchants in the eighteenth century to show that for these reasons 'a relatively small fortune like that of the Li family could be dissipated in two or three generations. A large fortune like that of the Ch'eng family might be fairly well levelled off in five generations'.[45]

But the arguments of these scholars need to be somewhat qualified. For there is, in fact, evidence that Chinese kinship ties can be the basis of large scale enterprise. Mark Elvin has described the case of a sixteenth-century merchant of Huizhou who built a big fortune together with his 'clan' members:

He gathered together the worthy persons in his clan, thus obtaining some ten persons, and each of them contributed three hundred strings of cash for their common use. They traded in Hsin-shih in Wu-hsing. At that time the Ch'eng clan was prosperous, and the young blood vied with each other in wasteful expenditure. Ch'eng Sou made a pact with his ten associates that they should reject such behaviour and face up to hardship...In the course of time their undertakings prospered and the ten became wealthy beyond measure.[46]

Even when co-operation is kept purely within the *jia*, there is the example of the Rong family which created a huge textile venture in modern China. In the 1930s this family possessed nine spinning mills with a total of 500,000 spindles or over one fifth of the total spindleage of Chinese-owned mills. By 1947 its industrial assets had increased to 625,278 spindles or about 23 per cent of all privately owned Chinese spindleage.[47] This example demonstrates that there is nothing inherent in the Chinese family structure to limit the size of an enterprise.

As for the alleged aversion of family firms to expansion, D. W. Stammer, who has studied the financial structure of Hong Kong, would disagree. 'The very fact that much of commerce and industry consists of family-owned businesses and not public companies means that a high proportion of profits can be retained for reinvestment. Some sizeable, progressive businesses have for some years, used *all* their profits to finance expansion.'[48] As data on the use of profit by Chinese companies are hard to obtain, it is not possible to determine the degree of accuracy of Stammer's statement. But it is conceivable that he is describing the behaviour of family firms in a favourable economic climate while Landes' analysis applies to a less prosperous time. Moreover, Chinese family firms in Hong Kong did tap outside capital supplies such as bank loans without relinquishing their exclusive ownership. But most important, the scale and growth potential of family enterprises should be seen developmentally in terms of the family life cycle which merits close examination.

The Chinese family has a number of features which affect its conduct as a unit of industrial ownership. One is the principle of patrilineal descent which means that relatively discrete and enduring corporate kinship units can be constituted for the management of economic resources. Another is the rule of equal inheritance among male heirs. The third is the process of family division which occurs in several stages. As a rule, the first asset to be divided is the profit derived from the family estate. Then come the right of utilization and the right of transferral of the *jia* property respectively. Whereas demands for the division of profit can be made by the heirs after their marriage, the division of utilization and transferral must wait till the retirement or death of the family head.

Whether these demands are pressed depends very much on the nature of the family property. When the property takes the form of industrial assets involving economies of scale, team work, a business reputation, and financial borrowings, it is generally in the interests of the heirs to defer the physical fragmentation of the *jia* estate.

Table 6.5. Developmental Phases of Chinese Family Firms

	Aspects of Family Firm		
Phases	Estate	Management	Profit
Emergent	+	+	+
Centralized	+	+	−
Segmented	+	−	−
Disintegrative	−	−	−

Note: + means unity.
     − means division.

With these features in mind, a better understanding of the Chinese family firm can be achieved by positing four significant phases in its development as shown schematically in Table 6.5. These phases tend to coincide with generational shifts inside the *jia* so that the profit, management, and estate of the family enterprise are progressively fragmented.

During the emergent phase, the pater-entrepreneur is usually involved in a venture with several partners. He uses his family savings as the capital share, and the well-being of his *jia* provides the main spur to his business activities. A Chinese family head, as mentioned earlier, acts as a trustee of the *jia* property. But a distinction should be made between inherited *jia* property and that which is acquired by the pater-entrepreneur himself.[49] The latter carries with it greater freedom of manoeuvre, social recognition and esteem, as well as the gratitude of his offspring. In a religious sense, the pater-entrepreneur's 'salvation' or immortality also depends on the continuation and glorification of his family line. All of these are powerful incentives for his endeavour to create an endowment.

Partnerships in Chinese business are notably unstable. Most individuals apparently enter this form of business alliance as an expedient, fully aware that they must fend for themselves. As a result, this type of economic organization is generally under-capitalized. Partners typically defer paying up on their shares and demand maximum returns for their investments. The Dai Sheng Cotton Mill founded by Zhang Jian, for instance, had to pay 8 per cent

'guaranteed dividend' annually to all partners before actual production started.[50] In the absence of mutual trust, factions and
cliques tend to be rife with each partner attempting to place his own
men inside the firm. If the business manages to take off despite
these obstacles, then there occurs an asymmetrical growth in the
distribution of shares. Some partners are in a more advantageous
position than others to increase their portion of ownership. The
usual method is to capture the key managerial positions as these
carry an entitlement to extra 'red' shares as an incentive to effort.[51]
Those who have close relatives among the partners will have an obvious edge over others as they can act jointly. This could explain
why teams of brothers are so common at this precarious stage.[52]

Once a shareholder is successful in capturing the majority shares
of the partnership or in accumulating enough capital from that venture to set up on his own, the family enterprise can be said to enter
the second phase of centralization. As he acquires the estate
himself, the pater-entrepreneur has the authority to make use of the
assets as he sees fit. Before the division of the *jia* estate, he does
not need the consent of his sons for the investment of family
funds.[53]

Decision-making power is thus highly centralized in the hands of
the pater-entrepreneur during this phase. This power is sometimes
written into the article of association of the companies. In Mill 3,
for example, there were two kinds of stocks — founder's shares
and ordinary shares. Only the chairman held the 100 founder's
shares, and this entitled him to be both the governing director and
permanent director of the mill. The 100 founder's shares were
equal in voting power to all of the 99,900 ordinary shares put
together. This made the chairman the incontestable leader with the
ability to veto any decision of the board of directors or the general
meeting of the company.

The combination of such power and the urge to enlarge the *jia*
estate tends to make the pursuit of vigorous growth and a forceful,
highly personalized style of leadership the hallmarks of this second
phase of the family enterprise. Such a style of leadership has two
major implications for capital formation. The possibility of the
retention and reinvestment of profits is much enhanced. In addition, funds can also be freely transferred from one line of business
to another for lateral expansion and mutual sustenance. Capital is
mobile within the family group of enterprises because it belongs to
an essentially unified *jia* budget. Managerially, the style of leader-

ship involves a low degree of delegation of authority as well as a reluctance of the pater-entrepreneur to abdicate power. Retirement from the family business will remove the very basis on which his social status in the wider community is built. Although some of the mills had a fixed age of retirement compulsory for executives, none of the owner-directors were bound by these regulations. As long as they held some shares, they would remain directors with the right to intervene in company affairs.

The chairman of Mill 6, for example, was in his eighties and had been paralysed by a stroke for several years, but his directorship was still annually renewed. Accustomed to undisputed authority and closely identified with the founding of the firm, the pater-entrepreneur must find the process of giving up control a painful one. The difficult adjustment that the chairman of Mill 3 had to make can well be imagined when, in 1971, a special resolution was passed by the board of directors to abolish the founder's shares. This indicated that his eldest son had taken control at a point when the chairman was suffering from poor health. Each of the 100 founder's shares was converted into an ordinary share, with an additional financial compensation of HK$30,000 for the chairman. Yet at the time of the interview, he still went to the office every day for a few hours. When asked what types of activity took up most of his working day, he told me 'I oversee everything. When there are problems, they will come to me.'

The founder, it appears, will continue to overshadow his successors as long as he lives even though a formal transfer of responsibility might have taken place. Nevertheless, this formal change-over does mark the beginning of the third phase of the family enterprise. Although the problem of succession has naturally attracted the attention of most observers, it does not, in fact, constitute a major crisis. Most difficulties, such as the transfer of staff loyalty from the founder to the successor, the conflict between a young leader imbued with new ideas and experienced employees set in their ways, are problems general to managerial transition irrespective of the form of ownership.

Only two features may be unique to the succession process of Chinese family firms. The first is that an inheritor *per se* is not esteemed. In the Chinese system of values, a strong emphasis on social mobility leads to a high regard for the self-made man. An inheritor of wealth is not socially respected until he can prove his worth. That is why nearly all of the second-generation spinners interviewed admitted some initial reluctance to join the family enterprise.[54] The remarks made by a director of Mill 33 were striking. He was called in to talk to me by his uncle. His first reaction to his uncle's summons was 'I am not suitable [for the interview]. I am a good-for-nothing son'. Although he obviously meant it as a joke, it is significant that his self-deprecation should take this form.

The second feature is the rule of equal inheritance by sons which was universally followed by the mill owners. An apparent exception will prove this rule. In Mill 8, shares had already been allotted to the five sons of the founder in 1953, the year of establishment. For some reason, the fourth son was given a bigger portion. He held 1,000 shares while the other brothers had only 250 each. In later years the differential was narrowed but not completely erased. By 1977 he had 9,636 or about 2,000 shares more than his brothers. The founder also had another company dealing in various textile-related businesses. In that firm, the fourth son did not own any shares until 1972, while the other sons each had 10,000 shares. In 1972, when he finally acquired 66,180 shares, the other brothers' portions had already been increased to 103,680. The basic rule is, therefore, still parity of ownership among brothers with a smaller allotment in one company being balanced by a bigger one in another.[55]

Equal inheritance has been blamed for fragmenting the family estate and dissipating capital. This might have been the case for families engaging in agriculture in late imperial China, but is certainly not relevant to Hong Kong's cotton spinning industry. Equality in legal claims to the *jia* estate does not mean physical division of industrial property. Most family-owned mills have company regulations designed to keep their capital intact. Shares cannot be freely sold to outsiders. If family members want to give up company ownership, they must first offer the shares to existing shareholders 'at fair value'. Company regulations usually provide a further safeguard empowering the board of directors to refuse to register transfer of shares. There are also strong deterrents against an heir selling his portion of inheritance. Besides the possible charge of unfilial and unfraternal conduct, it is economically disadvantageous for him to do so, since his inheritance includes company assets as well as debts. After the deduction of outstanding debts, the 'fair value' of his shares will be substantially lower than the nominal value.[56] He will also forsake the steady income that his shares may yield in future years.

Thus the pressure towards fission is not very great during the third phase of development of the family firm. Nonetheless, tension builds up around the competitive relations among the brothers. Though all brothers have equal claims to ownership, only one can occupy the highest managerial position. The eldest, by virtue of his age, stands a much better chance of inheriting that status. This will create discontent among the younger brothers as they have not been brought up to submit to their eldest sibling. Margery Wolf points out that the brittle relationship among Chinese brothers probably originates in child training practices within the family:

As children, the elder is required to yield to his younger brother's demands in all things, some of which are outrageous when the younger is still small... Younger brothers learn very early and very concretely that older brothers yield to younger brothers, and yet as adults the expectation is exactly the reverse — the younger is expected to yield to his older brother's decisions and guidance, a situation for which he has been poorly prepared.[57]

Sibling rivalry was hardly disguised among the respondents, as shown in the following remarks by the younger brother of the managing director of Mill 32. When asked for his opinion on family enterprises, he replied:

In terms of succession, the older generation is still around and the 'dynastic change' has not yet occurred on a large scale. As a rule, sons get more than daughters, and again the eldest son gets more than the rest. Even when the father intends to give equal shares to the sons, the very fact that the eldest enters the business earlier and gets more shares as a result gives him a head start over the rest. Then the younger sons may decide not to come back.

The relative ownership position among the brothers in Mill 3, summarized in Table 6.6, shows how the fortune of brothers begins to diverge once the transfer of managerial power has taken place. It demonstrates the edge that the eldest son has over the others. He naturally is the first to have the opportunity to work in the family firm and accumulate experience. This prepares him to take over the mantle of chief executive when succession occurs. Once he inherits the leadership role, he will see his assets increased relative to his brothers' as he is usually entitled to more bonus shares to reward him for his contribution. Brothers who are non-executive owners

Table 6.6 Shareholdings of the Founder's Sons in Mill 3 (in 1,000 shares)

Birth order	1957	1962	1964	1971	1973	1976
Eldest son	1.5	3	6	10	10	56.4
Second son	1.5	3	6	10	0	0.0
Third son	1.5	3	6	10	10	43.4
Fourth son	1.5	3	6	10	10	43.4

Source: Record of Mill 3, Company Registry, Hong Kong.

are at a disadvantage. Their shares will remain more or less the same even when the company prospers.

How, then, are tensions arising from sibling rivalry and the jostling for managerial control contained? A common arrangement is for the brothers to agree on different spheres of responsibility. In Mill 8, for example, three brothers had different posts and separate offices. The eldest was the chairman. He was responsible for running a holding company owning the mill, and his main activity was in real estate. The second brother was the managing director of the mill in charge of business and personnel. Production within the mill was the preserve of the third brother who had the title of general manager and director.

This separation of spheres of responsibility to give maximum independence to participating brothers means a proliferation of departments, factory plants, or subsidiary companies within the family concern. Outwardly, there tends to be physical expansion; but internally, the organizational structure becomes less unified.

Centralized decision-making is more and more untenable, which decreases the possibility for the new chief executive to exercise strong leadership. Institutional restraints are sometimes set up to limit the autonomy of the chief executive. Finding his hands tied, he may gradually resign himself to the role of a caretaker instead of an innovator. This tendency was clearly manifested in the history of the Heng Feng Mill. After the death of the founder, a family council was set up consisting of the widow and her sons. The council drew up a fixed formula for the distribution of future profits, with the result that the son who became the managing director could not invest as he saw fit.[58] Reduction in reinvestment therefore tends to accompany the physical expansion and segmentation of the company.

The mutual watchfulness among brothers in a segmented family firm is very similar to the relationship among partners during the emergent phase. The same opportunity for asymmetrical growth in shareholding is present. In some cases, therefore, a brother in a segmented family firm might be able to build up a majority stake so that the enterprise is taken over by his *fang* (branch). The firm will then re-enter the centralized phase.

If this does not happen and the brothers remain in partnership until it is their turn to yield to their own offspring, then the family enterprise will pass into the final phase of disintegration. When the sons of the brothers succeed in their turn, the number of members in the family economy has greatly increased so that discord over the running of the enterprise is likely to multiply. In addition, the economic considerations against the sale of family shares is less inhibitive. The value of individual shareholding will have become much smaller due to the subdivision, which will have reduced the attraction of the regular income derived from the shares. Moreover, since it is unlikely for brothers to have the same number of children, inheritance by the third generation will create unequal ownership among the shareholders. Brothers may still co-operate on a more or less equal footing as owners, but cousins with unbalanced portions of shares have fewer reasons for doing so. Those in a weaker bargaining position may decide to break off the economic ties with the family enterprise, especially if they have been brought up with little emotional attachment to it. When I asked the younger brother of the managing director of Mill 32 whether he expected his children to join the family business, he said: 'I doubt it very much. The company is actually owned by several families, and I am not the eldest son'. Family members as shareholders will then be more concerned with immediate, tangible benefits than with long term business prospects. From this stage onwards, the family firm will be crisis-ridden.

Thus looked at developmentally, the Chinese family firm behaves differently in the successive stages of its life cycle. It is not intrinsically conservative or lethargic. Relative to its Japanese counterpart, it is less durable. But compared to families constructed on the principle of bilineal descent, it is not short-lived particularly as it can avoid disintegration by shedding the alienated branches and re-entering the centralized phase. Even if it has disintegrated, the dispersed family units can quickly spawn new enterprises of their own. The competitive strengths of Chinese family firms are considerable. There exists a much stronger measure of trust among *jia* members than among unrelated business partners. Consensus is easier to attain. The need for mutual accountability is reduced. As a director of Mill 14 said, the drawback of a public company was 'too much documentation and paper work'. In his family-owned mill, 'problems can be solved immediately by several phone calls. There is greater efficiency.' Such rapid entrepreneurial responses are essential when economic and political instability prevail. The textile industry is unique in the frequent fluctuation in raw material prices and the cyclical pattern of trade. This may be why, in most countries, this industry has large numbers of family firms.[59] Besides the economic peculiarities of the textile industry, the uncertain political future of Hong Kong was never far from the minds of the entrepreneurs. The managing director of Hong Kong Textiles, Ltd. has said:

The border between Hong Kong and Communist China is only 21 miles from this building, and we know that the Communists could take Hong Kong some morning before breakfast if they really wanted to...We can earn good returns on our investments here in Hong Kong, but we can also buy AT and T bonds from the US brokerage firm on the second floor of this building.[60]

This political consideration alone will have persuaded many spinners to cling to the family form of ownership so that a swift transfer of company funds can be made if necessary.[61]

External Relations among Mills

Kinship constitutes a strong bond in the internal organization of the spinning mills, but only provides a weak framework for external business transactions. This view is contrary to those of some writers with regard to Chinese economic conduct. Levy thinks that '[employment] is not the only sphere in which the particularism bred by the "traditional" kinship structure is a hindrance to the development of modern industry in China. It is *equally* important in the relations of the organization with other organizations'.[62] Willmott also says that '[in] the external relations of Chinese business enterprise...there is a strong tendency to maintain traditional Chinese practises based upon family ties, personal contacts, and maximum independence'.[63] His claim is partly based on the alleged importance of kinship in facilitating credit among Chinese enterprises. He gives the following examples:

> [The] Tjan family made fairly large loans to less successful brothers, in order to get them started in business or to pull them out of difficulties. No interest is paid on such loans, and in some cases they are never repaid. One of the prominent Chinese productive enterprises of Semarang was established many years ago with capital borrowed from a close relative. The original borrower died, and his family have never mentioned repayment. The sum involved was large, and the lending family, though they would never think of asking for repayment, have not forgotten it.[64]

The accuracy of the information aside, two points are pertinent in interpreting the economic meaning of these cases. First, the financial obligations among family members are radically different before and after the division of the *jia* estate. Before division, an adult male member can draw on the common family fund for business capital. This is not considered borrowing as his business remains part of the *jia* economy. But after division, a man has no special financial claim on his brothers except in times of crisis. In the community of Lukang in Taiwan, Deglopper finds that '[no] one wants to be dependent on his brother and an able-bodied man should not expect his brother or kinsmen to make sacrifices for his sake...cooperation or special help in business affairs is not considered one of a brother's axiomatic obligations'.[65]

Second, it is important to clarify whether the money is regarded as a loan or as funds entrusted for investment in a kinsman's business. In the latter case, which is a common Chinese practice, interests and repayment are irrelevant because it is dividends that are expected. Although he is a relative, the 'lender' will be treated as any other shareholder.

Kinsmen, therefore, are not in a privileged credit position. Indeed, there appears to be a tendency to avoid financial dealings with one's relatives. According to Fei Xiao-tong, who conducted research in rural Yunnan, participants in the rotating credit associations there preferred to have non-kinsmen as partners. This was not because of pecuniary calculations, such as the charging of interest being forbidden between kith and kin, but because relatives would take liberties by delaying the payment of dues and increased the risk of bad debts thus jeopardizing the operation of the credit associations.[66]

Besides financial dealings, kinship reciprocity also tends to deter commercial transactions. The subtle considerations involved are vividly shown in Deglopper's ethnography:

Retailers are expected to give close kinsmen a lower price, but the kinsman is also expected to buy without a lot of quibbling. An unusually candid cloth retailer told me that he gave his close relatives a more 'honest' price. But they did not constitute any appreciable proportion of his clientele, and he did not make very much profit from selling to them. 'So I don't really care if they buy here or not; I don't get that much out of it anyway.' One old lady carefully avoided shopping at the mixed goods shop run by her sister's son because she would feel obligated to buy once she went in. If she wanted a blue thing and all they had were red ones, she would have to take a red one. So she went to the shop of a non-kinsman where she could carefully look for something that exactly suited her taste, walk out if she didn't find it, and bargain fiercely if she did.[67]

It can therefore be inferred that the use of the kinship bond to secure credit and custom is uncommon, if not completely shunned by Chinese businessmen. This proposition cannot be checked against direct evidence from the cotton spinners because I have refrained from probing into what they regarded as company secrets. Some indirect support can be obtained from examining the phenomenon of intermarriage and interlocking directorship among the mill owners. There were few signs of industrial endogamy. From my incomplete data on the occupations of respondents' fathers-in-law, only three spinners were found to have intermarried with other textile families (see Table 6.7). However, their wives' families were in dyeing or garment-making, and not in spinning. The majority had affinal ties with families engaged in trade or other industries such as machinery, battery, tobacco manufacture, or ship-building. It is, of course, possible that such kinship ties in other commercial and industrial fields were economically important, but it is more probable that they were useful mainly for business information and in emergencies, rather than for direct commercial transactions.

Systematic data are not available on the occupational background of the respondents' sons-in-law. Only one instance of industrial endogamy among the offspring of the spinners has come to my notice. That is the marriage between a grandson of

Table 6.7. Occupation of Fathers-in-Law of Spinners

Occupation	No.	Adjusted %*
Textile industrialist	3	14
Other industrialist	6	28
Merchant	8	38
Banker	1	5
Civil servant	1	5
Teacher	1	5
Landlord	1	5
Unknown	7	—
No response	12	—
Total	40	100

Note: Only those who gave a specific answer are included.

Source: Interviews, 1978.

the late founder of Mill 11 and the granddaughter of the late Rong De-sheng whose family owned several local mills. The cotton spinners as a whole did not seem to follow a consistent marriage strategy. Even had they wished to do so, the decline of the institution of arranged marriages and the inability of a family head to disinherit his children for disobedience would render such a strategy impracticable.

Where affinal ties were forged, they did not usually lead to the creation of formal alliances among the mills in the form of interlocking directorship. Affinal links existed among three pairs of mill owners. The first pair comprised the principal owners of Mill 18 and Mill 25, respectively, who were brothers-in-law. The former held no post in the latter's company, but the latter had been a director in the former's mill. This was apparently because the former's enterprise had been partly financed by his father-in-law, thus his brother-in-law was entitled to a seat in his board of directors. But in 1971 the seat had been given up. The second set consisted of the heads of Mill 17 and Mill 12, respectively. The two major partners of Mill 17 were brothers-in-law. They were related to the head of Mill 12 who was their father's (father-in-law's) brother's son-in-law. There was no overlapping between their boards of directors.

The owners of Mill 13 and Mill 26, respectively, formed the third set. The latter was the former's sister's son-in-law. Similarly, there were no joint directors between the two enterprises.

Clan and lineage links were equally weak in regulating economic relations among the mills. T'ien Ju-k'ang has discovered that 'Chinese rural economy in Sarawak hinges upon a framework of clanship'.[68] But the Chinese in Sarawak were in a rather special situation. The common surname of T'ien provided the widest possible basis for joint economic action among this small ethnic minority. The necessity for ritual reinforcement of their clanship tie testifies to its inherent weakness. One group of the T'iens came from Zhao An in Fujian and another one originated from 'Hweilai' in Guangdong. They had no demonstrable genealogical links. As they spoke different dialects, even the pronunciation of their shared surname was different in each group. To overcome these difficulties, they invented an ancestor as well as a kinship vocabulary:

At the Ch'ing Ming festival, for example, it is always a joint Chao An and Hweilai party that performs the ceremony of sweeping the ancestral tombs. It appears that this linkage was first made several years ago at the instigation of the Hweilai group who desired to cash in on their connexion with the rich and influential T'iens...in Kuching. As the two groups do not possess a common ancestor,...there cannot possibly be a common ancestral tomb. The difficulty was not insurmountable. In 1925 a special mock tomb — containing, of course, no corpse — was constructed in the Chao An cemetery. This monument was carefully inscribed with a reference to the origin of the T'ien surname group in China, and an expression of hope for continued prosperity 'by all the descendants who worshipped here together and erected this tomb in the 7th lunar month of the year 1923'...

A second external mark of the mutual solidarity of the two sections of the T'ien surname group in Sarawak is the habit by which members of both address each other in kinship terms. This goes beyond the mere attribution of clan brotherhood...All Chao An T'iens and all Hweilai T'iens know the order of generations within their own groups, and are thus able to refer to those of the next senior generation as 'uncles' and 'aunts', and those in the next junior generation as 'nephews' and 'nieces' and so forth. Chao An T'iens address Hweilai T'iens similarly, difference of dialect notwithstanding, but as actual relationships are untraceable questions of seniority are settled entirely by considerations of age and social prestige.[69]

Clan ties were far more tenuous for the cotton spinners, and there is no evidence that these ties shaped the external relations of the mills at all. Though clan associations exist in Hong Kong, none of the respondents named them when asked about their participation in community organizations. Entrepreneurs tended to have their social status confirmed by their clan associations, but not achieved through them. The lineage itself would not be expected to have much economic significance in cities as it is mainly a rural institution owing its corporate being to the control of land-based wealth.[70] The business conduct of the Hong Kong cotton spinners was not much influenced by lineage relationships.

To recapitulate, kinship is one of the important bases on which economic closure can be accomplished. It is similar to ethnicity in that both are related to an individual's sense of origin. When kin and ethnic categories overlap, the foundation for joint economic action will be much strengthened. But kinship differs from ethnicity in two major respects. The boundary of a kin group is more rigid, and kinship-related rights and obligations are more intense and specific so that they sometime militate against economic transactions and co-operation among kinsmen. In the case of the Chinese industrialists in general and the Shanghai cotton spinners in particular, kinship plays a more significant role in cementing the internal organization of firms than in regulating their external relations. By activating regional and familistic ties to exclude potential competitors, the selected group of Shanghai entrepreneurs, pruned by the process of migration, were able to maintain a high degree of economic concentration in Hong Kong's cotton spinning industry, an occupational niche which they first captured with a particular set of competitive skills and business attitudes.

7 Conclusion

HAVING heard the story of the Shanghai spinners in Hong Kong's post-war development, we can now return to the problems posed in the Introduction and assess the implications of this case study. What does this empirical example reveal about the characteristics of Chinese industrial entrepreneurship? What light does it shed on the phenomenon of ethnic concentration in economic niches?

Chinese Industrial Entrepreneurship

In Schumpeter's view, the entrepreneur is a glamorous adventurer. His innovative spirit is sustained by three main incentives:

First of all, there is the dream and the will to found a private kingdom, usually, though not necessarily, also a dynasty. The modern world really does not know any such positions, but what may be attained by industrial or commercial success is still the nearest approach to medieval lordship possible to modern man...Then there is the will to conquer; the impulse to fight, to prove oneself superior to others, to succeed for the sake, not of the fruits of success, but of success itself...

Finally, there is the joy of creating, of getting things done, or simply of exercising one's energy and ingenuity...Our type seeks out difficulties, changes in order to change, delights in ventures.[1]

Frederick Barth elaborates on this portrayal, specifying three behavioural tendencies of the entrepreneur:

(1) The entrepreneur's more single-minded concentration on the maximization of *one* type of value: 'profit'...
(2) The more experimental and speculative, less institutionalized character of the activity of the entrepreneur, who must act in terms of a *deductive prognosis* of results, rather than — as may the encumbents of institutionalized statuses — accumulated experience which gives empirically founded expectation of results...
(3) The entrepreneur's greater willingness to take risks, exemplified by his (i) committing a greater fraction of his total assets in a single venture, (ii) putting his trust in his own deductive reasoning as against common opinion, and perhaps even (iii) delighting in gambler's odds, leading to possible risk favouring departures from the mini-maxi principle, where

other actors might entertain a conservative, exaggerated fear of the risk of loss...[2]

If innovation is the essence of entrepreneurship, then the Shanghai spinners have a reasonable claim to be entrepreneurs as they have combined land, capital, and labour in ways which, previously, had not been effectively done in Hong Kong. In addition, they have pioneered new markets. Yet they do not quite fit into the theoretical mould constructed by Schumpeter and Barth. For the spinners extol the virtues of caution and self-restraint, rather than the speculative and adventurous spirit. In a booklet produced in 1975, introducing the industry to overseas buyers, the Hong Kong Cotton Spinners' Association proudly declared that '[the] Hong Kong cotton spinning industry may...derive some satisfaction from the policy of conservatism it has consistently adopted'. Cotton mills in Hong Kong, it said, have displayed 'moderation and self-discipline' as well as 'the spirit of collective responsibility'.[3]

During the interviews, I asked my respondents to describe the qualities of a good textile industrialist and also to account for the failure of spinning ventures. They showed a high degree of consensus as to what constituted the entrepreneurial role, which can be summarized in the following six features, arranged according to the frequency of their being mentioned.

First, they emphasized the ability to handle people. The phrase 'team work' recurred in their responses. A good industrialist must be able to lead a well-co-ordinated team. To achieve this, he needed the skill to spot talent and put it to maximum use. 'People are the most important', one of them said. 'Capital and machinery are dead things. You require good staff to make them work.' Conversely, mismanagement and personnel problems were the most often cited cause for the decline of a mill. These include 'too many partners', 'conflict among directors', 'factionalism within the mill', and 'inability to set up a system of administration'.

The second quality is dedication to the job. Hard work was regarded as a prerequisite for industrial success. One must not shirk difficulties and should apply oneself unsparingly to tackle substantive tasks. 'In industry, problems occur every day and you have to solve them', one respondent said. 'If you do not like that, you should not get into industry.' Associated with the value placed on hard work was an emphasis on frugality and asceticism. Two contrasting examples were cited, by the directors of Mill 22 and Mill 1 respectively, to show that frugality led to success and conspicuous consumption resulted in failure. The first was that of an eighty-year-old spinner who had started his career as a labourer without much formal education. His mill prospered, it was said, because he was industrious and careful with money. The second was that of a carpenter in one of the mills who 'made some money several years ago' and set up on his own. 'He had a Rolls Royce and several Benzes' and soon went bankrupt, said the director of Mill 1.

Good market judgement was mentioned as the third quality essential to success. A spinner must have foresight based on familiarity with world affairs and the textile trade. Since the price of raw materials made up nearly 70 per cent of the cost of yarn production, accurate timing in the purchase of cotton in the midst of wide price fluctuations was crucial. This high degree of market uncertainty actually militated against risk-taking. 'Over-expansion', 'speculation', and 'trying to do too much in too short a time' were seen as the ingredients for disaster. The merits of restraint and circumspection were extolled. The chairman of Mill 22, one of the most successful textile conglomerates, said, 'Don't trust to luck. One must know one's limits and never go beyond them. If there is no hope of success, I would not do it. I would only go ahead where there is a 70 per cent chance of success.'

The fourth necessary quality was technical proficiency and reputation. The ideal cotton spinner should have a firm grasp of the technical aspects of production and pay particular attention to maintaining the quality of his products.

Fifth, he must be honest and level-headed, and not be tempted by short cuts. The reputation of trustworthiness was seen as the most precious asset. Thus an industrialist has to be meticulous in honouring contracts and to be punctual with deliveries.

Long-term perspective was the last quality cited by the spinners. The ideal entrepreneur would not go after immediate profit. Keenness for short-term benefits was regarded as inimical to the sound development of an enterprise. Industrialists should aim at sustained financial reward instead of the highest profit at a particular moment. Important gains and losses were often 'invisible' and one should be far-sighted in the approach to profit. The managing director of Mill 4 told me:

Some of us do not see the invisible losses. Therefore they hesitate to scrap equipment. Cantonese businessmen usually let tangible losses cloud their vision. They are more inclined towards gambling. So they show two traits. First, they hesitate to give up machinery that has outlived its utility. Second, they try to manage with as few personnel as possible.

These six characteristics are not compatible with the prevalent theoretical image of the entrepreneur as a profit-maximizer, experimenter, and risk-taker. Although it is possible that my respondents deviate from the norm, there are both empirical and theoretical grounds for believing otherwise. A significant finding of McClelland on the high '*n*-achievers', those he holds to be potential entrepreneurs, is that they tend to avoid high risks. They prefer tackling tasks with a calculated and moderate chance of success 'where their efforts or skills can make a difference in the outcome'. In McClelland's words, '[they] are not impractical "dreamers" overestimating their chances of success at everything; instead they rely on facts so far as they are available, and then fall back on generalized self-confidence'.[4] Some economists have discovered through empirical research that many industrialists are pursuing adequate instead of 'maximum' profit. As P.W.S. Andrews observes, 'Businessmen want the quiet life'.[5] This discovery suggests that there are at least two types of entrepreneurs — the 'snatchers' who go after immediate profit, and the 'stickers' who plan on the basis of steady rewards from long-term competition.[6] His personal knowledge of British industry leads J. P. Nettl to argue that the centre of big business in the United Kingdom in the 1960s was occupied by 'consensus' figures whose life-style and values were similar to those of senior civil servants. The 'rugged entrepreneurs' usually belong to the periphery of the company hierarchy, their role and their style preventing them from reaching the top. In compensation, according to Nettl, they were often 'shunted into the expense account world'.[7]

Gerschenkron has provided a theoretical explanation for these phenomena. He points out that the behaviour of entrepreneurs is moulded by the nature of their field of activity. Modern industry, on account of its structure, calls for behavioural patterns in its decision-makers which are different from those in trade and crafts. He argues that manufacturing activities require participants to adopt a long-term horizon, to regard their pursuit as lifetime occupation, and to maintain high standards of commercial honesty.[8]

Thus the industrial world expects to be led by planners and consensus figures, not gamblers and rugged individualists.

Now we begin to see why the collective self-image of the Shanghai spinners is at odds with the dominant theoretical model of the entrepreneur. Schumpeter and his followers have adopted the framework of perfect competition for their analysis. In particular, they assume that industries are arenas for open competition. New entrepreneurs are not barred from entry. Under such conditions, how will innovation occur? Why should an individual be an innovator if his imitators can reap similar profit and avoid the higher opportunity costs of experimentation? Schumpeter acknowledges the problem without giving a satisfactory answer:

new businesses are continually arising under the impulse of the alluring profit...Consequently, the surplus of the entrepreneur in question and his immediate followers disappears. Not at once, it is true, but as a rule only after a longer or shorter period of progressive diminution. Nevertheless, the surplus is realized, it constitutes under given conditions a definite amount of net returns even though only temporary.[9]

His model is clearly useful in understanding cases where the entry barriers are very low and economic closure is nearly impossible to attain. Under these circumstances, the entrepreneur has to accept a state of open competition and be content with short term profits. But the limited explanatory range of this theoretical model becomes obvious when it is confronted with most instances of industrial entrepreneurship in which imperfect competition is the rule and an element of power is integral to economic relations.[10] Seen in the light of imperfect competition, the dynamics of industrial innovation look different. The possession of talent is not sufficient for the entrepreneur to create a new combination of productive factors. He will not develop his ideas and put them into practice unless he is able to restrict the encroachment of imitators and prevent them from diluting his profits. This means that an essential part of the entrepreneurial role is the ability to raise the entry barrier to transform an open economic niche into a relatively closed one. Thus strivings for industrial innovation and closure are inherently connected.

Closure, in turn, is often achieved by activating particularistic ties such as ethnicity and kinship. These ties, therefore, should not be too readily seen as obstacles to economic development. Unless perfect competition is held to be the only route to economic development, it should be recognized that particularistic ties are effective in situations of imperfect competition.[11]

One of the distinguishing features of the entrepreneur is his strong desire for autonomy. In order to innovate, he must have the urge to do things in his own way. But on its own such a desire for autonomy is inimical to the formation of organizations and hierarchies essential to successful industrial competition. The entrepreneur cannot function effectively by himself. He must be supported by a team of managers and executives who have competence and commitment. Yet the glamour of the entrepreneur often overshadows his assistants, and the lack-lustre 'organizational men' who form the supporting cast in the drama of industrialization seldom get the academic attention they deserve. Most studies of entrepreneurship tend to look at the entrepreneur in isolation and try to define his essence. The role set in which the entrepreneur is embedded is usually neglected. In order to understand entrepreneurship fully, it is necessary to have a balanced view by taking into account the orientation and behaviour of the people on whom the entrepreneur depends, in particular his executives and assistants. In his essay on the Protestant ethic, Max Weber noted in passing: 'The power of religious asceticism provided him [the entrepreneur] in addition with sober, conscientious, and unusually industrious workmen, who clung to their work as to a life purpose willed by God'.[12]

When we look at the role set of the Chinese entrepreneur, it appears that a striking feature of Chinese private industry is that it is strong in entrepreneurship but weak in management. The supply of entrepreneurs outstrips the supply of managers and executives. The Chinese who enter into industrial competition, as exemplified by the Shanghai spinners, take pride in proprietorship but disdain salaried employment. They pursue technical expertise, but not managerial professionalism. The emphasis they place on the ability to handle people and the importance of team-work in industrial success underscores their awareness that the weakest chink in their armour is management.

The strong drive towards autonomy and proprietorship is generated by a pervasive economic ethos which I shall call 'entrepreneurial familism'. Such an ethos involves the family as the basic unit of economic competition. The *jia* provides the impetus for innovation and the support for risk-taking. Entrepreneurial familism, in the Hong Kong context, entails a peculiar style of economic organization with several distinguishing features. Economic hierarchy tends to be fluid. There exists a centrifugal force fostered by the widespread desire of employees to set up on their own. Consequently, decision-making within the firm tends to be highly centralized with very limited delegation of authority.

This pattern of entrepreneurial familism has its own competitive strengths as well as weaknesses. It has its share of problems, most of which are however not insurmountable. The internal centrifugal force, for instance, has led to the evolution of a system of subcontracting, with the production process being divided up and undertaken by multiple, interdependent units. Such a system obviously calls for co-ordination through economic networks, hence the important role of regional ties. At present, however, this system, and particularly the details of its constitution and operation, are not fully understood. Nevertheless, there is little doubt that such a system has enhanced Hong Kong industry's flexibility and responsiveness to fluctuations in the international market.

Studies in Taiwan, showing that very similar values are found there, have indicated that the ethos of entrepreneurial familism might not be unique to Hong Kong, and may, indeed, constitute a peculiar Chinese style of entrepreneurship. Susan Greenhalgh, for example, has pointed out that '[family] networks undergird both the sociey and the economy of Taiwan...with virtually all small-scale commercial and service enterprises run by families, and an estimated 97 per cent of private industrial firms (urban and rural) organized along familial lines'.[13] She further notes that working-class families in Taiwan 'are driven by a strong cultural emphasis on "being your own boss" (*dang laoban*)', an observation which has been confirmed by other researchers.[14]

Why does Chinese entrepreneurship take such a form? A comparison between the social structures of China and Japan during the late traditional period might throw some light on this problem. As Marion Levy has pointed out, Tokugawa Japan was a feudal society while Qing China was a bureaucratic one.[15] This structural difference doubtless shaped the subsequent development of industrial enterprises in the two countries in several important ways. The closed stratification system of Tokugawa Japan was probably conducive to the emergence of a stable and dedicated middle managerial stratum, while the open stratification system of Qing

China, with its associated value on upward social mobility tended to reduce the supply of dependable executives to staff modern enterprises. The importance of the *samurai* in Japan's industrialization may not be in their potential as entrepreneurs.[16] Their code of honour, their willingness to observe regulations, and their devotion to the service of their feudal lords probably prepared them to become loyal and competent industrial bureaucrats. The *samurai* has no obvious counterpart in late imperial China.

In addition, the feudal institutions of the fiefs and manors in Japan might be more readily convertible into modern industrial corporations with managerial hierarchies as their hallmark.[17] In China there was a relative scarcity of strong intermediary organizations similar to the fiefs mediating between the imperial bureaucracy and the local kin groups. This could have limited the range of organizational possibilities for the formation of Chinese industrial enterprises and led to the sharp bifurcation of public enterprises modelled on the imperial bureaucracy and private firms modelled on the family.

The bifurcation of public bureaucratic enterprises and private family firms provides us with a clue to the understanding of another special feature of Chinese industrial competition noted in Chapter 4. This is the relative absence of oligopolistic groupings similar to the *zaibatsu* in Japan and the cartels in Europe. The formation of oligopolistic groupings requires the existence of relatively permanent corporate entities and the tolerance of political authorities towards economic alliances. In the Chinese case, private enterprises are generally not durable because the family on which they are modelled has an inherent tendency towards segmentation. Just as each son in the family is a potential *pater*, each heir in the firm is a potential entrepreneur. The Chinese state, for its part, was particularly watchful of attempts by families and kin groups to form alliances, as it was feared that these would challenge its authority and upset the system of political integration. The strong hostility to private enterprise expressed by both the Guomindang and Communist administrations in recent times could represent the continuation of this attitude.

I have suggested connections between facets of Chinese industrial entrepreneurship and China's bureaucratic past. The hypotheses are generated from my study of Shanghai spinners who may not be representative of Chinese industrialists as a whole. In the present state of knowledge, the question of regional variations in Chinese entrepreneurship cannot be directly tackled here, but it can serve as a convenient point of departure for the examination of the phenomenon of ethnic concentration in economic niches.

Ethnic Concentration

Numerous propositions have been put forward by sociologists to account for ethnic concentration in various economic enclaves in a society. These propositions may be grouped into two theoretical clusters which I shall call cultural and structural explanations respectively. The former seeks the cause in either the heritage or future orientation of the ethnic group itself, while the latter emphasizes the nature of the host society which provides the context for competition. Key concepts employed by the cultural theorists include 'achievement syndrome', 'withdrawal of status respect', 'serfdom's legacy', 'handling of money', and 'homeward bound orientation'.[18] The structural theorists, on the other hand, tend to highlight contextual factors such as 'social blockage', 'status gap', and 'internal colonialism'.[19]

However, these propositions deal only with limited facets of the problem and their insights are partial. An adequate explanation of the concentration of ethnic members in particular spheres of economic activity should be able to establish the interconnections among three important aspects of the phenomenon. The first aspect is the processes by which individuals with common ethnic attributes enter and then hold on to an occupational enclave. Most existing theories try to account for the *emergence* of the kind of economic concentration but little attention has been paid to its *persistence*. Ethnic consciousness is the second aspect. The relevant issues are the formation, expression, and transmission of this consciousness. The last aspect concerns the waxing and waning of hostility between the ethnic groups. The theoretical model implicit in the foregoing analysis of the Shanghai spinners is an attempt to elucidate the way in which these three features are related to one another. The outline of this model is presented in Fig. 7.1 and I shall discuss the significance of a few of these factors as most linkages in the theoretical scheme should by this point require no further elaboration.

Fig. 7.1   A Model of Ethnic Concentration in Economic Niches

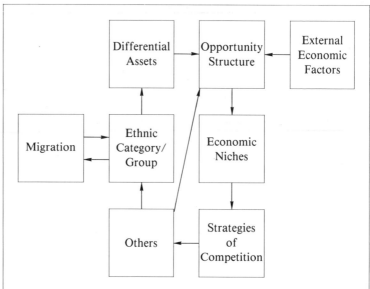

Types of Migrants

The factor of migration and the classification of migrants should first be looked at. A migrant may be a voluntary one in that he chooses to leave for better prospects or for a more congenial environment. Or he may be an involuntary migrant, compelled to depart because he has lost control over his own fate or is threatened with persecution. Having left home, a migrant may regard his stay abroad as permanent, and will sever his home ties, becoming uprooted and transplanted. Or he may consider his stay as temporary, though it can last for decades or even a lifetime. He will then retain his original roots and look upon himself as an outsider in the host society. With these distinctions, it is possible to derive four ideal types of migrants (as shown in Table 7.1), each with its own distinctive pattern of economic behaviour.

The settlers migrate intending to embrace a new identity and abandon the old one. Though they may use their original social network to facilitate their transition, it can be predicted that they will quickly relinquish it in order to establish new ties with the in-

Table 7.1. Typology of Migrants

Types	Volition in Departure	Permanence of Stay Abroad
Settlers	+	+
Sojourners	+	−
Refugees	−	+
Captives	−	−

Note: + means positive.
        − means negative.

digenous residents. As they try to become accepted in the host community, their ethnic network shrinks and non-ethnic links increase. They may succeed economically on an individual basis, but the phenomenon of ethnic concentration does not emerge because they seldom activate their former ethnic bonds.

The sojourners regard their stay abroad as transient. They are drawn to a foreign land primarily by the promise of rewards and remunerations which can ultimately better their livelihood and status at home. For them, their destination is merely a place for work and for obtaining economic benefits. Their lack of commitment to the host society is embodied in the persistence of their homeward ties. Compared with the settlers, the sojourners are likely to visit their native places more often, send remittances or letters home at more regular intervals, have more fellow sojourners as friends in non-work situations, and even maintain absentee membership in associations at home so that they can return and resume their social position.[20] This homeward orientation, some sociologists suggest, has several economic effects.[21] William Willmott has noted that among the Overseas Chinese in South-east Asia, 'the desire to return to China motivated the emigrants, at least at the outset, to enter a profession that would involve a minimum of fixed investment in the host country, and a maximum of liquid assets that could be returned to China'.[22] Occupations promising quick returns such as that of trader, money lender, dealer and broker are preferred. Thus the typical sojourner is a middleman displaying commercial, but not industrial, entrepreneurship. Besides liquidity, he will aim at high profits. Since he is not fully integrated in the host community, he can afford to ignore indigenous social norms and take up ventures that are despised locally but are remunerative. In his chosen profession, he is willing to exert himself and to defer gratification. He will minimize consumption and actively save in order to return home. Bonacich argues that 'this "future orientation" enables them to accumulate capital' but simultaneously arouses the hostility of the host society over the sojourners' divided loyalty. The hostility in turn perpetuates the reluctance of the sojourners to assimilate completely.[23]

In contrast to the sojourners, the refugees are not attracted to their destinations but are forced to leave home by the threat of persecution. As with the Shanghai spinners, it is self-preservation, not economic betterment that causes their flight. Some, such as the Hungarian refugees in 1956, had little control over their final destination. As they were assigned by relief agencies to various countries that were prepared to accept them, it was unlikely that they would form ethnic neighbourhoods and occupational clusters.[24] Only the more fortunate or more resourceful refugees can manage their own passage to a safer shore, and thereby retain or even strengthen a web of social ties during the process of exodus.

In his study of the Hindu and Sikh refugees in the Punjab-Haryana region of India, Keller finds that the refugees had become innovators. They were more adventurous in their choice of occupation, and a significant number had established new enterprises. Many had tried a variety of jobs, showing a high rate of occupational mobility.[25] According to Keller, the violence, danger and suffering accompanying their departure had induced in them a profound psychological change. The trauma of losing nearly everything led them first to wonder why they had been spared, and then to the belief that they must be special in some way. This gave rise to 'a sense of invulnerability'. Having reached rock bottom, nothing worse could happen to them. Thus Keller argues that they had a strong desire to start all over again, and were willing to push toward uncharted territories where others dared not tread.[26]

However, interviews with the Shanghai spinners suggest to me that the refugees' entrepreneurial behaviour can be better understood in terms of a deeply felt insecurity rather than a sense of 'invulnerability'. Having had to abandon most of their possessions, they have learnt that they must start to maximize their economic flexibility. They can be expected, therefore, to make maximum use of other people's money and to invest in human capital that can be easily transferred. They will also attempt to diversify their investments. Their concern for liquidity links them to the sojourners. But the refugees differ from the sojourners in two crucial respects. First, they tend to reinvest and expand their enterprises continually, seeking ever greater success. For, unlike the sojourners, they cannot return home. Without homeward ties and obligations, their savings will not be drained at periodic intervals during home visits.[27] In addition, they are deprived of the safety net available to the sojourners in times of economic adversity. With no haven to return to, they must depend on themselves. Their ultimate insurance for safety is mutual assistance and their own wealth and skills which cannot easily be taken from them.

The second feature that distinguishes the refugees from the sojourners is their different social composition resulting from selective migration. In general, sojourners are ambitious individuals from economic backwaters.[28] Since opportunities at home do not match their aspirations, they leave. However, as they come from peripheral regions of an economy, their hopes are high but skills low. The refugees, by contrast, are normally the native élites who flee because they have much to lose after political changes. They tend to be far better endowed in competitive resources than the sojourners. For these reasons, the refugees on the whole are the most cohesive and enterprising of the four types of migrants.

Finally, there are migrants who are captives and whose emigration is forced. The captives are either bought or abducted, and then transported to an alien place into social and economic subordination. In that process, their original social networks are completely shattered. They suffer from what Orlando Patterson calls 'natal alienation'. He writes: 'It was this alienation of the slave from all formal, legally enforceable ties of "blood", and from any attachment to groups or localities other than those chosen for him by the master, that gave the relation of slavery its peculiar value to the master.'[29] Stripped of significant kinship and ethnic linkages, the captives cannot mobilize these social relationships for economic competition. Their migration has given them a severe handicap and they are generally confined to the bottom of the social hierarchy.

Ethnic Consciousness

After moving to a new environment, immigrants find themselves among strangers of different origins. Their awareness of ethnicity is consequently heightened. In order to comprehend how ethnicity is handled and manifested by the immigrants as well as by the host population, it is useful to make a distinction between an ethnic category and an ethnic group.[30] The distinction marks a difference in the level of analysis. The former refers to the cultural sphere of cognition, or how individuals order their perception of their surroundings. The latter points to the structural aspect of relations, or how individuals organize their social action. The counterparts of this distinction can be found in the study of social class between 'class in itself' and 'class for itself', and in the analysis of stigma between the 'discreditable' and the 'discredited'.[31] In ethnic categories, class in itself, or the discreditable, there are some common attributes to be found among collectivities of people. But it is only when such attributes are used as the basis of social action that the collectivities become ethnic groups, class for itself, and the discredited. The conversion of an ethnic category into an ethnic group involves a process of subjective identification, of 'self-ascription and ascription by others'.[32] To be consistent with the terminology of class analysis, I shall call this process the emergence of ethnic consciousness. Since this process is not automatic, as an investigation of the discrepancy between the expressed attitude and the actual practice of racial discrimination has forcefully demonstrated,[33] the significant research question is the condition under which ethnic consciousness will wax and wane.

In Chapter 5, I have argued that when economic actors begin to be concerned about protecting their established interests and try to create a situation of imperfect competition, it is likely that ethnic consciousness will emerge. But as the example of the Shanghai spinners has shown, ethnicity can be expressed either stridently or in muted forms. The intensity and expression of ethnic consciousness are influenced by a number of factors. One of them is social visibility. A projected ethnic identity has to be accepted by other people before it can become a basis of interaction. This involves a negotiation process during initial contact.[34] When ethnic cues are highly conspicuous, such as facial features or distinctive styles of dress, the scope for manoeuvre is restricted. Thus, whether they like it or not, the Shanghai spinners will be readily identified as Chinese under most circumstances. However, regional differentiation among the Chinese is far less visible, and dialect is almost the only dependable guide. As a result, ethnic jokes among the Chinese generally involve word play directed at the linguistic peculiarities of other groups.[35] During the course of my research, I was frequently asked by respondents and informants alike whether I was a Shanghainese. That they could not readily judge for themselves means that without the dialect, a Chinese can easily disguise his regional origin and pass as a member of another group.

It is fair to assume that an individual will only try to pass for what he is not when there is some benefit to be gained by doing so. The weaker the bargaining position of his own ethnic group, the greater the appeal such an option will have for the individual. Bargaining positions can be affected by the numerical size of the group, the second determinant of the intensity of ethnicity. This is an important factor leading to dissimilar rates of assimilation among people of identical origins settling in different communities. The significance of this dimension has apparently been neglected by Orlando Patterson in his analysis of the contrasting patterns of ethnic allegiance among the Chinese in Jamaica and Guyana. As his data indicate, the Chinese made up 1.2 per cent of the population of Jamaica which stood at 1.8 million in the early 1970s. About 20,000 strong, the Chinese there had the numerical strength to staff an entire retail trade and to resist assimilation. But the demographic situation of the Guyanan Chinese was different. They constituted a mere 0.6 per cent of a population of 714,000. A minority of about 4,200 people had little chance of survival if they did not merge with the majority and took up whatever jobs were available. Their numbers were far too small for them to imitate their Jamaican cousins in maintaining cultural exclusiveness.[36] For similar reasons, the overall adaptive behaviour of the Shanghainese in Hong Kong, consisting of less than 4 per cent of the population, necessarily diverges from that of the Chaozhou, who are a large minority of about 11 per cent. The absence of a Shanghainese organization parallel to the Chaozhou Chamber of Commerce is thus not surprising.

Of course, size is not just a question of absolute numbers in the population. Relative numerical balance in a specific sphere of competition is also important. Thus the degree of residential or economic concentration of co-ethnics should also be taken into account. With the dual dimensions of size and economic concentration, we can derive the following four ideal typical situations:

Fig. 7.2 Size of Ethnic Group and Economic Concentration

Economic Concentration in a Niche	Size of Ethnic Group in the Whole Population	
	Large	Small
High	I	II
Low	III	IV

The likelihood of preserving and mobilizing ethnic ties steadily decreases as we go from type I to type IV. The Shanghai spinners belong to type II, indicating that they will be more ethnically conscious than the Shanghainese diffused in other occupations in a type IV situation.

Power is the third determinant of the intensity of ethnic consciousness. The relative position of various groups in the power structure will affect their idiom of competition. In his analysis of class conflict, Frank Parkin argues that divergent strategies of closure are employed by members of the upper and lower classes. The former typically adopt the approach of 'exclusion', to resist the permeation of personnel and ideas from the lower social echelons. The latter, on the other hand, try to advance their class interest through 'solidarism', to join together in order to challenge inequity.[37] The concepts of exclusion and solidarism are equally applicable to the study of ethnic groups. Powerful ethnic groups try to exclude, while disadvantaged ones attempt to achieve solidarity. Each strategy entails its own form of justification for action.

In most modern societies, except probably those upholding explicit racist ideologies, ethnicity constitutes a political liability for the élites because parochial allegiance is divisive and undermines authority. In order to preserve the integration of the social system as well as their own privileged position, it is imperative for the élites to disavow specific ethnic identification.[38] Thus ethnic groups with power will generally try to maintain exclusiveness with universalistic justifications. They will assert that people of other groups simply lack the proper capabilities or qualifications to fill vacancies in their midst. Ethnicity, in this situation, is being utilized *covertly*.

For groups in a weak power position, the consideration is different. It is in their interest to interpret the élites' behaviour in terms of ethnic self-serving, thus exposing the latter to charges of hypocrisy and duplicity. They will flaunt their own ethnic symbols, taking pride in a common bond which causes them suffering and humiliation so as to forge solidarity. In their case, ethnicity must be mobilized *overtly*.

Therefore the processes of exclusion and solidarism are closely related to covert and overt use of the idiom of ethnicity. But so far we are treating the dimension of power in isolation. If we introduce the variable of group size, we can differentiate cases giving rise to various degress of overtness or covertness in ethnic competition. The interplay of power position and group size yields the following four types of ethnic situation:

Fig. 7.3 Size of Ethnic Group and Power Position

	Size of Ethnic Group	
Power Position	Large	Small
Strong	I	II
Weak	III	IV

Types I and IV form a combination commonly found in ethnically heterogeneous societies. The ethnic majority is in a strong power position. They are confident and are often not particularly aware of their own ethnicity. Thus the white Protestants in the United States, for example, are not usually considered as an ethnic group. As Ulf Hannerz observes, 'they are non-ethnic "real Americans", while those usually thought of as "ethnic" are the later immigrants'.[39] Their secure power basis permits them to discriminate against minorities on explicitly ethnic grounds. They can be less covert in their ethnic behaviour.

The combination of types II and III usually appears in colonial societies. The Shanghai spinners who wielded economic power constituted a type II group. Being outnumbered demographically, they were in a more precarious position than type I groups. Consequently, they consciously projected a cosmopolitan image and suppressed outward signs of ethnic affiliation. This explains the low self-ascription as Shanghainese, the use of Mandarin in the schools they sponsored and so forth. Their behaviour, as if they were not ethnics, was appropriate within the confines of Hong Kong. But in the context of the world economy, the power position of these spinners was reversed. They found themselves in a type IV situation in relation to Western textile men. Therefore in international textile negotiations and conferences, they would underline their identity as industrialists of developing regions. They attempted to form a common front with other developing Asian countries such as Korea, Malaysia and Indonesia to oppose trade restrictions imposed by the economically advanced nations. In the world context, they belonged to a weak minority, and solidarism was the more effective strategy.

The last factor affecting the intensity of ethnicity is the structural characteristics of the occupational niche. The idea of opportunity structure has been used by scholars to explain the economic adjustments of ethnic minorities. Enclaves in an opportunity structure are often thought of as high or low in occupational prestige. This generates the crude model of economic succession among ethnic groups where an immigrant minority will enter the structure at the bottom rung, then gradually move upwards as other newcomers take over their original employment. Length of settlement and occupational ranks are believed to be positively correlated. Otherwise, enclaves are regarded as either occupied or unoccupied. This gives rise to the hypothesis of 'blocked' opportunity. Since most rewarding jobs are already held by the host population, immigrants have to explore new economic horizons or take up socially despised careers. But other than the high status/low status and occupied/unoccupied dimensions, few distinctions are made among the niches. This blunts our analysis of the phenomenon that people with similar origins often handle their ethnic identity differently when they are not engaged in the same kind of economic activity. It is essential to examine the structural aspects of an economic enclave, the most important of which is the entry barrier.

The hypothesis is put forward in Chapter 5 that when the economic barrier to entry to an enclave is low, compensatory action will be taken by industrial incumbents to raise the barrier. Such an action frequently involves the mobilization of particularistic ties such as ethnicity and kinship. Therefore we may expect more overt expressions of ethnicity in industrial competition involving economic niches with low entry barriers.

Ethnic Conflict

The competitive strategies adopted by an ethnic group will have a direct impact on its relations with others in the same society. Bonacich has used the notion of 'host hostility' to describe the reaction of other groups toward the sojourners.[40] However, this notion is misleading on two counts. First, it over-simplifies reality by creating a false image of homogeneity among the host population which fails to distinguish a variety of possible reactions. For example, the Shanghainese arriving in Hong Kong encountered a spectrum of 'others' — administrators of the colonial government, Western businessmen, indigenous Cantonese residents, and migrants from other parts of China. The relationship ranged from direct conflict of economic interests, accommodation and symbiosis, to peaceful coexistence. Second, the argument that host hostility is aroused because an immigrant group refuses to assimilate and retains a homeward orientation is not convincing. It can be asserted with equal plausibility that the host population will be more tolerant precisely because the sojourners will not remain as permanent competitors and because they usually provide a useful service.

The role of the homeward orientation of an ethnic group in the development of ethnic conflict is at best secondary. The root cause of ethnic tension lies in the strategies of economic closure. The logical sequence for hostility to occur can be stated baldly as follows: innovation and entrepreneurship require substantial profits as rewards; this calls for economic closure to prevent the dilution of profit; closure is best attained by mobilizing particularistic ties such as ethnic ones; exclusion of potential competitors on ethnic grounds creates a sense of injustice among outsiders; other groups seek to retaliate and ethnic conflicts ensue. A vicious circle is formed.

Hostility tends to strengthen ethnic boundaries and influence the transmission of ethnic consciousness to the younger generation. When conflict is intense, groups will try to manipulate the opportunity structure to seal off economic spheres. Once rigid ethnic and occupational barriers are erected, erosion of ethnic identity is unlikely to happen. Children of the migrants hoping for acculturation might suffer the shock of unanticipated discrimination. Ethnic consciousness might be rekindled when they enter into active employment and are treated unfairly. The younger generation will then be reintegrated into the ethnic fold. If channels for occupational mobility are restricted, then sojourners and refugees are not only unable to become settlers in the second or third generation, but also migrants with a settler mentality may rear children with sojourning attitudes. In these circumstances, second-step migration or even forced repatriation of entire ethnic groups can happen.

Therefore, it appears that economic concentration and ethnic tension are inherent processes of economies marked by innovation and competition. When the external environment is favourable and the economy is booming, communal strife will remain latent as opportunities for material gain proliferate. But in times of recession, when economic opportunities contract, attempts at preserving existing interests by closure will become more explicit and ethnic conflict will be more strident. Alternatively, when the opportunity structure is relatively stable and economic spheres have already been clearly divided, a temporary truce may prevail among ethnic groups. But if the opportunity structure is suddenly rearranged, as after the overthrow of a colonial system, then economic territories will have to be redrawn and ethnic discord is bound to erupt.[41]

Limitations and Further Research

It is to be hoped that the foregoing analysis of the Shanghainese cotton spinners in Hong Kong has demonstrated the basic validity of my theoretical model for understanding the congregation of co-ethnics in an economic sphere. However, a single case study obviously cannot provide a broad enough empirical foundation to determine the validity of all the model's propositions. Therefore, in the final sections, I shall set out the main limitations of the case study, and indicate the types of future research required to specify more rigorously the relationship between ethnicity and economic behaviour.

One possible way of testing the model against more empirical evidence is by reanalysing the existing ethnographic data with a bearing on the problem of ethnic concentration in economic niches. Some of those studies may be examined afresh using the conceptual scheme already formulated. The merit of the model will rest on its ability to arrange the data more neatly and to point to new and more convincing interpretations of the facts. Cohen's investigation of the Hausa cattle traders in West Africa readily suggests itself for such an exercise, and it would be interesting to compare the strength of his analytical framework with that of mine on the same field-work material.[42]

Most existing studies, including the present one, are concerned with situations where persistently high levels of ethnic occupational concentration prevail. Because they are striking, these extreme instances of ethnic 'monopoly' tend to attract the attention of most researchers. But for the sake of theory-building, it is essential to look for a wider range of situations. Examples of high ethnic concentration provide information about how such a phenomenon comes into being. Consequently, research efforts can be easily led into a preoccupation with the processes of migration and the use of differential assets in economic competition. However, as the entrepreneurs are successful in capturing the niches, they often do not have to mobilize their ethnic ties overtly. As a result, the mechanisms of ethnic group formation and economic closure are not readily observable. Other cases are needed with a lesser degree of concentration to lay bare these mechanisms. Ethnic groups that succeed in gaining access to an enclave but subsequently fail to maintain their dominance constitute one such type of case. It would be instructive to study the strategies they adopt for competition and discover why these are ineffective in excluding outsiders. Another type of situation is where several ethnic groups coexist in an enclave, none having as yet attained economic dominance. One example is Hong Kong's weaving industry where the means of production are more or less equally shared between Cantonese and Shanghainese entrepreneurs. Under such conditions, it can be predicted that strategies of ethnic group formation and economic closure will be pursued more explicitly with greater vigour. Investigations into these cases might shed more light on the consolidation of ethnic concentration and economic power, a process which I can only dimly detect among the Shanghainese cotton spinners.

It is clear that my treatment of business ideology as one of the differential assets held by members of an ethnic group raises more questions than it answers. Do the Shanghainese entrepreneurs have an ideology different from that of Cantonese, Chaozhou, or Sichuan industrialists? How important is the opportunity structure of a society in shaping entrepreneurial attitudes? What is the influence of the nature of the economic niche on these attitudes? Is the instability in cotton and yarn prices, for example, crucial in making the Shanghainese spinners cautious and conservative? Three kinds of comparative studies could be designed to unravel the effects of ethnicity, opportunity structure and characteristics of occupational niches on business ideology. First, an industry under multi-ethnic ownership, such as the Hong Kong garments or electronics industry, could be chosen for study. The second format would be to compare the norms and beliefs of entrepreneurs with the same ethnic background engaging in the same industry in different societies. The Shanghainese spinners operating in Taiwan, Indonesia, and different parts of Africa and South America would provide one instance. The third approach would be to look at the ideologies of industrialists of common ethnic affiliation, but active in different occupations in the same community. Examples would be, for instance, Shanghainese owners in the manufacture of enamelware, in shipping, in the insurance business, and in the different lines of textile production in Hong Kong.

However, ignorance in the field of business ideology is not confined to the Chinese entrepreneurs, but also extends to the Chinese government officials. There are few comprehensive studies on the attitudes and policies toward industry of recent successive Chinese governments. I have touched on what appears to be a strong anti-private enterprise sentiment in the Nationalist administration. However, the lack of systematic analyses of this topic means that the theme of the relationship between government and industry cannot be developed fully with reference to the Shanghainese cotton spinners. Thus my treatment of the variable of 'others' in this case study is not as substantial as is desirable. Incidentally, the economic ideology of Chinese governments raises a new issue in the debate on the 'retardation' of China's modernization. How have capitalistic *ideas*, such as concepts of private property and profit, impersonal corporations, industrial authority, and continual reinvestment been received in modern China? This area has been neglected even though a good deal of material has already been collected on the institutional set-up and development of both foreign and Chinese-owned enterprises in China.

The last major limitation of this study that I am aware of is the relative absence of ethnic conflicts. This is in line with the prediction of my model that conflicts are most likely to occur during prolonged economic recessions or radical transformations of the social and economic order. Neither of these conditions has yet appeared in Hong Kong. It is necessary to search for cases with more intensive communal hostility to compare with the present study of the Shanghai spinners in order to have an adequate understanding of the interrelationship among strategies of closure, external economic influences, and ethnic tension.

8 Epilogue

THE narrative part of the story of the Shanghai spinners ends in 1978. Since then three events have taken place that have significant bearing on the future orientation of these industrialists. The first was the depression of the spinning industry between 1980 and 1982. The second was the initiation of economic reforms by the leadership of the People's Republic of China. The third and most important event was the Sino-British negotiations over the future of Hong Kong.

The Depression (1980–1982)

The depression of the spinning industry coincided with a property boom in Hong Kong. The spindleage of the members of the Hong Kong Cotton Spinners' Association contracted by 21 per cent in 1981 as against the productive capacity of the previous year. The associated reductions in monthly output and employment were 22 and 25 per cent respectively.[1] Eight mills were reported to have closed down during 1980 and 1981.[2] Some of them had sold their plant to real estate developers. This turn of events had led commentators in the local press to lament that the spinning industry was in decline and might eventually disappear from the economic scene.

Their pessimism proved to be unjustified as they had failed to appreciate the cyclical nature of the industry and the vocational commitment of the spinners. The more resilient spinners proceeded, during the depression, to re-equip their factories with more sophisticated machinery and tried to reorganize their production to cater more closely to the needs of the flourishing local garment industry.[3] By the end of 1983, the number of spinning mills had stabilized at 27. Total spindleage and employment had dropped further, by 13 and 12 per cent respectively, against the figures for the previous year. But the number of rotors in the industry had increased by 6 per cent, and export volume and export value had risen by 20 and 30 per cent respectively.[4] The Nan Fung Textiles Ltd., one of the largest companies in the industry, merged its plants and expanded its production capacity from 251,000 bales in 1981 to a projected 360,000 bales in 1984.[5] Thus it appears that the spinning industry emerged from the depression more streamlined and more efficient than before. Ownership had become more concentrated and with no new entrants into the industry, the dominance of the Shanghai spinners remained unchallenged.

China's Economic Reform

The second event with an impact on the industrial behaviour of the Shanghai spinners is the economic reform launched in China since the late 1970s. In the industrial sphere, the Chinese leadership is adopting an 'open door' policy. Special economic zones have been created in which joint ventures with industrialists outside China are encouraged. In these ventures, China for the most part provides land and labour while the outside partners supply machinery and technical expertise.

Some Hong Kong industrialists, including several spinners, have responded to China's new economic initiative. In 1978 the managing director of the Textile Corporation of Hong Kong Ltd., Mr Eric L. C. Chen, invested in a textile joint venture in Canton.[6] In 1981 Mr H. C. Tang, a director of the Winsor Corporation and chief executive of two cotton spinning mills and a worsted factory in Hong Kong, set up, jointly with the Chinese government, a wool processing factory in Xinjiang and a worsted factory in Shanghai.[7]

The spinners invest in the Chinese special economic zones for a number of reasons. By transferring part of the manufacturing process to China where land and labour are cheaper, they can lower the cost of production. In some cases, the joint ventures can secure for them raw materials in scarce supply. The wool processing factory in Xinjiang, for instance, will be able to tap the supply of cashmere at its source. There is also the consideration of political goodwill. A number of the spinners apparently believe that industrial co-operation with China will contribute to the future stability of Hong Kong. Those who have parents and other family members living in the mainland may also hope that the well-being of their close relatives will be enhanced through their direct participation in China's industrial development.[8]

However, China's open door policy is unlikely to lure many Shanghai spinners back to their homeland in the foreseeable future. Most of them are pragmatists, not easily moved by nationalistic appeals. As refugees, few of them still have close family in China. As cautious industrialists, they have yet to be convinced that the reform policy of the Chinese government will persist. They are also keenly aware that the economic benefits to be gained from the joint ventures are at best transient. The contracts for these ventures usually last no more than four to five years, at the end of which the factories will have to be turned over to the Chinese government. When that happens, as one of the spinners has warned, 'China will have the mills, the equipment and the expertise learned from Hong Kong operators, in addition to land and low-cost labour. There's no way Hong Kong can compete.'[9]

The Sino-British Negotiations

The most momentous event influencing the orientation of the Shanghai spinners was, of course, the Sino-British negotiations over the future of Hong Kong. During the negotiations, some of the spinners openly expressed their apprehension. 'Communist ideas and politics would kill the Hong Kong system', said Liu Hong-tong, chairman of Unisouth and South Textiles Ltd.[10] 'The minute this place turns communist', declared Alex Woo, executive director of Central Textiles Ltd., 'I'll go'.[11] They are, as shown in previous chapters, well prepared for that eventuality. From soon after their arrival in the colony, most of them diversified their investments, acquired foreign passports, and educated their children abroad.

The Chinese government seems to take them very seriously and has made a special effort to coax them to stay. Soon after the start of the Sino-British negotiations, the People's Republic of China changed the key personnel of the Hong Kong branch of the New China News Agency, which has served as its unofficial diplomatic organ in the colony. In place of middle level cadres from Guangdong, high ranking officials were sent from the Shanghai region to lead the Agency. Xu Jia-tun, the First Party Secretary of Jiangsu, who had been engaged in the administration of that province for nearly thirty years, arrived in Hong Kong in 1983 to become the new director of the New China News Agency.[12] He was accompanied by Li Shu-wen, head of the Foreign Affairs Office of Shanghai, who took up the post of deputy director of the Agency.[13] One of Hong Kong's local leftist magazines has pointed out that these new assignments were partly 'a reflection of the importance attached by the Chinese Communist Party to linkages with the "Shanghai clique" in Hong Kong'.[14] In an apparent move to strengthen such linkages, the Chinese government dispatched a Shanghai regional theatrical group to perform in Hong Kong in the wake of Xu Jia-tun's arrival. Six Shanghainese notables including three spinners were invited to host the cultural event.[15]

The Chinese and British governments reached an agreement in 1985 over the future of Hong Kong. China will recover sovereignty over the territory in 1997. Under a 'one country, two systems' formula, Hong Kong will retain its social and economic system as a 'special administrative region' of China for a period of fifty years. This provision has met the major demand of the spinners and other groups in Hong Kong who wanted, above all else, to preserve 'a free-enterprise system' and 'freedom of movement of the people and of assets'.[16] In order further to calm the nerves of the Shanghainese entrepreneurs, the Chinese government quickly organized a Basic Law Drafting Committee to design the future constitutional make-up of Hong Kong in which the Shanghainese were given a prominent role. T. K. Ann, chairman of the Winsor Industrial Corporation, was named a deputy director of the committee while Cha Chi-ming, managing director of New Territories Textiles Ltd., was appointed a committee member.

There are no signs at present that an exodus of the Shanghai spinners is imminent. To a certain extent, they may have been reassured by the Chinese government's gestures of good will. But being level-headed businessmen mindful of the past record of the Chinese Communist Party in its treatment of private industrialists, the spinners will most probably take the Sino-British Agreement for what it is — a declaration of intention. What is attracting them to stay in Hong Kong during the coming transitional period is not so much the promises of the Chinese leadership, but rather the economic opportunity assured by the textile quota system. As long as Hong Kong can preserve its independent share of quotas under the international Multi-Fibre Arrangement, the spinners will have a stake there too valuable to forsake.[17] Moreover, many of them have reached an age when they are reluctant to undertake a second-step migration. 'Many older people here hope to die before any drastic changes take place', one of the spinners said. Yet they are concerned for their children and grandchildren. 'We are looking for a better world for the younger generation who have no idea of Shanghai.'[18] That better world could still be Hong Kong. But it could well be elsewhere. They are keeping their options open.

Notes

Notes to Chapter 1

1. G. W. Skinner (1957), *Chinese Society in Thailand* (Ithaca, Cornell University Press), p.315.

2. F. D. Cloud (1906), *Hangchow: The 'City of Heaven'* (Shanghai, Presbyterian Press), pp.9–10. W. T. Rowe has discussed in detail the significance of sub-ethnic or local origin groups in Hankou in the late imperial period. See Rowe (1984), *Hankow: Commerce and Society in a Chinese City, 1796–1889* (Stanford, Stanford University Press). In this study, I shall use the generic term 'ethnic group' to refer to groups such as the Shanghainese and the Cantonese. By ethnicity, I refer to a principle of social organization based on shared origins, either biological or territorial in nature. I do not adopt the term 'sub-ethnic group' mainly because of its unwarranted assumption that the 'racial' identity of being Han Chinese is of primary importance and that regional differences are of secondary significance.

3. E. H. P. Brown (1971), 'The Hong Kong Economy: Achievement and Prospects', in K. Hopkins (ed), *Hong Kong: The Industrial Colony* (Hong Kong, Oxford University Press), p.13.

4. Commerce and Industry Department, Hong Kong Government (1973), 'Memorandum for the Trade and Industry Advisory Board: Land for Industry' (Hong Kong, The Department, mimeo. paper), p.2.

5. D. Podmore, 'The Population of Hong Kong', in Hopkins (ed), *Hong Kong*, p.26

6. World Bank (1982), *World Development Report, 1982* (New York, Oxford University Press), p.111.

7. United Nations, *Economic and Social Survey of Asia and The Far East, 1969*, p.4; United Nations, *Economic Survey, 1976*, p.3; and World Bank, *World Development Report, 1982*, p.111.

8. Far Eastern Economic Review (1978), *Asia 1978 Yearbook* (Hong Kong, The Review), p.193. See also J. Riedel, *The Industrialization of Hong Kong* (1974), (Tübingen, J. C. B. Mohr), pp.7–11.

9. G. W. Skinner (1977), 'Regional Urbanization in Nineteenth-century China', in Skinner (ed), *The City in Late Imperial China* (Stanford, Stanford University Press), pp.221–49. J. Chesneaux observes that the Chinese proletariat in the early twentieth century were distributed in 'six clearly defined regions'. See Chesneaux (1968), *The Chinese Labor Movement 1919–1927* (Stanford, Stanford University Press), p.43.

10. Skinner, 'Regional Urbanization', pp.213–14.

11. *Provincial Atlas of the Peoples's Republic of China* (1974), (Beijing, Ditu Chuban She), p.48. This area is roughly equivalent to what was traditionally known as the *sanwu* area.

12. Yuen Ren Chao (1976), *Aspects of Chinese Sociolinguistics* (Stanford, Stanford University Press), pp.22–3.

13. Jiangsu & Zhejiang Residents' (H.K.) Association, *Special Publication of the Jiangsu & Zhejiang Residents' Association* (Hong Kong, The Association, n. d.), p.32.

14. Hong Kong Ningbo Residents' Association (1977), *Commemorative Volume on The Tenth Anniversary of The Association* (Hong Kong, The Association), p.56.

15. As above, p.17; Kiangsu & Chekiang Residents' (H.K.) Association (1979), *Directory of Presidents, Advisors and Directors, No. 20, 1977–1979* (Hong Kong, The Association, 1979).

16. Shanghai Fraternity Association (1978), *Chinese Opera in Mandarin for Raising Charity Fund* (Hong Kong, The Association, 1978).

17. See *Xingdao Ribao*, 31 July 1978, for the funeral notices of Mr Zhu. E. Honig has described the split between female textile workers originating from Jiangnan [Southern Jiangsu] and Subei [Northern Jiangsu] in pre-war Shanghai in her book *Sisters and Strangers* (1986), (Stanford, Stanford University Press), Chapter 3.

18. Jiangsu & Zhejiang Residents' (H.K.) Association (1961), *Collected Publication of The Jiangsu & Zhejiang Residents' Association, The Jiangsu & Zhejiang Secondary School, and The Jiangsu & Zhejiang Primary School* (Hong Kong, The Association), p.48.

19. K. M. A. Barnett, *Hong Kong Report on The 1961 Census* (Hong Kong, Government Printers, no date), Vol. 1, p.xxvii.

20. As above, Vol. 2, Table 132, p.43.

21. I use the following formula to arrive at an estimate of the number of local-born Shanghainese:

$$\text{No. of Cantonese speakers} \times \frac{\text{No. of Shanghainese speakers}}{\begin{array}{c}\text{No. of Shanghainese, 'Hoklo'}\\\text{and Mandarin speakers}\end{array}}$$

$$= 50,837 \times \frac{64,190}{64,190 + 21,769 + 10,882} = 33,697$$

22. *Hong Kong 1978* (1978), (Hong Kong, Government Printers), p.11.

23. HKCSA (1973), *Twenty Five Years of The Hong Kong Cotton Spinning Industry* (Hong Kong, The Association), p.50.

24. V. F. S. Sit, S. L. Wong, and T. S. Kiang (1979), *Small Scale Industry in a Laissez-Faire Economy: A Hong Kong Case Study* (Hong Kong, University of Hong Kong, Centre of Asian Studies), p.25.

25. For detailed information on the external markets of the Hong Kong textile industry, see M. C. H. Mok (1968), 'The Development of Cotton Spinning and Weaving Industries in Hong Kong, 1946–1966', M. A. thesis (University of Hong Kong), Chapter 7; HKCSA, *Twenty Five Years*; and *Hong Kong External Trade: Report and Tables*, various years.

26. The number of mills does not include those which were closed down before 1978 as it is not possible to obtain systematic information about them.

Notes to Chapter 2

1. *The Hong Kong Government Gazette*, 15 February 1873, p.57; 24 February 1877, p.85; *Hong Kong Government Sessional Papers*, No. 30/91, p.382; No. 26/97, p.482; No.39/1901, p.16; No. 17/1911, p.103; No. 15/1921, p.205; No. 5/1931, pp.127–8. The 1941 census gave no breakdown of Chinese by regional origin. See *Hong Kong Government Sessional Papers*, 3/1941, p.7.

2. Jiangsu & Zhejiang Residents' Association, *Special Publication*, p.35; Tu Yun-pu and Jiang Shu-liang (eds) (1940), *Travel Guide to Hong Kong* (Shanghai, China Travel Service), pp.120–2.

3. Jiangsu & Zhejiang Residents' Association, *Special Publication*, p.35.

4. *FEER*, 11 December 1946, p.8.

5. *DGB*, 6 December 1948.

6. The demand for hotel accommodation was so acute that a 'Hotels Bill' was introduced in the Legislative Council in 1949 to control provision and charges. See Hong Kong Government, *Hansard* (1949), pp.38–47.

7. *DGB*, 6 December 1948.

8. J. L. Espy, 'Hong Kong Textiles, Ltd.' in L. C. Nehrt, G. S. Evans, and L. Li, (eds), *Managerial Policy, Strategy and Planning for Southeast Asia* (Hong Kong, Chinese University Press, 1974), p.275. The name of the company is fictitious.

9. *RQS*, Vol. 2, pp.23–4; p.647.

10. A. Feuerwerker (1968), *The Chinese Economy, 1912–1949* (Ann Arbor, University of Michigan, Center of Chinese Studies), p.22.

11. *RQS*, Vol. 2, pp.304–11.

12. Shanghai Shi Shanghui (ed) (1947), *Textile Industry* (Shanghai, Shangye Yuebao She), section L., pp.1–32; Lin Bin (1948), 'Dissecting The China Textile Industries Inc.', *Jingji Daobao* 55, pp.22–3; 56, pp.21–3; 57 and 58, pp.28–31; 59, pp.20–3; and A. Chung (1953), 'The Development of Modern Manufacturing Industry in China, 1928–1948', Ph.D thesis (University of Pennsylvania), pp. 260–1.

13. See A. D. Barnett (1963), *China On The Eve of The Communist Takeover* (New York, Frederick A. Praeger), p.73.

14. See P. M. Coble Jr. (1980), *The Shanghai Capitalists and The Nationalist Government 1927–1937* (Cambridge, Harvard University Press).

15. *Da Gong Bao [Shanghai]*, 26 May 1948, quoted in Ji Chong-wei, 'The Present Condition and Future Prospect of the Cotton Spinning Industry', *Fangzhi Zhoukan*, 9 (1948), p.302.

16. *RQS*, Vol. 2, pp.608–15; pp.647–9.

17. Espy, 'Hong Kong Textiles', p.275.

18. See R. H. Lee (1960), *The Chinese in The United States of America* (Hong Kong, Hong Kong University Press), pp.12–26; and M. G. Tan, *The Chinese in the United States: Social Mobility and Assimilation* (1971), (Taipei, Orient Cultural Service), pp.41–59.

19. See F. H. Golay, R. Anspach, M. R. Pfanner, and E. B. Ayal, (1969), *Underdevelopment and Economic Nationalism in Southeast Asia* (Ithaca and London, Cornell University Press); W. E. Willmott, *The Chinese in Cambodia* (1967), (Vancouver, University of British Columbia Press); G. W. Skinner, *Chinese Society in Thailand: An Analytical History* (1957), (New York, Cornell University Press); S. Spectre (1958), 'The Chinese in Singapore', in M. Fried (ed.), *Colloquium on Overseas Chinese* (New York, Institute of Pacific Relations), pp.22–5.

20. *Hong Kong Hansard* (1949), p.233.

21. *Hong Kong Hansard* (1949), pp.240–1.

22. *DGB*, 11 March 1950. Similar conditions prevailed in countries such as Indonesia and Singapore, as discovered by the delegation of Hong Kong industrialists looking for investment opportunities in South-east Asia during the depression created by the Korean War. See *DGB*, 12 June; 8 November; 11 November; 21 November 1951.

23. *RQS*, Vol. 2, p.662. For the biography of Wellington Koo, see H. L. Boorman and R. C. Howard (eds) (1968), *Biographical Dictionary of Republican China* (New York, Columbia University Press), pp.255–9. An obituary of Koo was published in *The New York Times*, 16 November 1985.

24. *DGB*, 7 April 1949.

25. J. C. Ingram (1971), *Economic Change in Thailand 1850–1970* (Stanford, Stanford University Press), p.121. See also *DGB*, 6 October 1949.

26. *RQS*, Vol. 2, p.663.

27. *RQS*, Vol. 2, p.649.

28. S. P. S. Ho (1978), *Economic Development of Taiwan, 1860–1970* (New Haven and London, Yale University Press), p.105; J. H. Power, G. P. Sicat, and

M. H. Hsing (1971), *The Philippines and Taiwan: Industrialization and Trade Policy* (London, Oxford University Press), p.151, note 1.

29. Power, Sicat and Hsing, *The Philippines and Taiwan,* p.151, Table 1.2.

30. F. H. Chaffee, G. E. Aurell, H. A. Barth, A. S. Cort, J. H. Dombrowski, V. J. Fasano, and J. O. Weaver, (1969), *Area handbook for The Republic of China* (Washington, The American University Foreign Area Studies), p.293.

31. See Power et al., *The Philippines and Taiwan*, pp.201–5; and H. D. Fong (1968), 'Taiwan's Industrialization, with Special Reference to Policies and Controls', *Journal of Nanyang University*, 2, pp.365–426.

32. E. Hambro (1955), *The Problem of Chinese Refugees in Hong Kong* (Leyden), p.148.

33. During the Japanese occupation there had been a good deal of emigration from Hong Kong. The population in 1945 was estimated to be between 500,000 and 600,000 persons. See Podmore, 'Population of Hong Kong', pp.24–5.

34. This change in orientation of the Chinese immigrants was not recognized by the Hong Kong government at first. As Grantham, the then Governor, wrote in his memoir, 'To begin with, little for them was done since we predicted, wrongly as it turned out, that as soon as the new regime in China had settled down and things got back to normal, they would return to their native villages.' See Grantham, *Via Ports*, p.155.

35. Confidential memorandum from Joint Chiefs of Staff Secretaries, W. G. Lalor and J. H. Ives, 21 October 1949, quoted in D. Tsang, 'Home Truths from History', *FEER*, 14 July 1978, p.29.

36. *FEER*, 11 May 1949, p.1.

37. For the story of a Chinese industrialist continuing normal business in the French Concession of Shanghai throughout the Anti-Japanese War, see H. C. Ting (1974), *Truth and Facts: Recollection of A Hong Kong Industrialist* (Hong Kong, Kader Industrial Company Ltd.), pp.50–3.

38. *Hong Kong Hansard* (1949), pp.59–60.

39. *Hong Kong Hansard* (1949), p.6.

40. *Hong Kong Hansard* (1949), p.73.

41. HKCSA (1973), 'Annual Report of the General Committee' (Hong Kong, The Association, mimeographed), p.5; and N. J. Miners (1981), *The Government and Politics of Hong Kong* (Hong Kong, Oxford University Press) pp.357–9.

42. *Hong Kong Hansard* (1948), p.7.

43. See for example Chen Zhen and Yao Luo (eds)(1957), *Source Materials on The Modern Industry of China* (Beijing, Sanlian Shudian); Cong Han-xiang (1962), 'On The Problem of the Primitive Accumulation of National Capital in China', *Lishi Yanjiu*, 2, pp.26–45.

44. Fan Bei-chuan (1955), 'On the Various Components of the Chinese Bourgeoisie', *Zhongguo Kexue Yuan Lishi Yanjiu Suo Disan Suo Jikan*, 2, pp.99–128.

45. M. Bergère (1969), 'The Role of The Bourgeoisie', in M.C. Wright (ed), *China in Revolution: The First Phase, 1900–1913* (New Haven & London, Yale University Press), p.249. On the basis of his study of the competition between the British-American Tobacco Company and the Nanyang Brothers Tobacco Company in China, S. Cochran maintains that the distinction between national and comprador capitalists, though imprecise, is a useful one because 'it calls attention to an urgent dilemma that Chinese who were engaged in Sino-foreign rivalries frequently faced: to merge or not to merge with one's foreign competitors.' See Cochran (1980), *Big Business in China: Sino-Foreign Rivalry in the Cigarette Industry, 1890–1930* (Cambridge, Harvard University Press), p.210.

46. A Feuerwerker (1958), *China's Early Industrialization: Sheng Hsuan-huai (1844–1916) and Mandarin Enterprise* (Cambridge, Harvard University Press).

47. See Shanghai Shi Shanghui (ed), *Textile Industry*, section L, pp.1–32.

48. H. D. Fong, 'Private Enterprise Should Start With the China Textile Industries Inc.', in *Textile Industry*, section A, p.74; 'Report on the Work of the China Textile Indutries Inc. for 1946', in *Textile Industry*, section L, p.26.

49. Lin Bin (1948), 'China Textile Industries Inc.', *Jingji Daobao*, 59, pp.20–2.

50. *DGB*, 16 June 1949.

51. Fong, 'Taiwan's Industrialization', p.383.

52. Zhongguo Wenshi Yanjiu Xuehui (ed), *Biographies of New China* (Hong Kong, Zhongguo Wenshi Yanjiu Xuehui, no date), pp.153–5.

53. *DGB*, 15 May 1950.

54. *Huaqiao Ribao*, 21 and 31 December 1948; *DGB*, 24 December 1948.

55. Zhao Zhong-sun (1977), 'An Interview with The National Bourgeoisie in The Chinese Mainland', *Qishi Niandai*, 91, pp.45–6. In an apparent reference to Rong De-sheng's family, Robert Loh says that four of the sons were by the wife while three were from a concubine. 'Before the Communists captured Shanghai, the legitimate sons left hurriedly. . . The concubine's sons found themselves in charge of the family empire'. See Loh (1962), *Escape From Red China* (New York, Coward McCaan), p.52.

56. *DGB*, 11 March 1978; W. Bartke (1987), *Who's Who in The People's Republic of China* (München, K. G. Saur, 2nd edn.), pp.392–3.

57. HKCSA, *Twenty Five Years*, pp.95–104.

58. Taeuber, 'Migrants and Metropolis', p.6.

59. See F. L. K. Hsu (1971), *Under The Ancestor's Shadow* (Stanford, Stanford University Press, revised edition), p.108; pp.301–2; M. Freedman (1958), *Lineage Organization in Southeastern China* (London, The Athlone Press), p.135.

60. G. W. Skinner (1966), 'Filial Sons and Their Sisters: Configuration and Culture in Chinese Families' (unpublished paper), cited in A. Speare Jr., 'Migration and Family Change in Central Taiwan', in G. W. Skinner and M. Elvin (eds) (1974), *The Chinese City Between Two Worlds* (Stanford, Stanford University Press), p.325.

61. Speare, 'Migration', p.326.

62. *DGB*, 4 April 1950; 19 March 1978.

63. For the funeral notice of Wu Kun-sheng, see *Xingdao Ribao*, 4 December 1975.

64. Reported in *DGB*, 15 June 1950.

65. *DGB*, 11 March 1978.

66. *RQS*, Vol. 2, p.23.

67. *RQS*, Vol. 2, p.665.

68. Rong Hong-yuan, for instance, vacillated in selling one of his Shanghai mills in 1949 when he had already moved to Hong Kong. He tried to withdraw the sale that had verbally been agreed upon, giving as his reason that the Communist advance might halt at the Yangzi River and that there might still be a future for textile manufacture in Shanghai under Nationalist rule. See *RQS*, Vol. 2, p.648.

69. *SCMP*, 29 May 1981; 17 June 1981; 13 March 1982; and *DGB*, 2 June 1981; 3 June 1981.

70. See the funeral notice in *Xingdao Ribao*, 25 December 1965.

71. See the funeral notice in *Xingdao Ribao*, 4 May 1965.

72. *Huaqiao Ribao*, 22 July 1978.

73. *Huaqiao Ribao*, 4 July 1978.

Notes to Chapter 3

1. L. W. Pye, 'Foreword', in C. Howe (ed) (1981), *Shanghai: Revolution and Development in An Asian Metropolis* (Cambridge, Cambridge University Press), p.xv.

2. R. Murphey (1953), *Shanghai: Key to Modern China* (Cambridge, Harvard University Press), p.3; Quan Han-sheng, 'The Role of Shanghai in the Industrializa-

tion of Modern China', in Quan (1972), *Essays on Chinese Economic History* (Hong Kong, The Chinese University of Hong Kong, New Asia Research Institute), p.698. For an assessment of the economic development of pre-war Shanghai, see D. K. Lieu (1936), *The Growth and Industrialization of Shanghai* (Shanghai, China Institute of Pacific Relations).

3. Grantham, *Via Ports*, pp.104–5.

4. *FEER*, 17 November 1946, p.10.

5. *FEER*, 7 January 1948, p.5.

6. *DGB*, 14 October 1948.

7. *DGB*, 29 July 1948.

8. Y. C. Jao (1974), *Banking and Currency in Hong Kong: A Study of Postwar Financial Development* (London, Macmillan).

9. *DGB*, 29 July 1948.

10. Wong Po-shang (1958), 'The Influx of Chinese Capital into Hong Kong since 1937' (University of Hong Kong, paper read at the Contemporary China Seminar, 15 May 1958), p.5.

11. *Huaqiao Ribao*, 17 April 1950.

12. Szczepanik, *Economic Growth*, p.142.

13. *Economic Growth*, p.143.

14. *FEER*, 7 April 1948, pp.336–7. Two contradictory figures were given concerning the total investment. In the table on p.336, the investment was said to be HK$4 million, but in the text, it was cited as HK$10 million. In the article 'Hong Kong' published in *Asian Textile Survey 1969–70,* L. C. Chung apparently adopted the latter figure and stated that the investment of the first spinning mill was 625,000 pounds sterling (p.77, evidently at the exchange rate of 1 pound to 16 Hong Kong dollars). But judging from the cost of spindles at that time, HK$10 million was too large a sum to be plausible and it was most probably a misprint.

15. These were the Wyler Cotton Mill, the Nan Yang Cotton Mill, the Tai Yuan Cotton Mill, and the Kowloon Cotton Mill. The Shen Xin Textile Company reported in the late 1950s that the four mills had a total of 113,600 spindles which were estimated to cost US$10 million. See *RQS*, Vol. 2, p.671.

16. HKCSA, *Twenty Five Years*, p.118.

17. *DGB*, 14 May 1949; *Jingji Daobao*, 72(1948), p.3.

18. United Nations Industrial Development Organization (1968), *Report of Expert Group Meeting on the Selection of Textile Machinery in the Cotton Industry* (Vienna, UNIDO), p.49; cited in Y. Nihei, H. S. R. Kao, D. A. Levin, M. E. Morkre, M. Ohtsu, and J. B. Peacock, (1979), *Technology, Employment Practices and Workers: A comparative study of ten cotton spinning plants in five Asian countries* (Hong Kong, University of Hong Kong, Centre of Asia Studies), p.29.

19. *FEER*, 6 July 1950, p.3. According to the HKCSA, the spindleage at the end of 1950 was 132,000 (see *Twenty Five Years*, 118). But this figure only covered those mills which were members of the Association. In late 1950 the China Engineers Ltd., which was closely related to the financing of the industry, recorded a total of 190,000 spindles in the colony (see *FEER*, 21 September 1950, p.346).

20. *Huaqiao Ribao*, 3 April 1951.

21. Szczepanik, *Economic Growth*, p.14.

22. On the prosperity of the spinning industry at the beginning of the war, see R. W. Barnett, *Economic Shanghai: Hostage to Politics, 1937–1941* (New York, Institute of Pacific Relations, 1941), pp.107–10.

23. Shanghai Shi Shanghui, *Textile Industry*, section A, p.43; *FEER*, 21 May 1947, p.11; 7 April 1948, p.336. On the post-war profits of various plants of the Shen Xin Textile Company, see *RQS*, Vol. 2, p.437, p.455, and p.512.

24. Shanghai Shi Shanghui, *Textile Industry*, section C, p.14; *FEER*, 21 May 1947, p.11.

25. For detailed accounts of the inflation, see A. N. Young (1965), *China's Wartime Finance and Inflation, 1937–1945* (Cambridge, Harvard University Press); S. H. Chow (1963), *The Chinese Inflation, 1973–1949* (New York, Columbia University Press); and Chang Kia-ngau (1958), *The Inflationary Spiral: The Experience of China, 1939–1950* (Cambridge, M.I.T. Press).

26. *FEER*, 2 July 1947, p.132.

27. *DGB*, 9 January 1949.

28. *DGB*, 21 August 1949; *FEER*, 1 September 1949, p.268.

29. *FEER*, 25 June 1947, p.120.

30. *Jingji Tongxun*, 72 (1948), p.2.

31. J. K. Chang (1969), *Industrial Development in Pre-Communist China* (Edinburgh, Edinburgh University Press), p.105.

32. *FEER*, 26 November 1947, pp.628–9.

33. See the report by H. Stott, mill manager of the Calico Printers' Association in *FEER*, 21 September 1950, p.346; and the opinion of the British experts invited by the Hong Kong government to survey the spinning and weaving industry of Hong Kong, reported in *DGB*, 22 May 1949, and 21 July 1949.

34. A. S. Pearse (1955), *Japan's Cotton Industry* (Cyprus, Kyrenia, 1955), pp.122–3.

35. See Wong, 'Influx of Chinese Capital', pp.6–12.

36. E. Mansfield has found for the steel, petroleum, and rubber tyre industries that 'smaller firms often tend to have higher and variable growth rates than larger firms'. See Mansfield (1973), 'Entry, Exit and Growth of Firms', in B. S. Yamey, *Economics of Industrial Structure* (Harmondsworth, Penguin Education), p.94.

37. *FEER*, 6 July 1950, p.4; 21 September 1950, p.356; *DGB*, 3 March 1951.

38. *FEER*, 21 September 1950, p.346; the price dropped further in 1952, see *DGB*, 3 April 1952.

39. *DGB*, 24 January 1953.

40. A similar statement was quoted in A. Y. C. King and D. H. K. Leung (1975), 'The Chinese Touch in Small Industrial Organization' (The Chinese University of Hong Kong, Social Research Centre, mimeographed paper), p.38.

41. 'Native Banking in Shanghai' (1926), *The Chinese Economic Monthly*, 3, pp.168–83; J. C. Ferguson (1906), 'Notes on Chinese Banking System in Shanghai', *Journal of Royal Asiatic Society North China Branch*, 37, pp.55–82; A. L. McElderry (1976), *Shanghai Old Style Banks (Ch'ien-chuang), 1800–1935* (Ann Arbor, Center of Chinese Studies, University of Michigan).

42. S. M. Jones, 'The Ningpo *Pang* and Financial Power at Shanghai', in Skinner and Elvin (eds), *The Chinese City Between Two Worlds*, pp.74–96; Y. Shiba, 'Ningpo and Its Hinterland', in Skinner (ed), *The City in Imperial China*, p.436; Zhong Shu-yuan (1948), 'The Pillar of the Jiangsu-Zhejiang Financial Syndicate — The Ningbo *Bang*', *Jingji Daobao*, 67, p.6.

43. J. Ahler (1964), 'Postwar Banking in Shanghai', *Pacific Affairs*, 19, p.391.

44. As above, pp.384–93.

45. Chen Zhen and Yao Luo (1957) (eds), *Source Materials on The Modern Industry of China* (Beijing, Sanlian Shudian), p.761

46. Kang Chao (1977), *The Development of Cotton Textile Production in China* (Cambridge, Harvard University Press), p.143.

47. Calculated from the figures provided in *RQS*, Vol. 2, pp.315 and 317.

48. J. L. Espy (1970), 'The Strategies of Chinese Industrial Enterprises in Hong Kong', D. B. A. Thesis (Harvard), p.137.

49. P. A. Graham, 'Financing Hong Kong Business', *FEER*, 17 April 1969, p.152.

50. See W. K. K. Chan (1977), *Merchants, Mandarins, and Modern Enterprise in Late Ch'ing China* (Cambridge, Harvard University Press), p.147.

51. *RQS*, Vol. 2, p.153.

52. M. Oksenberg, 'Management Practices in the Hong Kong Cotton Spinning and Weaving Industry' (Columbia University, Seminar on Modern East Asia, mimeographed paper, 15 November 1972), p.10. I wish to thank Professor Oksenberg for permitting me to quote from his unpublished paper.

53. F. H. H. King (1953), *Monetary System of Hong Kong* (Hong Kong, Weiss); Szczepanik, *Economic Growth*, pp.18-21.

54. Wang Chu-ying (ed) (1947), *Survey of Hong Kong Factories* (Hong Kong, Nanqiao Xinwen Qiye Gongxi).

55. Chao, *Cotton Textile Production*, p.148.

56. *RQS*, Vol. 2, p.209; pp.432-3.

57. Chao, *Cotton Textile Production*, pp.144-9.

58. *RQS*, Vol. 2, pp.51-5.

59. *RQS*, Vol. 2, pp.317-19.

60. *SCMP*, 31 August 1973.

61. *RQS*, Vol. 2, p.56.

62. As above, p.57.

63. As above, p.545.

64. *SCMP*, 17 November 1981.

65. *DGB*, 20 July 1984.

66. N. H. Neff (1978), 'Industrial Organization and Entrepreneurship in the Developing Countries: The Economic Group', *EDCC*, 26, p.663.

67. Chen Zhen and Yao Luo (eds), *Modern Industry*, p.350.

68. For an organizational chart of the Rong family enterprises, see *Modern Industry*, p.390.

69. Winsor Industrial Corporation (1978), *1977-78 Annual Report* (Hong Kong, The Corporation), p.25.

70. See Chen Zhen and Yao Luo (eds), *Modern Industry*, p.423.

71. Yang Yin-pu (1930), *On Chinese Exchanges* (Nanjing, National Central University Publication), p.37.

72. *On Chinese Exchanges*, pp.36-7.

73. *On Chinese Exchanges*, p.37; Xu ji-qing (1932), *The Recent History of Finance in Shanghai* (Shanghai, no publisher), p.296.

74. Liang, 'Cotton Manufacturers in China', p.167.

75. Both the managers of the Hongkong and Shanghai Bank and the Chartered Bank had commented on this reluctance to use the stock-market. See M. G. Carruthers, 'Financing Industry', *FEER*, 24 February 1966, p.8; P. A. Graham, 'Financing Hong Kong Business', *FEER*, 17 April 1969, p.148.

76. Yan Zhong-ping (1963), *A Draft History of the Chinese Cotton Textile Industry* (Beijing, Kexue Chuban She), pp.1-14; Elvin, 'High-Level Equilibrium Trap'.

77. Elvin, *Pattern of Chinese Past*, pp.286-7.

78. Zhongguo Shiye Bu, Guoji Maoyi Chu (1933), *Industrial Survey of Jiangsu Province* (Shanghai, Zhongguo Shiye Bu), p.5.

79. M. J. Levy, Jr. (1949), 'The Social Background of Modern Business Development in China', in Levy and Kuo-heng Shih, *The Rise of Modern Chinese Business Class* (New York, Institute of Pacific Relations), p.5.

80. For a general assessment of the compradors as industrial investors, managers, and entrepreneurs, see Yen-P'ing Hao (1970), *The Comprador in Nineteenth Century China: Bridge Between East and West* (Cambridge, Harvard University Press), pp.120-53.

81. As above; Levy, 'Contrasting Factors'; Jacobs, *Capitalism and Asia*, pp.118-21.

82. A. Gerschenkron (1966), 'The Modernization of Entrepreneurship', in M. Weiner (ed), *Modernization: The Dynamics of Growth* (New York and London, Basic Books), p.253.

83. Weber, *Religion of China*, p.53.

84. Ping-ti Ho (1962), *The Ladder of Success in Imperial China* (New York, Columbia University Press), pp.46–52.

85. Elvin, *Pattern*, pp.289–94.

86. See L. S. Yang (1970), 'Government Control of Urban Merchants in Traditional China', *The Tsing Hua Journal of Chinese Studies*, 8, pp.186–209; T. Metzger (1966), 'Ch'ing Commercial Policy', *Ch'ing-shih Wen-t'i*, 1, pp.4–10.

87. See the Biography of Zhang Qian in Chen Zhen et al. (ed), *Modern Industry*, pp.348–9.

88. R. Wilhelm (1947), *Chinese Economic Psychology* (New York, Institute of Pacific Relations), p.43. On the rise of merchant status in modern China, see Chan, *Merchants*, pp.39–46.

89. Jiang Meng-lin (1971), *Western Tide* (Hong Kong, Shijie Shuju), pp.192–3.

90. HKSCA, 'Annual Report of the General Committee for the Year ended 30th June, 1975', p.7. See also the editorials of the *SCMP*, 14 and 19 June 1975, as well as the records of the debate in the Legislative Council of the Hong Kong government, 18 June 1975.

91. Chao, *Cotton Textile Production*, p.141; and the autobiography of H. C. Ting, in Ting, *Truth and Facts*, pp.22–6; pp.34–7; p.82.

92. In a survey of the Hong Kong textile industry published in the 1960s, a similar view was expressed. 'The mechanical equipment of the Hong Kong Cotton Spinning Industry comes from many countries, seldom do we find a local cotton spinning mill equipped with units of machinery from one country alone. This cosmopolitan nature accounts for the success of the mechanical equipment of the Hong Kong cotton spinning industry as the experienced local spinners have chosen the best machinery of each country.' See *Federation of Hong Kong Cotton Weavers 1961–1962 Year Book* (Hong Kong, The Federation, 1962), p.44.

93. *Hong Kong Standard*, 21 October 1968.

94. J. G. Lutz (1971), *China and the Christian Colleges, 1850–1950* (Ithaca, Cornell University Press).

95. *DGB*, 16 November 1948.

96. Interviews with the directors of Mill 3 and Mill 32; *DGB*, 23 and 24 January 1949; and *China Mail*, 27 December 1961.

97. Nihei et al., *Technology*, p.58.

98. *DGB*, 23 January 1949; 25 January 1949; and 20 February 1952.

99. Shanghai Shi Shanghui, *Textile Industry*, section M, pp.29–36.

100. HKCSA, *Twenty Five Years*, pp.88–92; HKCSA, 'Annual Report of the General Committee for the Year Ended 30th June, 1976', pp.6–7.

101. A. Wright (ed) (1908), *Twentieth Century Impression of Hong Kong, Shanghai, and Other Treaty Ports of China* (Lloyd's Greater Britain Publishing Co. Ltd.), p.236.

102. As above, pp.236–8.

103. Yan, *Chinese Textile Industry*, p.338; Hong Kong Government, *Hong Kong Administrative Report for the Year 1914* (1915), (Hong Kong Government Printer), p.16; *Commercial and Industrial Hong Kong: A Record of 94 Years of Progress of the Colony in Commerce, Trade, Industry and Shipping (1841–1935)* (Hong Kong, The Bedikton Co., 1935), p.45.

104. F. Leeming (1975), 'The Early Industrialization of Hong Kong', *Modern Asian Studies*, 9, pp.338–9.

105. A Shanghainese specialist in management recalled that during a lecture given by Dr Teele, then Dean of Harvard Business School, in Hong Kong in 1961, 'one distinguished friend asked why was training necessary for the managerial class' while

others at the meeting 'objected to using the word "Training" and said that only animals were trained'. See Pan, 'Management and Maintenance', p.1. Richman thinks that Chinese industrial managers were weakest in their management skills. See Richman (1967), 'Capitalists and Managers in Communist China', *Harvard Business Review*, January–February, p.70.

106. Massachusetts Institute of Technology, News Office, 'Tang Residence Hall Dedicated at M. I. T.' (M. I. T. news release, 2 June 1973).

107. This separation of the business office and the production plant was quite common in Republican China, and F. Schurmann believes that it represented a 'policy-operations dichotomy'. See Schurmann (1966), *Ideology and Organization in Communist China* (Berkeley, University of California Press), p.227.

108. HKCSA, *Twenty Five Years*, p.51.

109. Hong Kong Productivity Centre (1978), *Textiles Industry Data Sheet* (Hong Kong, The Centre), p.12; and various interview data, 1978.

110. *DGB*, 23, 25 and 28 January 1949.

111. See the files on Mill 12 and Mill 13 in the Labour Relations Service Section, Labour Department, Hong Kong.

112. Xue Ming-jian (1935), 'My Experience in Handling Workers' Activities in the Shen Xin Third Mill', *Jiaoyu Yu Zhiyu*, 165, p.336; *DGB*, 24 November 1949.

113. Reports on joint consultation promotion visits to Mill 30 in May 1973; to Mill 3 in 1968; to Mill 12 in 1972. Similar reactions were recorded for Mill 13 and Mill 6. See files in Labour Relations Service Section of the Labour Department.

114. Report on a visit to Mill 5 in August 1971. See the file in Labour Department, Labour Relations Service Section.

115. Espy, 'Chinese Industrial Enterprise', p.*i*.

116. M. I. T., 'Tang Hall', p.1.

117. Wong Siu-kuan (1966), 'An Interview with a Shanghai Capitalist', *Eastern Horizon*, 5, pp.11–12.

118. *FEER*, 16 October 1946, p.2.

Notes to Chapter 4

1. Glazer and Moynihan, *Ethnicity*, p.17, original emphasis.

2. For the handful of studies that exist, see E. Ryan (1969), 'The Value System of a Chinese Community in Java', Ph.D. thesis (Harvard University), pp.13–36; King and Leung, 'The Chinese Touch', pp.33–50; S. M. Olsen, 'The Inculcation of Economic Values in Taipei Business Families', in Willmott (ed), *Economic Organization*, pp.261–96; and Bergère, 'Role of Bourgeoisie', pp.242–57.

3. By 'bourgeoisie', I follow Marx's usage to refer to 'the class of modern capitalists, owners of the means of social production and employers of wage labour'. See K. Marx and F. Engels, 'Manifesto of the Communist Party', in H. J. Laski (1948), *Communist Manifesto: Socialist Landmark* (London, George Allen and Unwin), p.119, note 1.

4. R. Bendix (1959), 'Industrialization, Ideologies, and Social Structure', *ASR*, 25, p.615.

5. Marx and Engels, *Manifesto*, p.123.

6. *Manifesto*, p.123.

7. A. Fox (1966), 'Managerial Ideology and Labour Relations', *British Journal of Industrial Relations*, 4, p.372.

8. Bendix, 'Industrialization', p.615.

9. T. Nichols (1969), *Ownership, Control and Ideology* (London, George Allen and Unwin).

10. R. Bendix (1956), *Work and Authority in Industry* (New York, Wiley); Bendix (1954), 'Industrial Authority and Its Supporting Value System', in R. Dubin (ed) (1969), *Human Relations in Administration* (Englewood Cliffs, Prentice-Hall, 2nd edn.), pp.270–6; Bendix, 'Industrialization'.

11. K. Mannheim, *Ideology and Utopia* (London, Routledge and Kegan Paul, 1936), pp.49–53.

12. This includes studies such as F. X. Sutton (1956), *The American Business Creed* (New York, Schocken); R. Heilbroner (1964), 'The View From the Top: Reflection on a Changing Business Ideology', in E. Cheit (ed), *The Business Establishment* (New York, Wiley), pp.1–36; T. Christ (1970), 'A Thematic Analysis of the American Business Creed', *Social Forces*, 49, pp.239–45; M. S. Seider (1974), 'American Big Business Ideology: A Content Analysis of Executive Speeches', *ASR*, 39, pp.802–15.

13. Nichols, *Ownership*, pp.52–7.

14. H. Smith (1966), *John Stuart Mill's Other Island: A Study of the Economic Development of Hong Kong* (London, the Institute of Economic Affairs); N. C. Owen, 'Economic Policy in Hong Kong', in Hopkins (ed), *Hong Kong*, p.141. For a more sophisticated view of the Hong Kong government as practising 'macroeconomic laissez-faire and microeconomic intervention', see B. Glassburner and J. Riedel (1972), 'Government in the Economy of Hong Kong', *Economic Record*, 48, pp.58–75.

15. Hsiao-tung Fei (1946), 'Peasantry and Gentry: An Interpretation of Chinese Social Structure and Its Changes', *AJS*, reprinted in R. Bendix and S. M. Lipset (eds), *Class, Status and Power: A Reader in Social Stratification* (Glencoe, The Free Press, 1st edn., 1953), pp.646–7.

16. Oksenberg finds the industrialists in the cotton spinning and weaving industries to be 'not civic minded men' but men motivated by 'unbridled avarice'. See Oksenberg, 'Management Practices', p.6.

17. Nichols, *Ownership*, Appendix III, pp.254–5.

18. The shortcoming of this approach is that it assumes that the three statements in a particular area are mutually exclusive and of roughly equal ideological distance to one another. It is better to ask the respondent to react to each statement and indicate his agreement or disagreement with it along a three point or five point scale. This can avoid the problem of unwarranted assumptions, and make possible the application of more sophisticated statistical techniques to extract information from the data. But for the sake of comparability, I follow Nichols' approach in the present study.

19. Nichols' sample includes 65 directors and senior managers in 15 private companies employing over 500 workers in 'Northern City'. These companies were engaged in various lines of manufacture — chemicals, heavy engineering, light engineering, pharmaceutical, flour milling and animal foodstuffs, distribution and allied business, and packaging. See Nichols, *Ownership*, Appendix I, pp.247–8.

20. *Ownership*, p.179.

21. *Ownership*, pp.189–90.

22. *Ownership*, p.198.

23. The same phenomenon is discovered by Nichols, see *Ownership*, pp.182 and 186–7.

24. The distrust of government intervention is widespread among Chinese businessmen and their children. See Sit, Wong and Kiang, *Small Scale Industry*, p.332; Olsen, 'Inculcation', p.292.

25. HKCSA, 'Annual Report of the General Committee for the Year Ended 30th June, 1973', p.5.

26. Marx and Engels, 'Manifesto', p.125.

27. Quoted in Heilbroner, 'View From the Top', p.5.

28. See Seider, 'American Business Ideology', p.807; Heilbroner, 'View', pp.30–1; R. G. Stokes (1974), 'The Afrikaner Industrial Entrepreneur and

Afrikaner Nationalism', *EDCC*, 22 (1974), pp.557–79; and S. L. Wong (1975), 'Economic Enterprise of the Chinese in Southeast Asia', B. Litt. thesis (Oxford University), pp.117–20.

29. See another spinner's account of how his company sold all of its products to South Korea 'at a good price' during the Korean War, in Espy, 'Hong Kong Textiles', p.276.

30. Bergère, 'Role of Bourgeoisie', p.246. Fei also notes a 'lack of political responsibility' among the new gentry in his article 'Peasantry and Gentry', p.648. Shih observes that early Chinese businessmen, 'being in an inferior social position. . . had a psychological weakness in regard to their own status role'. See Shih, 'Chinese Business Class', p.49.

31. For the report of a management seminar using the 'role playing' technique to explore this theme between Western and Chinese excutives in Hong Kong, see A. S. Chin (1972), 'Hong Kong Managerial Styles: Chinese and Western Approaches to Conflict Management' (Chinese University of Hong Kong, Social Research Centre, mimeographed paper).

32. J. England and J. Rear (1975), *Chinese Labour Under British Rule: A Critical Study of Labour Relations and Law in Hong Kong* (Hong Kong, Oxford University Press), pp.89–90.

33. Fox makes this distinction in his article 'Managerial Ideology', p.368 and p.371. Solomon has suggested that at the core of Chinese political culture is a fear of chaos and disorder. But I do not think it is necessary to resort to psychological reductions to understand the attitude of the spinners. See Solomon (1971), *Mao's Revolution and the Chinese Political Culture* (Berkeley, University of California Press).

34. Olsen, 'Inculcation', p.289.

35. The statements are (1) Competition among local mills is needed to encourage people to do their best. This is the ultimate guarantee of the survival and prosperity of the industry; (2) Competition among local mills is not necessary because there is enough scope for everybody to grow and develop together; (3) Local textile mills should combine to overcome external difficulties instead of competing among themselves. These three statements are not distinctly different, especially the second and third. What the last two statements highlight is the problem of the formation of oligopolistic groups versus a preference for peaceful co-existence with each firm going its own way.

36. Olsen, 'Inculcation', pp.288–9. Original quotation marks.

37. My attention was first drawn to such a contrast during a conversation with Dr Mark Elvin in 1979.

38. D. C. McCleland (1963), 'Motivational Pattern in Southeast Asia with Special Reference to the Chinese Case', *Journal of Social Issues*, 19, pp.6–17.

39. King and Leung, 'Chinese Touch', p.34. Similar findings are reported in Sit, Wong and Kiang, *Small Scale Industry*, pp.297–310; Olsen, 'Inculcation', p.291; Ryan, 'Value System', pp.20–1; J. A. Young (1971), 'Industrial Networks and Economic Behaviour in a Chinese Market Town', Ph.D. thesis (Stanford University), pp.195 and 199.

40. D. J. Munro (1969), *The Conception of Man in Early China* (Stanford, Stanford University Press), pp.1–22.

41. See T. T. Chü (1957), 'Chinese Class Structure and Its Ideology', in J. K. Fairbank (ed), *Chinese Thought and Institutions* (Chicago, Chicago University Press), pp.235–50; Ho, *Ladder*, pp.1–91.

42. Cited by a Fujianese industrialist in his autobiography as the motivation behind his enterprise. See Gui Hua-shan (1975), *The Memoir of Gui Hua-shan at Eighty* (Hong Kong, no publisher), p.35. A Cantonese entrepreneur, Chien Yü-chieh of the Nanyang Brothers Tobacco Company, also used this expression as a guideline for his decisions. See Cochran, *Big Business*, p.89.

43. Pan, 'Management', pp.4–5.

44. Chin, 'Managerial Style', p.17.

45. Espy, 'Hong Kong Textiles', p.279.

46. The name of the founder has been changed to protect the identity of the mill.

47. K. Mayer (1953), 'Business Enterprise: Traditional Symbol of Opportunity', *British Journal of Sociology*, 4, pp.160–80.

48. Li Quo-wei proposed giving shares as incentives to the senior executives in Shen Xin Fourth Mill in 1942, but this was strongly opposed by Rong De-sheng, his father-in-law. Rong maintained that rewards should be given in cash and not in shares. The scheme was finally dropped. See *RQS*, Vol. 2, pp.198–302.

Notes to Chapter 5

1. J. A. Schumpeter (1934), *The Theory of Economic Development* (Cambridge, Harvard University Press), p.66.

2. As above, p.89.

3. M. Weber (1968), *Economy and Society* (New York, Bedminster Press), p.342.

4. The existence of this 'dualistic ethic' has been commented on by Weber in *The Sociology of Religion* (London, Methuen, 1963), p.250. See also Rinder, 'Stranger', p.255.

5. W. F. Wertheim has advanced this argument to explain the ethnic hostility between the overseas Chinese and the host populations in South-east Asia. See Wertheim (1964), *East-West Parallels: Sociological Approaches to Modern Asia* (The Hague, W. Van Hoeve Ltd.), pp.39–82.

6. The distinction between 'abode' and 'residence' is discussed in G. W. Skinner (1971), 'Chinese Peasants and the Closed Community: An Open and Shut Case', *Comparative Studies in Society and History*, 13, p.275.

7. Fei Xiao-tong (1948), *Xiangtu Zhongguo (Rural China)* (Shanghai, Guancha She), pp.79–80.

8. Zhongwen Da Cidian Bianzuan Weiyuan Hui (ed), *The Encyclopedic Dictionary of the Chinese Language* (Taibei, The Institute of Advanced Chinese Studies), Vol. 25, pp.125–6.

9. Jones, 'The Ningpo *Pang*', p.96.

10. L. W. Crissman (1967), 'The Segmentary Structure of Urban Overseas Chinese Communities', *Man*, 2, p.190.

11. J. B. Jacobs (1979), 'A Preliminary Model of Particularistic Ties in Chinese Political Alliances: *Kan-ch'ing* and *kuan-hsi* in a Rural Taiwanese Township', *China Quarterly*, 78, p.244.

12. Oksenberg, 'Management Practices', p.5.

13. *DGB*, 28 January 1949.

14. *Hong Kong Industry 1951: The 9th Exhibition of Hong Kong Products* (Hong Kong, Blue Bird Publishing Co., 1951), no pagination.

15. Nihei et al., *Technology*, p.72.

16. See the file on this mill in the Labour Relations Section, Labour Department, as well as *Dongfang Ribao*, 30 March 1977.

17. On this phenomenon, see for example, *RQS*, Vol. 1, pp.133–6; and Chesneaux, *The Chinese Labour Movement*, p.128, p.223, and p.411.

18. B. E. Ward, 'A Small Factory in Hong Kong', in Willmott (ed), *Economic Organization*, p.380.

19. Gui Hua-shan, *Memoir*, p.72.

20. Company record of Mill 10 filled with the Company Registry, Hong Kong. For another illustration, see the bitter quarrel within the Chien family who owned the Nanyang Brothers' Tobacco Company over a proposed merger with the British-American Tobacco Company. One of the Chien brothers objected to the proposal

because the Western directors of the British-American Tobacco Company, 'not being members of our race, do not think like us' and thus could not be trusted. See Cochran, *Big Business*, pp.88–9.

21. Interview with the Chinese banker, 6 May 1977. See also *RQS*, Vol. 2, p.665.

22. *DGB*, 2 August 1951.

23. *DGB*, 18 July 1950; *FEER*, 21 September 1950, p.346; W. C. Gomersall (1957), 'The China Engineers Ltd. and Textile Trade', in J. M. Braga (ed), *Hong Kong Business Symposium* (Hong Kong, South China Morning Post), p.513.

24. *DGB*, 2 August 1951; 16 August 1951.

25. On the role of the Bank of China in financing the Chinese textile industry in the pre-war period, see R. C. Bush III (1978), 'Industry and Politics in Kuomintang China: The Nationalist Regime and Lower Yangtze Chinese Cotton Mill Owners 1927–1937', Ph.D. thesis (Columbia University), pp.199–200.

26. These biographical details are drawn from Pan Fu-shuo (ed) (1948), *Who's Who in Shanghai* (Beijing, Zhanwang Chuban She), p.61; *Jingji Tongzun*, 1 (1947), p.1040; and *RQS*, Vol. 2, p.627.

27. Tang You-yong (1954), 'How much has the cotton spinning industry borrowed from the banks?', *The Hong Kong Industry Monthly*, No. 1, p.23.

28. Oksenberg, 'Management Practices', p.8.

29. Cochran, *Big Business*, pp.72 and 76.

30. *RQS*, Vol. 2, p.257.

31. On the problem of entry barriers in industrial competition, see for example J. S. Bain (1956), *Barriers to New Competition: Their Character and Consequences in Manufacturing Industries* (Cambridge, Harvard University Press); G. J. Stigler (1968), *The Organization of Industry* (Richard D. Irwin); and M. Porter (1980), *Competitive Strategy: Techniques for Analyzing Industries and Competitors* (New York and London, The Free Press).

32. H. M. Mann, 'Entry Barriers in Thirteen Industries', in Yamey (ed), *Industrial Structure*, pp.67–77.

33. For more details, see Hongkong and Shanghai Banking Corporation, *The Quota System September 1977: Hong Kong Textiles and Garment Export Restrictions* (Hong Kong, The Corporation, 1977).

34. S. J. Ting, 'Does Hong Kong's Textile Industry Permit Unlimited Investment?', *Federation of Hong Kong Cotton Weavers 1961–1962 Year Book*, p.37.

35. HKCSA, 'Annual Report of the General Committee for the Year Ended 30th June 1961, Supplementary Note', p.1.

36. As above.

37. Company record of Mill 6 at Company Registry; interview with a director of Mill 22, one of the Cantonese directors now working in the Winsor Corporation.

38. S. C. Fang, 'How to Treasure Our Achievements?', *Federation of Hong Kong Cotton Weavers 1961–1962 Year Book*, p.39.

39. *Textile Asia*, July 1976, p.10.

40. Qi Yi-zheng et al. (1980), *Biographies of the Super-rich in Hong Kong* (Hong Kong, Wenyi Shuwu), p.156.

41. *SCMP*, 23 October 1980.

42. *SCMP*, 25 August 1981.

43. For a biographical profile of Mr Deacon Chiu, see *SCMP*, 22 June 1982.

44. H. Blumer (1977), 'Industrialization and Race Relations', in J. Stone (ed), *Race, Ethnicity and Social Change* (Cambridge, Duxbury Press), p.160, original emphasis.

45. See Crissman, 'Overseas Chinese Communities'; and H. J. Lethbridge, 'The Social Structure, Some Observations', in D. Lethbridge (ed) (1980), *The Business Environment of Hong Kong* (Hong Kong, Oxford University Press), pp.52–3.

46. H. J. Lethbridge (1969), 'Hong Kong Under Japanese Occupation: Changes

in Social Structure', in Jarvie and Agassi (eds), *Hong Kong: A Society in Transition* (London, Routledge and Kegan Paul), p.124.

47. This method had been widely used by the Chinese spinners at the outbreak of the Sino-Japanese War. See *RQS*, Vol. 2, pp.42–8, and p. 106. The Cantonese founder of the Nanyang Brothers' Tobacco Company had also followed this approach when he acquired Japanese citizenship purportedly for business reasons. See Cochran, *Big Business*, p.64.

48. *RQS*, Vol. 2, pp.664–8.

49. Database Publishing (ed) (1984), *Who's Who in Hong Kong* (Hong Kong, Database Publishing), p.179.

50. C. Smith (1972), 'English-educated Chinese Élites in Nineteenth Century Hong Kong', in M. Topley (ed), *Hong Kong: The Interaction of Traditions and Life in the Towns* (Hong Kong, Royal Asiatic Society Hong Kong Branch), pp.65–96.

51. See for example HKCSA, *Twenty-Five Years*; *A Glance at the Hong Kong Cotton Spinning Industry*; and *Federation of Hong Kong Cotton Weavers 1961–1962 Year Book*.

52. See HKCSA, 'Annual Report of the General Committee', 1955–79.

53. As above, 1970, p.9.

54. See *DGB*, 20 April 1982.

55. *Ming Bao*, 31 March 1985. For the biographies of Peter Tsao and Sally Leung, see Database Publishing (ed), *Who's Who in Hong Kong*, pp.370 and 231.

56. See W. C. G. Kowles's article in *Federation of Hong Kong Cotton Weavers 1961–1962 Year Book*, pp.8–9. Kowles was the chairman of the Hong Kong General Chamber of Commerce.

57. See the Chinese General Chamber of Commerce of Hong Kong (1958), *Members of the Twentieth Committee 1956–58* (Hong Kong, The Chamber).

58. Chen Da-tong (ed) (1956), *Chinese General Chamber of Commerce, An Account of All Previous Elections* (Hong Kong, no publisher).

59. Gongshang Guancha She (1958), *A Critical Note on The Chinese General Chamber of Commerce of Hong Kong* (Hong Kong, Gongshang Guancha She), p.26, and pp.31–2; and The Hong Kong Chinese Manufacturers' Union (1957), *Classified Directory of Members, 1956–57* (Hong Kong, The Union).

60. Wang Ling (1949), *A Compendium on The Chaozhou Sojourners in Hong Kong* (Hong Kong, no publisher), pp.1–4.

61. HKCSA, *Twenty-Five Years*, p.51.

62. Shanghai Fraternity Association, *Chinese Opera*.

63. Jiangsu and Zhejiang Residents' (H.K.) Association, *Collected Publications*, p.49.

64. Jiang Hou-qu (1976), 'Reports on Two Graduation Ceremonies', *Da Cheng*, 35, p.42.

65. Grantham, *Via Ports*, pp.104–5.

66. Ting, *Truth and Facts*, p.86.

67. *Hong Kong Hansard*, 1948, p.80, emphases added.

68. *Hong Kong Hansard*, 1965, p.152, emphases added.

Notes to Chapter 6

1. Smelser, *Sociology of Economic Life*, p.57.

2. M. Freedman (1957), *Chinese Family and Marriage in Singapore* (London, Her Majesty's Stationery Office), p.87.

3. As above, p.88.

4. Jacobs, 'Particularistic Ties', p.247.

5. D. E. Willmott (1960), *The Chinese of Semarang: A Changing Minority Community in Indonesia* (Ithaca, Cornell University Press), p.47.

6. M. I. Barnett (1960), 'Kinship as a Factor Affecting Cantonese Economic Adaptation in the United States', *Human Organization*, 19, p.45.

7. As above, p.46.

8. Oksenberg, 'Management Practices', p.7.

9. R. Silin (1976), *Leadership and Values: The Organization of Large-Scale Taiwanese Enterprises* (Cambridge, Harvard University Press), p.66.

10. There is a good example in the novel by Mao Tun, *Midnight* (1957), (Beijing, Foreign Language Press), pp.58-9. For a similar phenomenon in Latin America, see T. C. Cochran, 'Cultural Factors in Economic Growth', in H. G. J. Aitken (ed) (1967), *Explorations in Enterprise* (Cambridge, Harvard University Press), pp.130-1.

11. Sik-nin Chau (1970), 'Family Management in Hong Kong', *Hong Kong Manager*, 6, p.21.

12. Barnett, 'Kinship', p.46.

13. F. C. Deyo (1978), 'The Cultural Patterning of Organizational Development: A Comparative Study of Thai and Chinese Industrial Enterprise', *Human Organization*, 37, p.69.

14. M. J. Levy, Jr. (1949), *The Family Revolution in Modern China* (Cambridge, Harvard University Press), p.354.

15. Levy, 'Business Development in China', p.12.

16. Chao, *Cotton Textile Production*, p.154. See also Gu Zheng-gang (1935), 'The State of China's Cotton Spinning Industry as Reflected in the Incident Concerning Shen Xin Seventh Mill', *Zhongguo Shiye Zashi*, 1, p.583.

17. See for example, D. K. Lieu (1926), 'The Social Transformation of China', *Chinese Social and Political Science Review*, 1917, reprinted in C. F. Remer (ed), *Readings in Economics for China* (Shanghai, The Commercial Press), pp.68-9; and Levy 'Business Development', p.12.

18. J. C. Pelzel, 'Japanese Kinship: A Comparison', in Freedman (ed), *Family and Kinship in Chinese Society* (Stanford, Stanford University Press), pp.228-9.

19. Levy, *Family Revolution*, p.355.

20. Espy, 'Chinese Industrial Enterprise', Table 10.2, p.174.

21. Sit, Wong, and Kiang, *Small Scale Industry*, Table 15.3, p.353.

22. Ward, 'A Small Factory', p.364.

23. M. L. Cohen, 'Development Process in the Chinese Domestic Group', in Freedman (ed), *Family and Kinship*, p.27.

24. Lieu, 'Social Transformation', p.70.

25. Freedman, 'Introduction', in Freedman (ed), *Family and Kinship*, pp.13-14.

26. Espy, 'Chinese Industrial Enterprise', p.175.

27. Sit, Wong, and Kiang, *Small Scale Industry*, Table 15.3, p.353.

28. Willmott, *Chinese of Semarang*, p.50. Willmott goes on to note that the company's ownership and top management were still kept within the Oei family in the 1940s. Thus it appears that a non-nepotistic personnel policy can co-exist with the family mode of ownership.

29. Freedman, *Family in Singapore*, p.88.

30. Ryan, 'Chinese in Java', p.37.

31. Sit, Wong, and Kiang, *Small Scale Industry*, p.355.

32. Kang Chao (1975), 'The Growth of a Modern Cotton Textile Industry and the Competition with Handicrafts', in D. H. Perkins (ed), *China's Modern Economy in Historical Perspective* (Stanford, Stanford University Press), pp.167-202.

33. Lee Sheng Yi, 'Business Élites in Singapore', in P. S. J. Chen and H. Evers

(eds) (1978), *Studies in ASEAN Sociology: Urban Society and Social Change* (Singapore, Chopman Enterprises), p.39.

34. Espy, 'Chinese Industrial Enterprise', p.174. For high growth rate companies, four had no family members as employees while seven had. Among low growth rate companies, the corresponding figures were five and seven.

35. Espy, 'Hong Kong Textiles', p.280.

36. D. H. Perkins, 'Introduction: The Persistence of the Past', in Perkins (ed), *China's Modern Economy in Historical Perspective* (Stanford, Stanford University Press), p.14.

37. Perhaps this is why the Chinese term for reliable aides, *qinxin*, is a combination of the characters for kinship and trust.

38. Sit, Wong, and Kiang, *Small Scale Industry*, p.355.

39. Huang is a pseudonym.

40. J. Schumpeter (1951), *Imperialism and Social Classes* (New York, Augustus M. Kelly), p.148.

41. D. S. Landes (1951), 'French Business and the Businessmen: A Social Cultural Analysis', in E. M. Earle (ed), *Modern France: Problems of the Third and Fourth Republic* (Princeton, Princeton University Press), reprinted in Aitken (ed), *Explorations in Enterprise*, p.185.

42. As above, pp.186–7.

43. Willmott, *Chinese of Semarang*, p.50.

44. As above, p.52.

45. Ping-ti Ho (1954), 'The Salt Merchants of Yang-chou: A Study of Commercial Capitalism in Eighteenth-Century China', *Harvard Journal of Asiatic Studies*, 17, p.167.

46. Elvin, *Pattern*, p.295. W. A. Lewis writes in general that '[in] societies where men cannot rely on strangers to give faithul service, the family may be the most appropriate unit for large-scale enterprise', in Lewis (1955), *The Theory of Economic Growth* (London, George Allen and Unwin), p.115.

47. Yao Song-ling (1978), 'Short Biographies on Personalities of the Republican Period: Rong Zhong-jing, 1873–1938', *Chuanji Wenxue*, 33, p.142; and *RQS*, Vol. 2, p.558.

48. D. W. Stammer, 'Money and Finance in Hong Kong', Ph.D. thesis (Australian National University, 1968), pp.261–162, quoted in Brown, 'Hong Kong Economy', p.10, original emphasis.

49. Sung Lung-sheng (1981), 'Property and Family Division', in E. M. Ahern and H. Gates (eds), *The Anthropology of Taiwanese Society* (Stanford, Stanford University Press), pp.361–78.

50. S. C. Chu (1965), *Reformer in Modern China: Chang Chien, 1853–1926* (New York and London, Columbia University Press), p.29.

51. For an illustration of the distribution of these 'red' shares, see Y. H. Lin (1947), *The Golden Wing: A Sociological Study of Chinese Familism* (London, Kegan Paul, Trench, Trubner and Co.), p.99.

52. Examples include the Nanyang Brothers' Tobacco Company, the Shaw brothers in film-making, the Rong brothers in textiles, and the Kwok [Guo] brothers who founded the Wing On Group.

53. S. Shiga (1978), 'Family Property and the Law of Inheritance in Traditional China', in D. C. Buxbaum (ed), *Chinese Family Law and Social Change* (Seattle and London, University of Washington Press), pp.128–33.

54. See the ambivalence expressed by Mr S. K. Chang as reported in Espy, 'Hong Kong Textiles', p.280.

55. M. Topley says that in Hong Kong, 'the English doctrine of freedom of alienation appears to have been accepted and acted upon in the urban area. Some Chinese

now make wills to determine the distribution of their property. . .'. See Topley, 'The Role of Savings and Wealth among Hong Kong Chinese', in Jarvie and Agassi, *Hong Kong*, p.206. However, this has not yet caused the cotton spinners to abandon the strict Chinese custom of equal inheritance by sons.

56. For an illustration, see the description on inheritance in Shanghai Academy of Social Sciences, Institute of Economic Research (1958), *The Establishment, Development and Transformation of the Heng Feng Cotton Spinning Mill* (Shanghai, Shanghai Renmin Chuban She), p.35.

57. M. Wolf, 'Child Training and the Chinese Family', in Freedman (ed), *Family and Kinship*, p.53.

58. See Shanghai Academy of Social Sciences, *Heng Feng Mill*.

59. Kindleberger, *Economic Growth*, pp.120–1.

60. Espy, 'Hong Kong Textiles', p.282.

61. For a similar analysis of the 'family particularism' in Latin American economies, see S. M. Lipset (1967), 'Values, Education, and Entrepreneurship', in S. M. Lipset and A Solari (eds), *Elites in Latin America* (New York, Oxford University Press), pp.16–17.

62. Levy, *Family Revolution*, p.357, emphasis added.

63. Willmott, *Chinese of Semarang*, p.66.

64. As above, pp.65–6

65. D. R. Deglopper, 'Doing Business in Lukang', in Willmott (ed), *Economic Organization*, p.318.

66. Fei, *Rural China*, p.81. On the price of credit paid by kinsmen to kinsmen in traditional China, see Freedman, *Lineage Organization*, p.18.

67. Deglopper, 'Doing Business', p.319.

68. T'ien, *Chinese of Sarawak*, p.35.

69. As above, pp.25–6.

70. H. R. Baker, 'Extended Kinship in the Traditional City', in G. W. Skinner (ed), *City in Imperial China*, p.502. See also E. Wolf (1966), 'Kinship, Friendship, and Patron-client Relation', in M. Banton (ed), *The Social Anthropology of Complex Societies* (London, Tavistock Publications), p.6.

Notes to Chapter 7

1. J. A. Schumpeter (1934), *The Theory of Economic Development* (Cambridge, Harvard University Press), p.66.

2. F. Barth (ed) (1963), *The Role of The Entrepreneur in Social Change in Northern Norway* (Bergen, Universitetsforlaget), pp.7–8, original emphases.

3. HKCSA (1975), *A Glance at the Hong Kong Cotton Spinning Industry* (Hong Kong, HKCSA, 1975), pp.5–7.

4. D. C. McClelland (1961), *The Achieving Society* (Princeton, Van Nostrand), p.221 and p.223. I should note here that Schumpeter has maintained that the entrepreneur 'is never the risk bearer. . . The one who gives credit comes to grief if the undertaking fails. For although any property possessed by the entrepreneur may be liable, yet such possession of wealth is not essential, even though advantageous. But even if the entrepreneur finances himself out of former profits, . . . the risk falls on him as capitalist or as possessor of goods, not as entrepreneur. Risk-taking is in no case an element of the entrepreneurial function. Even though he may risk his reputation, the direct economic responsibility of failure never falls on him.' See Schumpeter, *Economic Development*, p.173. I do not find this claim convincing because he is making an artificial distinction between the roles of an individual as entrepreneur and as

capitalist which can hardly be separated when a risk of failure is involved. If it was different individuals performing these two roles, then he begs the question of why the capitalist should finance the entrepreneur when it was he alone who would bear the economic consequences.

5. P. W. S. Andrews (1964), *On Competition in Economic Theory* (London, Macmillan), p.36. See also Andrews and Brunner (1962), 'Business Profits and the Quiet Life', *Journal of Industrial Economics*, 11, pp.72–8.

6. J. R. Hicks (1954), 'The Problem of Imperfect Competition', *Oxford Economic Papers*, 1, pp.42–54.

7. J. P. Nettl (1965), 'Consensus or Élite Domination: The Case of Business', *Political Studies*, 14, p.35.

8. Gerschenkron, 'Modernization of Entrepreneurship', pp.247–9.

9. Schumpeter, *Economic Development*, pp.131–2.

10. A few scholars have made germane but laconic remarks in this vein. For example, Baumol cites Lewis' observation that 'the entrepreneur is doing something new and is therefore to some extent a monopolist... We have no good theory of entrepreneurship because we have no good theory of monopoly'. See Baumol (1968), 'Entrepreneurship in Economic Theory', *American Economic Review*, 58, p.69, note 4. Gerschenkron has commented that 'an approach which managed to ignore so thoroughly the categories of power and interest inevitably failed to explain the phenomenon of successful entrepreneurial activities in the most intriguing historical situations.' In 'The Entrepreneur — Discussion', *American Economic Review*, 58 (1968), p.96.

11. I have elaborated on this point in my essay, 'The Applicability of Asian Family Values to Other Socio-Cultural Settings', in P. Berger and M. Hsiao (eds), *In Search of An East Asian Development Model*, forthcoming.

12. M. Weber (1930), *The Protestant Ethic and The Spirit of Capitalism* (London, Unwin), p.177.

13. S. Greenhalgh (1984), 'Networks and Their Nodes: Urban Society on Taiwan', *The China Quarterly*, 99, p.529 and p.532.

14. As above, p.541. See also S. Harrell (1985), 'Why Do the Chinese Work So Hard?', *Modern China*, 11, pp.203–26; R. W. Stites (1985), 'Industrial Work as an Entrepreneurial Strategy', *Modern China*, 11, pp.227–46; and I. Numazaki (1986), 'Network of Taiwanese Big Business', *Modern China*, 12, pp.487–534.

15. M. Levy Jr. (1955), 'Contrasting Factors in the Modernization of China and Japan', in S. Kuznet, W. E. Moore, and J. J. Spengler (eds), *Economic Growth: Brazil, India, Japan* (Durham, Duke University Press), pp.496–536.

16. See J. Hirschmeier (1964), *The Origins of Entrepreneurship in Meiji Japan* (Cambridge, Harvard University Press, 1964); K. Yamamura (1974), *A Study of Samurai Income and Entrepreneurship* (Cambridge, Harvard University Press).

17. See A. D. Chandler, Jr. (1977), *The Visible Hand: The Managerial Revolution in American Business* (Cambridge, Harvard University Press); A. D. Chandler, Jr., and H. Daems (eds) (1980), *Managerial Hierarchies: Comparative Perspectives on the Rise of Modern Industrial Enterprise* (Cambridge, Harvard University Press).

18. See B. C. Rosen (1959), 'Race, Ethnicity, and The Achievement Syndrome', *ASR*, 24, pp.47–60; E. E. Hagen (1964), *On The Theory of Social Change: How Economic Growth Begins* (London, Tavistock Publication); C. Schooler, 'Serfdom's Legacy: An Ethnic Continuum', *AJS*, 81 (1975–76), pp.1265–86; M. Freedman (1959), 'The Handling of Money: A Note on The Background to the Economic Sophistication of the Overseas Chinese', *Man*, 19, pp.64–5; I. H. Light (1972), *Ethnic Enterprise in America* (Berkeley, University of California Press); P. Mayer (1962), 'Migrancy and the Study of Africans in Towns', *American Anthropologist*, 64, pp.576–92; W. E. Willmott (1966), 'The Chinese in Southeast Asia', *Australian*

Outlook, 20, pp.252–62; P. C. P. Siu, 'The Sojourner', *AJS*, 58 (1952–53), pp.35–44; and E. Bonacich (1973), 'A Theory of Middleman Minorities', *ASR*, 38, pp.583–94.

19. See H. M. Blalock, Jr. (1967), *Toward a Theory of Minority Group Relations* (New York, John Wiley); J. S. Furnivall (1956), *Colonial Policy and Practice* (New York, New York University Press); I. D. Rinder (1959), 'Strangers in The Land: Social Relations in the Status Gap', *Social Problems*, 6, pp.253–60; and M. Hechter (1974), 'The Political Economy of Ethnic Change', *AJS*, 79, pp.1151–78.

20. A typical example is the Xhosa migrants to East London in Africa. See Mayer, 'Migrancy', p.584.

21. See Siu, 'Sojourner', p.43; and Bonacich, 'Middleman Minorities', p.585.

22. Willmott, 'Chinese in Southeast Asia', p.254.

23. Bonacich, 'Middleman Minorities', pp.589–93.

24. W. G. Kuepper, G. L. Lackey, and E. N. Swinerton (1975), *Ugandan Asians in Great Britain: Forced Migration and Social Absorption* (London, Croom Helm), pp.10–11.

25. S. L. Keller (1975), *Uprooting and Social Change* (New Delhi, Ramesh C. Jain), p.86.

26. As above, pp.82–5.

27. For an illustration of how a thrifty, shrewd Chinese in the United States turned into a generous, ineffective businessman in his Chinese home town, see Siu, 'Sojourner', p.40.

28. C. Erickson (1972), *Invisible Immigrants: The Adaptation of English and Scottish Immigrants in 19th Century America* (London, Leicester University Press), p.401.

29. O. Patterson (1982), *Slavery and Social Death: A Comparative Study* (Cambridge, Harvard University Press), p.7.

30. J. C. Mitchell (1970), 'Tribe and Social Change in South Central Africa: A Situational Approach', *Journal of Asian and African Studies*, 5, p.85; H. S. Morris (1968), 'Ethnic Group', in *International Encyclopedia of The Social Sciences* (New York, Macmillan and The Free Press), p.168.

31. E. Goffman (1968), *Stigma: Notes on the Management of Spoiled Identity* (Harmondsworth, Penguin), p.57.

32. F. Barth (ed) (1969), *Ethnic Groups and Boundaries* (Bergen, Universitets Forleget), p.13.

33. R. T. La Pierre (1934), 'Attitude vs Action', *Social Forces*, 12, pp.230–7.

34. S. M. Lyman and W. A. Douglass (1973), 'Ethnicity: Strategies of Collective and Individual Impression Management', *Social Research*, 40, pp.344–65.

35. For illustrations, see E. N. Anderson, Jr. (1967), 'Prejudice and Ethnic Stereotypes in Rural Hong Kong', *Kroeber Anthropological Society Papers*, 37, p.95.

36. O. Patterson, 'Context and Choice in Ethnic Allegiance: A Theoretical Framework and Caribbean Case Study', in Glazer and Moynihan (eds), *Ethnicity*, pp.305–49. The population figures are drawn from his table on p.321.

37. F. Parkin (1974), 'Strategies of Social Closure in Class Formation', in Parkin (ed), *The Social Analysis of Class Structure* (London, Tavistock Publications), pp.1–18.

38. See the discussion on the political significance of 'tribalism' in Africa in Mitchell, 'Tribe and Social Change', pp.97–100.

39. U. Hannerz (1974), 'Ethnicity and Opportunity in Urban America', in A. Cohen (ed), *Urban Ethnicity* (London, Tavistock), p.46.

40. Bonacich, 'Middleman Minorities'.

41. For some case studies, see United Nations Educational, Scientific and Cultural Organization (1977), *Race and Class in Post-Colonial Society* (Paris, UNESCO).

42. Cohen, *Custom and Politics*.

Notes to Chapter 8

1. *DGB*, 5 February 1982.

2. *DGB*, 30 October 1981; 5 February 1982.

3. See 'Severe Shake-up to Beat Hong Kong's Spinning Slump', *SCMP*, 14 June 1981; and Alexander C. H. Woo's letter to the editor, *SCMP*, 17 November 1981.

4. See Jingji Daobao (1984), *Hong Kong Economic Yearbook 1984* (Hong Kong, Jingji Daobao), section 2, pp.14–15.

5. See the advertisement 'Congratulations to Nam Fung Textiles Limited on the Expansion of their First Mill' published in *SCMP*, 23 May 1983.

6. *DGB*, 4 December 1980.

7. *DGB*, 16 June 1981.

8. In the meeting between Mr H. C. Tang and the deputy director of the People's Congress as well as the head of the United Fronts' Department of the Chinese Communist Party in Shanghai, it was reported that the parents of Mr Tang who were apparently living in Shanghai had also been invited to attend. See *DGB*, 4 August 1981.

9. Quoted in Richard Liu, 'China move may strangle local mills', *SCMP*, 26 November 1981.

10. Quoted in Mary Lee, 'Hong Kong hopes to avoid a "Shanghai"', *FEER*, 20 January 1983, p.37.

11. As above.

12. For the biography of Xu Jia-tun, see Database Publishing (ed) (1984), *Who's Who in Hong Kong* (Hong Kong, Database Publishing), p.413.

13. See *Guangjiao Jing* (Wide Angle), 16 June 1983, p.7.

14. *Guangjiao Jing*, 16 June 1983, p.7.

15. *DGB*, 31 October 1983.

16. *FEER*, 20 January 1983, p.37.

17. For a discussion of this issue in relation to the Sino-British negotiations, see the interview with Mr Kayser Sung, editor of *Textile Asia*, in *Jiushi Niandai* (The Nineties), May 1984, pp.53–5.

18. Quoted in *FEER*, 20 January 1983, p.37.

Bibliography

Ahlers, J. (1946), 'Postwar Banking in Shanghai', *Pacific Affairs*, 19, pp.384–93.

Allen, S., and Smith, C. (1974), 'Race and Ethnicity in Class Formation: A Comparison of Asian and West Indian Workers', in F. Parkin (ed), *The Social Analysis of Class Structure* (London, Tavistock Publications), pp.39–54.

Anderson, E. N. Jr. (1967), 'Prejudice and Ethnic Stereotypes in Rural Hong Kong', *Kroeber Anthropological Society Papers*, 37, pp.90–107.

Andrews, P. W. S. (1964), *On Competition in Economic Theory* (London, Macmillan).

Andrews, P. W. S., and Brunner, E. (1962), 'Business Profits and The Quiet Life', *Journal of Industrial Economics*, 11, pp.72–8.

Bain, J. S. (1958), *Barriers to New Competition: Their Character and Consequences in Manufacturing Industries* (Cambridge, Harvard University Press).

Baker, H. R. (1977), 'Extended Kinship in the Traditional City', in G. W. Skinner (ed), *The City in Late Imperial China* (Stanford, Stanford University Press), pp.499–518.

Balazs, E. (1964), *Chinese Civilization and Bureaucracy* (New Haven, Yale University Press).

Barnett, A. D. (1963), *China On The Eve of The Communist Takeover* (New York, Frederick A. Praeger).

Barnett, K. M. A. (n.d.), *Hong Kong Report on the 1961 Census* (Hong Kong, Government Printer).

Barnett, M. L. (1960), 'Kinship as a Factor Affecting Cantonese Economic Adaptation in the United States', *Human Organization*, 19, pp.40–6.

Barnett, R. W. (1941), *Economic Shanghai: Hostage To Politics 1937–1941* (New York, Institute of Pacific Relations).

Barou, N. (1945), *The Jews in Work and Trade* (London, Trade Advisory Council).

Barth, F. (ed) (1963), *The Role of The Entrepreneur in Social Change in Northern Norway* (Bergen, Universitets Forleget).

Barth, F. (ed) (1969), *Ethnic Groups and Boundaries* (Bergen, Universitets Forleget).

Bartke, W. (1987), *Who's Who in the People's Republic of China* (München, K. G. Saur, 2nd edn.).

Baumol, W. J. (1968), 'Entrepreneurship in Economic Theory', *American Economic Review*, 58, pp.64–71.

Bell, D. (1962), *The End of Ideology* (New York, The Free Press, revised edn.).

Bellah, R. N. (1963), 'Reflections on the Protestant Ethic Analogy in Asia', *The Journal of Social Issues*, 19, pp.52–60.

Belshaw, C. S. (1955), 'The Cultural Milieu of the Entrepreneur: A Critical Essay', *Explorations in Entrepreneurial History*, 7, pp.146–63.

Bendix, R. (1956), *Work and Authority in Industry* (New York, Wiley).

Bendix, R. (1957), 'A Study of Managerial Ideologies', *EDCC*, 5, pp.118–28.

Bendix, R. (1959), 'Industrialization, Ideologies and Social Structure', *ASR*, 25, pp.613–23.

Bendix, R. (1961), 'Industrial Authority and its Supporting Value Systems', in R. Dubin (ed), *Human Relations in Administration* (Englewood Cliffs, Prentice-Hall, 2nd edn.), pp.270–6.

Benham, F. C. (1956), 'The Growth of Manufacturing in Hong Kong', *International Affairs*, 32, pp.456–63.

Bergère, M. (1968), 'The Role of the Bourgeoisie', in M. C. Wright (ed), *China in Revolution: The First Phase, 1900–1913* (New Haven, Yale University Press), pp.229–95.

Black, R. B. (1965), *Immigration and Social Planning in Hong Kong* (London, China Society).

Blalock, H. M. Jr. (1967), *Toward A Theory of Minority-Group Relations* (New York, John Wiley and Sons).

Blumer, H. (1965), 'Industrialization and Race Relations', in G. Hunter (ed), *Industrialization and Race Relations* (London, Oxford University Press); reprinted in J. Stone (ed) (1977), *Race, Ethnicity and Social Change* (Cambridge, Duxbury Press).

Bodde, D. (1950), *Peking Diary: A Year in Revolution* (New York, Henry Schuman).

Bonacich, E. (1973), 'A Theory of Middleman Minorities', *ASR*, 38, pp.583–94.

Boorman, H. L., and Howard, R. C. (eds.) (1968–70), *Biographical Dictionary of Republican China* (New York and London, Columbia University Press).

Braga, J. M. (ed) (1957), *Hong Kong Business Symposium* (Hong Kong, South China Morning Post).

Brimmer, A. F. (1955), 'The Setting of Entrepreneurship of India', *Quarterly Journal of Economics*, 29, pp.553–76.

Broady, M. (1958), 'The Chinese in Great Britain', in M. H. Fried (ed), *Colloquium on Overseas Chinese* (New York, Institute of Pacific Relations).

Brown, E. H. P. (1971), 'The Hong Kong Economy: Achievements and Prospects', in K. Hopkins (ed), *Hong Kong: The Industrial Colony*, pp.1–20.

Bush, R. C., III (1978), 'Industry and Politics in Kuomintang China: The

Nationalist Regime and Lower Yangtze Chinese Cotton Mill Owners, 1927-1937', Ph.D. thesis (Columbia University).

Carroll, J. J. (1965), *The Filipino Manufacturing Entrepreneur* (Ithaca, Cornell University Press).

Carruthers, M. G. (1966), 'Financing Industry', *FEER*, 24 February, pp.367-70.

Chaffee, F. H., Anrell, G. E., Barth, H. A., Cort, A. S., Dombrowski, J. H., Fasano, V. S., and Weaver, J. O. (1969), *Area Handbook of the Republic of China* (Washington, The American University Foreign Area Studies).

Chan, W. K. K. (1977), *Merchants, Mandarins, and Modern Enterprise in Late Ch'ing China* (Cambridge, Harvard University Press).

Chang, J. K. (1969), *Industrial Development in Pre-Communist China* (Edinburgh, Edinburgh University Press).

Chang, K. N. (1958), *The Inflationary Spiral: The Experience of China, 1939-1950* (Cambridge, M. I. T. Press).

Chang, P. (1957), 'The Distribution and Relative Strength of the Provincial Merchant Groups in China, 1842-1911', Ph.D. thesis (University of Washington).

Chao, K. (1977), *The Development of Cotton Textile Production in China* (Cambridge, Harvard University Press).

Chao, Y. R. (1976), *Aspects of Chinese Sociolinguistics* (Stanford, Stanford University Press).

Chau, S. N. (1970), 'Family Management in Hong Kong', *Hong Kong Manager*, 6, pp.18-21.

Chen, D. T., 陳大同 (1956), 中總歷屆改選回憶錄 (*Chinese General Chamber of Commerce: An Account of All Previous Elections*) (Hong Kong, no publisher).

Chen, Y. C. (1978), 'A Hong Kong View', *The Textile Institute and Industry*, 6, pp.200-3; pp.237-9.

Chen, Z., and Yao Luo (eds.), 陳眞、姚洛（編）(1957), 中國近代工業史資料 (*Source Materials on the Modern Industry of China*) (Beijing, Sanlian Shudian).

Chesneaux, J. (1968), *The Chinese Labor Movement, 1919-1927* (Stanford, Stanford University Press).

Chin, A. S. (1972), 'Hong Kong Managerial Styles: Chinese and Western Approaches to Conflict Management' (Chinese University of Hong Kong, Social Research Centre, mimeo. paper).

Chinese Academy of Science, Shanghai Institute of Economic Research, Shanghai Academy of Social Science, Institute of Economic Research, 中國科學院上海經濟研究所，上海社會科學院經濟研究所 (1958), 恆豐紗廠的發生，發展與改造 (*The Establishment, Development and Transformation of the Heng Feng Cotton Spinning Mill*) (Shanghai, Renmin Chuban She).

Chinese General Chamber of Commerce of Hong Kong (1958), *Members of the Twentieth Committee 1956–58* (Hong Kong, The Chamber).

Chow, S. H. (1963), *The Chinese Inflation, 1937–1949* (New York, Columbia University Press).

Christ, T. (1970), 'A Thematic Analysis of the American Business Creed', *Social Forces*, 49, pp.239–45.

Chu, S. C. (1965), *Reformer in Modern China: Chang Chien, 1853–1926* (New York and London, Columbia University Press).

Chü, T. T. (1957), 'Chinese Class Structure and Its Ideology', in J. K. Fairbank (ed), *Chinese Thought and Institutions* (Chicago, Chicago University Press), pp.235–50.

Chung, A. (1953), 'The Development of Modern Manufacturing Industry in China, 1928–1949', Ph.D. thesis (University of Pennsylvania).

Chung, L. C., 'Hong Kong', *Asian Textile Survey 1969–70*, pp.77–100.

Coble, P. M. (1980), *The Shanghai Capitalists and the Nationalist Government, 1927–1937* (Cambridge, Harvard University Press).

Cochran, S. (1980), *Big Business in China: Sino-Foreign Rivalry in the Cigarette Industry, 1890–1930* (Cambridge, Harvard University Press).

Cochran, T. C. (1960), 'Cultural Factors in Economic Growth', *Journal of Economic History*, 20, pp.515–30.

Cohen, A. (1969), *Custom and Politics in Urban Africa: A Study of Hausa Migrants in Yoruba Towns* (London, Routledge and Kegan Paul).

Cohen, A. (ed) (1974), *Urban Ethnicity* (London, Tavistock Publications).

Cohen, M. L. (1970), 'Developmental Process in the Chinese Domestic Group', in M. Freedman (ed), *Family and Kinship in Chinese Society* (Stanford, Stanford University Press), pp.21–36.

Cohen, M. L. (1976), *House United, House Divided: The Chinese Family in Taiwan* (New York, Columbia University Press).

Cole, A. H. (1968), 'The Entrepreneur: Introductory Remarks', *American Economic Review*, 58, pp.60–3.

Commerce and Industry Department, Hong Kong (1973), 'Memorandum for The Trade and Industry Advisory Board: Land for Industry' (Hong Kong, The Department, mimeo. paper).

Commercial and Industrial Hong Kong (1935) (Hong Kong, The Bedikton Co.).

Commissioner of Labour, Hong Kong (various years), *Labour Department Report*.

Cong, H. X. 叢翰香 (1962), ‘關於中國民族資本的原始積累問題’ ('On the Primitive Accumulation of National Capital in China'), *Lishi Yanjiu*, 2, pp.26–45.

Crissman, L. N. (1967), 'The Segmentary Structure of Urban Overseas Chinese Communities', *Man*, 2, pp.185–204.

Deglopper, D. R. (1972), 'Doing Business in Lukang', in W. Willmott (ed), *Economic Organization in Chinese Society* (Stanford, Stanford University Press), pp.297–326.

Deyo, F. C. (1976), 'Decision-making and Supervisory Authority in Cross-Cultural Perspectives: An Exploratory Study of Chinese and Western Management Practices in Singapore' (University of Singapore, Sociology Working Paper No. 55).

Deyo, F. C. (1978), 'The Cultural Patterning of Organizational Development: A Comparative Case Study of Thai and Chinese Industrial Enterprise', *Human Organization*, 37, pp.68–73.

Dial, O. E. (1965), 'An Evaluation of the Impact of China's Refugees in Hong Kong on the Structure of the Colony's Government in the Period Following World War II', Ph.D. thesis (University of California, Claremont).

Ding, X. 鼎銘 (1959), '第一次世界大戰期間民族資本主義的發展' ('The Growth of Indigenous Capitalism in China During the First World War'), *Lishi Jiaoxue*, August, pp.376–82.

Doornbos, M. R. (1972), 'Some Conceptual Problems Concerning Ethnicity in Integration Analysis', *Civilizations*, 22, pp.263–83.

Eberhard, W. (1962), 'Social Mobility among Businessmen in a Taiwanese Town', *Journal of Asian Studies*, 21, pp.327–39.

Elvin, M. (1967), 'The Gentry Democracy in Shanghai, 1905–1914', Ph.D. thesis (University of Cambridge).

Elvin, M. (1972), 'The High-Level Equilibrium Trap: The Causes of the Decline of Invention in the Traditional Chinese Textile Industries', in W. Willmott (ed), *Economic Organization*, pp.137–72.

Elvin, M. (1973), *The Pattern of the Chinese Past* (London, Eyre Methuen).

England, J., and Rear, J. (1975), *Chinese Labour Under British Rule: A Critical Study of Labour Relations and Law in Hong Kong* (Hong Kong, Oxford University Press).

Epstein, A. L. (1978), *Ethos and Identity* (London, Tavistock Publications).

Erickson, C. (1972), *Invisible Immigrants: The Adaptation of English and Scottish Immigrants in 19th Century America* (London, Leicester University Press).

Espy, J. L. (1970), 'The Strategy of Chinese Industrial Enterprise in Hong Kong', D. B. A. thesis (Harvard University).

Espy, J. L. (1971), 'Hong Kong as an Environment for Industry', *Chung Chi Journal*, 10, pp.27–38.

Espy, J. L. (1974), 'Hong Kong Textiles Ltd.', in L. C. Nehrt, G. S. Evans, and L. Li (eds.), *Managerial Policy, Strategy and Planning for Southeast Asia* (Hong Kong, Chinese University of Hong Kong Press), pp.273–82.

Fan, B. C. 樊百川 (1955), '試論中國資產階級的各個組成部份' ('A Tentative Discussion on the Composition of the Chinese Bourgeoisie'), 中國科學院歷史研究所第三所集刊, 2, pp.99–138.

Fang, H. D. 方顯庭 (1949), '民營應自中紡開始' ('Private Enterprise Should Start with the China Textile Industries Inc.'), in Shanghai Shi Shanghui (ed), *Textile Industry*, Section A, p.74.

Fang, S. C., 'How to Treasure our Achievements?', *The Federation of Hong Kong Cotton Weavers 1961–62 Year Book*, pp.38–40.

Far Eastern Economic Review.

Far Eastern Economic Review (1978), *Asia 1978 Yearbook* (Hong Kong, The Review).

Federation of Hong Kong Cotton Weavers 1961–1962 Year Book.

Fei, H. T. (1946), 'Peasantry and Gentry: An Interpretation of Chinese Social Structure and Its Changes', *AJS*, pp.1–17; reprinted in R. Bendix, and S. M. Lipset (eds.) (1953), *Class, Status and Power: A Reader in Social Stratification* (Glencoe, The Free Press, 1st edn.), pp.631–50.

Fei, X. T. 費孝通 (1948), 鄉土中國 (*Rural China*) (Shanghai, Guancha She).

Ferguson, J. C. (1906), 'Notes on Chinese Banking System in Shanghai', *Journal of Royal Asiatic Society North China Branch*, 27, pp.55–82.

Ferguson, J. C. (1926), 'Native Banking in Shanghai', *The Chinese Economic Monthly*, 3, pp.168–83.

Feuerwerker, A. (1958), *China's Early Industrialization: Sheng Hsuan-huai (1844–1916) and Mandarin Enterprise* (Cambridge, Harvard University Press).

Feuerwerker, A. (1968), *The Chinese Economy, 1912–1949* (Ann Arbor, University of Michigan, Center of Chinese Studies).

Fong, H. D. (1968), 'Taiwan's Industrialization, with Special Reference to Policies and Controls', *Journal of Nanyang University*, 2, pp.365–426.

Fox, A. (1966), 'Managerial Ideology and Labour Relations', *British Journal of Industrial Relations*, 4, pp.366–78.

Freedman, M. (1957), *Chinese Family and Marriage in Singapore* (London, Her Majesty's Stationery Office).

Freedman, M. (1958), *Lineage Organization in Southeastern China* (London, The Athlone Press).

Freedman, M. (1959), 'The Handling of Money: A Note on the Background to the Economic Sophistication of the Overseas Chinese', *Man*, 19, pp.64–5.

Freedman, M. (1970), 'Introduction', in M. Freedman (ed), *Family and Kinship in Chinese Society* (Stanford, Stanford University Press), pp.1–20.

Galle, O. R., and Taeuber, K. E. (1966), 'Metropolitan Migration and Intervening Opportunities', *ASR*, 32, pp.5–13.

Geertz, C. (1963), *Peddlers and Princes: Social Development and Economic Change in Two Indonesian Towns* (Chicago and London, University of Chicago Press).

Gerschenkron, A. (1966), 'The Modernization of Entrepreneurship', in M. Weiner (ed), *Modernization: The Dynamics of Growth* (New York, Basic Books), pp.246–57.

Gerschenkron, A. (1970), *Europe in the Russian Mirror* (Cambridge, Cambridge University Press).

Glade, W. P. (1967), 'Approaches to a Theory of Entrepreneurial Formation', *Explorations in Entrepreneurial History*, 4, pp.245–59.

Glassburner, B., and Riedel, J. (1972), 'Government in the Economy of Hong Kong', *Economic Record*, 48, pp.58–75.

Glazer, N., and Moynihan, D. P. (eds.) (1975), *Ethnicity* (Cambridge, Harvard University Press).

Goffman, E. (1968), *Stigma: Notes on the Management of Spoiled Identity* (Harmondsworth, Penguin).

Golay, F. H., Anspach, R., Pfanner, M. R., and Ayal, E. B. (1969) (eds), *Underdevelopment and Economic Nationalism in Southeast Asia* (Ithaca, Cornell University Press).

Gomersall, W. C. (1957), 'The China Engineers Ltd. and the Textile Trade', in J. M. Braga (ed), *Hong Kong Business Symposium* (Hong Kong, South China Morning Post).

Gongshang Guancha She 工商觀察社 (1958), 責香港中華總商會 (*A Critical Note on The Chinese General Chamber of Commerce*) (Hong Kong, Gongshang Guancha She).

Graham, P. A. (1969), 'Financing Hong Kong Business', *FEER*, 17 April, pp.144–54.

Grantham, A. (1965), *Via Ports: From Hong Kong to Hong Kong* (Hong Kong, Hong Kong University Press).

Greenhalgh, S. (1984), 'Networks and Their Nodes: Urban Society on Taiwan', *The China Quarterly*, 99, pp.529–52.

Gui, H. S. 桂華山 (1975), 桂華山八十回憶 (*The Memoir of Gui Hua Shan*), (Hong Kong, the author).

Gumperz, J. J. (1968), 'The Speech Community', in *International Encyclopedia of the Social Sciences* (New York, Macmillan and Free Press), pp.381–6.

Habakkuk, H. J. (1955), 'Family Structure and Economic Change in Nineteenth-Century Europe', *Journal of Economic History*, 15, pp.1–12.

Hagen, E. E. (1960–1), 'The Entrepreneur as Rebel Against Traditional Society', *Human Organization*, 19, pp.185–7.

Hagen, E. E. (1964), *On the Theory of Social Change* (London, Tavistock Publications).

Hambro, E. (1955), *The Problem of Chinese Refugees in Hong Kong* (Leyden).

Hamilton, G. G. (1975), 'Cathay and the Way Beyond: Modernization, Regionalism and Commerce in Imperial China', Ph.D. thesis (University of Washington).

Hang Seng Bank 恒生銀行 (1964), 香港棉織品出口限制問題 (*The Problem of Restriction on Hong Kong's Textile Products*) (Hong Kong, The Bank).

Hannerz, U. (1974), 'Ethnicity and Opportunity in Urban America', in A. Cohen (ed), *Urban Ethnicity* (London, Tavistock Publications), pp.37–76.

Harrell, S. (1985), 'Why Do the Chinese Work So Hard?', *Modern China*, 11, pp.203–26.

Hazlehurst, L. W. (1965), 'Entrepreneurship and the Merchant Castes in a Punjabi City', Ph.D. thesis (University of California, Berkeley).

Hechter, M. (1973), 'The Persistence of Regionalism in the British Isles, 1955–1966', *AJS*, 79 (1973), pp.319–42.

Hechter, M. (1974), 'The Political Economy of Ethnic Change', *AJS*, 79, pp.1151–78.

Heidhues, M. F. S. (1974), *Southeast Asia's Chinese Minorities* (London, Longman).

Heilbroner, R. L. (1964), 'The View From the Top: Reflections on a Changing Business Ideology', in E. F. Cheit (ed), *The Business Establishment* (New York, John Wiley and Sons), pp.1–36.

Herman, H. V. (1979), 'Dishwashers and Proprietors: Macedonians in Toronto's Restaurant Trade', in S. Wallman (ed), *Ethnicity at Work* (London, Macmillan), pp.71–90.

Hicks, J. R. (1954), 'The Problem of Imperfect Competition', *Oxford Economic Papers*, 1, pp.41–54.

Hirschmeier, J. (1964), *The Origins of Entrepreneurship in Meiji Japan* (Cambridge, Harvard University Press).

Ho, P. T. (1954), 'The Salt Merchants of Yang-chou: A Study of Commercial Capitalism in Eighteenth-Century China', *Harvard Journal of Asiatic Studies*, 17, pp.130–68.

Ho, P. T. (1962), *The Ladder of Success in Imperial China: Aspects of Social Mobility, 1368–1911* (New York and London, Columbia University Press).

Ho, S. P. S. (1978), *Economic Development of Taiwan, 1860–1970* (New Haven and London, Yale University Press).

Hong Kong Administrative Report, various years.

Hongkong and Shanghai Banking Corporation (1977), *The Quota System September 1977: Hong Kong Textiles and Garment Export Restrictions* (Hong Kong, The Corporation).

Hong Kong Chinese Manufacturers' Union (1957), *Classified Directory of Members, 1956–57* (Hong Kong, The Union).

Hong Kong Cotton Spinners' Association (1955–79), 'Annual Report of the General Committee'.

Hong Kong Cotton Spinners' Association (1973), *Twenty Five Years of the Hong Kong Cotton Spinning Industry* (Hong Kong, The Association).

Hong Kong Cotton Spinners' Association (1975), *A Glance at the Hong Kong Spinning Industry* (Hong Kong, The Association).

Hong Kong External Trade: Report and Tables, various years.

Hong Kong Government Gazette, 1873–7.

Hong Kong Government Sessional Papers, 1891–1941.

Hong Kong Hansard, 1948–79.

Hong Kong Ningbo Residents' Association (1977), 寧波旅港同鄉會成立十周年紀念 (*Commemorative Volume on The Tenth Anniversary of the Ningbo Residents' Association*) (Hong Kong, The Association).

Hong Kong Productivity Centre (1978), *Industry Data Sheet, Textile Industry: Textile Spinning* (Hong Kong, The Centre).

Honig, E. (1986), *Sisters and Strangers: Women in the Shanghai Cotton Mills, 1919–1949* (Stanford, Stanford University Press).

Hopkins, K. (ed) (1971), *Hong Kong: The Industrial Colony* (Hong Kong, Oxford University Press).

Howe, C. (ed) (1981), *Shanghai: Revolution and Development in an Asian Metropolis* (Cambridge, Cambridge University Press).

Hsu, F. L. K. (1971), *Under the Ancestor's Shadow* (Stanford, Stanford University Press, 2nd edn.).

Huaqiao Ribao. 華僑日報 .

Jacobs, J. B. (1979), 'A Preliminary Model of Particularistic Ties in Chinese Political Alliances: *Kan-ch'ing* and *Kuan-hsi* in a Rural Taiwanese Township', *China Quarterly*, 78, pp.237–73.

Jacobs, N. (1958), *The Origin of Modern Capitalism in Eastern Asia* (Hong Kong, Hong Kong University Press).

Jao, Y. C. (1970), 'Financing Hong Kong's Textile Growth', *Textile Asia*, December, pp.23–5.

Jao, Y. C. (1974), *Banking and Currency in Hong Kong: A Study of Postwar Financial Development* (London, Macmillan).

Jiang, H. Q. 江厚垲 (1976), ' 先後媲美的兩個畢業典禮 ' ('A Report on Two Graduation Ceremonies'), *Da Cheng*, 35, pp.40–3.

Jiang, M. L. 蔣夢麟 (1971), 西潮 (*The Western Tide*) (Hong Kong, Shijie Shuju, reprinted edn.).

Jiangsu and Zhejiang Residents' (Hong Kong) Association, 蘇浙旅港同鄉會特刊 (*Special Publication of the Jiangsu and Zhejiang Residents' Association*) (Hong Kong, The Association, no date).

Jiangsu and Zhejiang Residents' (Hong Kong) Association, 蘇浙旅港同鄉會 (1961) 蘇浙公學蘇浙小學彙刊 (*Collected Publications of The Jiangsu and Zhejiang Residents' Association, the Jiangsu and Zhejiang Secondary School, and The Jiangsu and Zhejiang Primary School*) (Hong Kong, The Association).

Jingji Daobao (ed) (1984), 香港經濟年鑑 (*Hong Kong Economic Year Book 1984*) (Hong Kong, Jingji Daobao).

Jingji Daobao. 經濟導報 .

Jingji Tongxun. 經濟通訊 .

Johnson, G. E. (1970), 'Natives, Migrants and Voluntary Associations in a Colonial Chinese Setting', Ph.D. thesis (Cornell University).

Jones, S. M. (1972), 'Finance in Ningpo: The *Ch'ien-chuang* 1750–1880', in W. Willmott (ed), *Economic Organization*, pp.47–77.

Jones, S. M. (1974), 'The Ningpo *Pang* at Shanghai: The Changing Organization of Financial Power', in G. W. Skinner and M. Elvin (eds.), *The Chinese City Between Two Worlds* (Stanford, Stanford University Press), pp.73–96.

Kasden, L. (1965), 'Family Structure, Migration, and Entrepreneur', *Comparative Studies in Society and History*, 7, pp.345–57.

Keller, S. L. (1975), *Uprooting and Social Change* (New Delhi, Ramesh C. Jain).

Kiangsu and Chekiang Residents' (Hong Kong) Association (1979), *Directory of Presidents, Advisors and Directors, No. 20, 1977–1979* (Hong Kong, The Association).

Kilby, P. (ed) (1971), *Entrepreneur and Economic Development* (New York, The Free Press).

King, A. Y. C., and Leung, D. H. K. (1975), 'The Chinese Touch in Small Industrial Organization' (Chinese University of Hong Kong, Social Research Centre, mimeo. paper).

King, F. H. H. (1953), *The Monetary System of Hong Kong* (Hong Kong, Weiss).

Kroef, J. V. D. (1953–54), 'Entrepreneur and Middle Class in Indonesia', *EDCC*, 2, pp.297–325.

Kuepper, W. G., Lackey, G. L., and Swinerton, E. N. (1975), *Ugandan Asians in Great Britain: Forced Migration and Social Absorption* (London, Croom Helm).

La Pierre, R. T. (1934), 'Attitudes vs. Actions', *Social Forces*, 12, pp.230–7.

Lai, D. C. Y. (1963), 'Some Geographical Aspects of the Industrial Development of Hong Kong Since 1841', MA thesis (University of Hong Kong).

Lamb, H. B. (1955), 'The Indian Business Communities and the Evolution of an Industrial Class', *Pacific Affairs*, 23, pp.101–16.

Landes, D. S. (1951), 'French Business and the Businessman: A Social and Cultural Analysis', in E. M. Earle (ed), *Modern France: Problems of the Third and Fourth Republic* (Princeton, Princeton University Press); reprinted in H. G. J. Aitken (ed), *Explorations in Enterprise* (Cambridge, Harvard University Press), pp.184–209.

Lee, R. H. (1960), *The Chinese in The United States of America* (Hong Kong, Hong Kong University Press).

Lee, S. Y. (1978), 'Business Élites in Singapore', in P. S. J. Chen and H. Evers (eds), *Studies in ASEAN Sociology: Urban Society and Social Change* (Singapore, Chopman Enterprises), pp.38–60.

Leeming, F. (1975), 'The Early Industrialization of Hong Kong', *Modern Asian Studies*, 9, pp.337–42.

Leff, N. H. (1978), 'Industrial Organization and Entrepreneurship in the

Developing Countries: The Economic Group', *EDCC*, 26, pp.66–75.

Leibenstein, H. (1968), 'Entrepreneurship and Development', *American Economic Review*, 58, pp.72–83.

Lethbridge, H. J. (1969), 'Hong Kong Under Japanese Occupation: Changes in Social Structure', in I. C. Jarvie and J. Agassi (eds), *Hong Kong, A Society in Transition* (London, Routledge and Kegan Paul), pp.77–127.

Lethbridge, H. J. (1980), 'The Social Structure, Some Observations', in D. Lethbridge (ed), *The Business Environment in Hong Kong* (Hong Kong, Oxford University Press).

Levy, M. J., Jr. (1949), *The Family Revolution in Modern China* (Cambridge, Harvard University Press).

Levy, M. J., Jr. (1955), 'Contrasting Factors in the Modernization of China and Japan' in S. Kuznet, W. E. Moore, and J. J. Spengler (eds), *Economic Growth: Brazil, India, Japan* (Durham, Duke University Press), pp.496–536.

Levy, M. J., Jr., and Shih, K. H. (1949), *The Rise of the Modern Chinese Business Class* (New York, Institute of Pacific Relations).

Lewis, W. A. (1955), *The Theory of Economic Growth* (London, George Allen and Unwin).

Lyman, S. M., and Douglass, W. A. (1973), 'Ethnicity: Strategies of Collective and Individual Impression Management', *Social Research*, 40, pp.344–65.

Liang, L. S. (1955), 'Problems of the Cotton Manufacturers in China', Ph.D. thesis (University of Pennsylvania).

Lianho Chengxin So (ed), 聯合徵信所（編）(1947), 上海製造廠商概覽 (*Directory of Manufacturers in Shanghai*) (Shanghai, Lianho Chengxin So).

Lieu, D. K. (1917), 'The Social Transformation of China', *The Chinese Social and Political Science Review*, reprinted in C. F. Remer (ed), *Readings in Economics for China* (Shanghai, The Commercial Press, 1926), pp.66–80.

Lieu, D. K. (1936), *The Growth and Industrialization of Shanghai* (Shanghai, China Institute of Pacific Relations).

Light, I. H. (1972), *Ethnic Enterprise in America* (Berkeley, University of California Press).

Lin, B. 林彬 , ‘解剖中國紡織建設公司’ ('Dissecting The China Textile Industries Inc.'), *Jingji Daobao*, 55 (1948), pp.22–3; 56 (1948), pp.21–3; 57 and 58 (1948), pp.28–31; 59 (1948), pp.20–3.

Lin, Y. H. (1947), *The Golden Wing: A Sociological Study of Chinese Familism* (London, Kegan Paul, Trench, Trubner and Co.).

Lipset, S. M. (1967), 'Value, Education and Entrepreneurship', in S. M. Lipset and A. Solari (eds), *Élites in Latin America* (New York), pp.3–60.

Logan, J. R. (1978), 'Growth, Politics, and the Stratification of Places', *AJS*, 84, pp.404–16.

Loh, R. (1962), *Escape From Red China, as told to Humphrey Evans* (New York, Coward McCaan).

Lutz, J. G. (1971), *China and the Christian College, 1850–1950* (Ithaca, Cornell University Press).

Luzzato, R. (ed) (1958–60), *Hong Kong Who's Who: An Almanac of Personalities and Their History* (Hong Kong, Rola Luzzato).

McClelland, D. C. (1961), *The Achieving Society* (Princeton, Van Nostrand).

McClelland, D. C. (1963), 'Motivational Patterns in Southeast Asia with Special Reference to the Chinese Case', *The Journal of Social Issues*, 19, pp.6–19.

MacDonald, J. S., and MacDonald, L. D. (1964), 'Chain Migration, Ethnic Neighbourhood Formation and Social Network', *Milbank Memorial Fund Quarterly*, 42, pp.82–97.

Makler, H. M. (1976), 'The Portuguese Industrial Elite and Its Corporative Relations: A Study of Compartmentalization in an Authoritarian Regime', *EDCC*, 24, pp.495–526.

Mann, H. M. (1973), 'Entry Barriers in Thirteen Industries', in B. S. Yamey (ed), *Economics of Industrial Structure* (Harmondsworth, Penguin Education), pp.67–77.

Mannheim, K. (1936), *Ideology and Utopia* (London, Routledge and Kegan Paul).

Mao, T. (1957), *Midnight* (Peking, Foreign Language Press).

Marris, P., and Somerset, A. (1971), *African Businessmen: A Study of Entrepreneurship and Development in Kenya* (London, Routledge and Kegan Paul).

Massachusetts Institute of Technology, News Office (1973), 'Tang Residence Hall Dedicated at M. I. T.' (M. I. T. News Release, 2 June).

Marx, K., and Engels, F. (1948), 'Manifesto of The Communist Party', in H. J. Laski (eds.), *Communist Manifesto: Socialist Landmark* (London, George Allen and Unwin).

Mayer, K. (1953), 'Business Enterprise: Traditional Symbol of Opportunity', *British Journal of Sociology*, 4, pp.160–80.

Mayer, P. (1962), 'Migrancy and the Study of Africans in Towns', *American Anthropologist*, 64, pp.576–92.

Medhora, V. B. (1965), 'Entrepreneurship in India', *Political Science Quarterly*, 130, pp.558–80.

Metzger, T. (1966), 'Ch'ing Commercial Policy', *Ch'ing-shih wen-t'i*, 4, pp.4–10.

Metzger, T. (1969), 'The State and Commerce in Imperial China' (Hebrew University, Franz Oppenheimer Memorial Symposium Paper No. 10).

Miners, N. J. (1981), *The Government and Politics of Hong Kong* (Hong Kong, Oxford University Press).

Mitchell, J. C. (1956), *The Kalela Dance* (Manchester, The Rhodes-Livingstone Papers No. 27, Manchester University Press).

Mitchell, J. C. (1969), 'Structural Plurality, Urbanization and Labour Circulation in Southern Rhodesia', in J. A. Jackson (ed), *Migration* (Cambridge, Cambridge University Press), pp.156–80.

Mitchell, J. C. (1970), 'Tribe and Social Change in South Central Africa: A Situational Approach', *Journal of Asian and African Studies*, 5, pp.83–101.

Mitchell, J. C. (1974), 'Social Networks' in B. J. Siegel (ed), *Annual Review of Anthropology*, 3, pp.279–99.

Mitchell, J. C. (1974), 'Perception of Ethnicity and Ethnic Behaviour: An Empirical Exploration', in A. Cohen (ed), *Urban Ethnicity* (London, Tavistock Publications), pp.1–36.

Mitchell, J. C. (ed) (1969), *Social Networks in Urban Situations* (Manchester, Manchester University Press).

Mitchell, R. E. (1969), *Family Life in Urban Hong Kong* (Taipei, Asian Folklore and Social Life Monograph).

Moerman, M. (1968), 'Being Lue: Uses and Abuses of Ethnic Identification', in J. Helm (ed), *Essays on the Problem of Tribe* (Seattle and London, University of Washington Press), pp.153–69.

Mok, M. C. H. (1968), 'The Development of Cotton Spinning and Weaving Industries in Hong Kong, 1946–1966', M. A. thesis (University of Hong Kong).

Morrell, J. (1968), 'Two Early Chinese Cotton Mills', *Papers on China*, 21, pp.43–98.

Morris, H. S. (1968), 'Ethnic Group', in *International Encyclopedia of the Social Sciences* (New York, Macmillan and The Free Press), pp.167–72.

Moulder, F. V. (1977), *Japan, China and the Modern World Economy: Toward a Reinterpretation of East Asian Development ca. 1600 to ca. 1918* (London, Cambridge University Press).

Munro, D. J. (1969), *The Conception of Man in Early China* (Stanford, Stanford University Press).

Murphey, R. (1953), *Shanghai: Key to Modern China* (Cambridge, Harvard University Press).

Naboru, N. (1950), 'The Industrial and Commercial Guilds of Peking and Religion and Fellow-Countrymanship as Elements of Their Coherence', *Folklore Studies*, 9, pp.179–206.

Narroll, R. (1964), 'On Ethnic Unit Classification', *Current Anthropology*, 5, pp.283–312.

Narroll, R. (1968), 'Who the Lue Are', in J. Helm (ed), *Essays on the Problem of Tribe* (Seattle, University of Washington Press).

'Native Banking in Shanghai' (1926), *The Chinese Economic Monthly*, 3, pp.168–83.

Nettl, J. P. (1965), 'Consensus or Elite Domination: The Case of Business', *Political Studies*, 14, pp.22–44.

Nichols, T. (1969), *Ownership, Control, and Ideology: An Inquiry Into Certain Aspects of Modern Business Ideology* (London, George Allen and Unwin).

Nihei, Y., Kao, H. S. R., Levin, D. A., Morkre, M. E., Ohtsu, M., and Peacock, J. B. (1979), *Technology, Employment Practices and Workers: A Comparative Study of Ten Cotton Spinning Plants in Five Asian Countries* (Hong Kong, University of Hong Kong, Centre of Asian Studies).

Numazaki, I. (1986), 'Network of Taiwanese Big Business', *Modern China*, 12, pp.487–534.

Oksenberg, M. (1972), 'Management Practices in the Hong Kong Cotton Spinning and Weaving Industry' (Columbia University, paper read at seminar on Modern East Asia, 15 November).

Olsen, S. M. (1972), 'The Inculcation of Economic Values in Taipei Business Families', in W. Willmott (ed), *Economic Organization*, pp.261–96.

Owen, N. C. (1971), 'Economic Policy in Hong Kong', in K. Hopkins (ed), *Hong Kong: The Industrial Colony*, pp.141–206.

Pan, F. K. (1974), 'The Simple Truth of Management and Maintenance' (Hong Kong, a lecture delivered on 21 June, no publisher).

Pan, F. S. (ed) 潘孚碩（編）(1948), 上海時人誌 (*Who's Who in Shanghai*) (Beijing, Zhanwang Chuban She).

Papanek, G. F. (1971), 'Pakistan's Industrial Entrepreneurs — Education, Occupational Background, and Finance', in W. P. Falcon and G. F. Papanek (eds.), *Development Policy II — The Pakistan Experience* (Cambridge, Harvard University Press), pp.237–61.

Parkin, F. (1974), 'Strategies of Social Closure in Class Formation', in F. Parkin (ed), *The Social Analysis of Class Structure* (London, Tavistock Publications), pp.1–18.

Parsons, T., and Smelser, N. J. (1957), *Economy and Society: A Study in the Integration of Economic and Social Theory* (London, Routledge and Kegan Paul).

Patterson, O. (1975), 'Context and Choice in Ethnic Allegiance: A Theoretical Framework and Caribbean Case Study', in N. Glazer and D. P. Moynihan (eds), *Ethnicity*, pp.305–49.

Patterson, O. (1982), *Slavery and Social Death: A Comparative Study* (Cambridge, Harvard University Press).

Pearse, A. S. (1955), *Japan's Cotton Industry* (Cyprus, Kyrenia).

Pelzel, J. C. (1970), 'Japanese Kinship: A Comparison', in M. Freedman (ed), *Family and Kinship in Chinese Society* (Stanford, Stanford University Press), pp.227–48.

Pepper, S. (1978), *Civil War in China: The Political Struggle 1945–1949* (Berkeley, University of California Press).

Perkins, D. H. (1967), 'Government as an Obstacle to Industrialization: The Case of Nineteenth-Century China', *Journal of Economic History*, 27, pp.478–92.

Perkins, D. H. (1975), 'Introduction: The Persistence of The Past', in D. H. Perkins (ed), *China's Modern Economy in Historical Perspective* (Stanford, Stanford University Press), pp.1–16.

Podmore, D. (1971), 'The Population of Hong Kong', in K. Hopkins (ed), *Hong Kong: The Industrial Colony*, pp.21–54.

Porter, M. (1980), *Competitive Strategy: Techniques for Analyzing Industries and Competitors* (New York, The Free Press).

Power, J. H., Sicat, G. P., and Hsing, M. H. (1971), *The Philippines and Taiwan: Industrialization and Trade Policies* (London, Oxford University Press).

Qi, Y. Z., and Guo Feng 齊以正等 (1980), 香港超級巨富列傳 (*Biographies of The Super-rich in Hong Kong*) (Hong Kong, Wenyi Shuwu).

Quan, H. S. 全漢昇 (1972), '上海在近代中國工業化中的地位' ('The Role of Shanghai in the Industrialization of Modern China'), in H. S. Quan, 中國經濟史論叢 (*Essays on Chinese Economic History*), Volume 2 (Hong Kong, Chinese University of Hong Kong, New Asia Research Institute), pp.697–733.

Reynolds, B. L. (1975), 'The Impact of Trade and Foreign Investment on Industrialization: Chinese Textiles, 1875–1931', Ph.D. thesis (University of Michigan).

Richman, B. M. (1967), 'Capitalists and Managers in Communist China', *Harvard Business Review*, January to February, pp.57–78.

Riedel, J. (1974), *The Industrialization of Hong Kong* (Tübingen, J. C. B. Mohr).

Rinder, I. D. (1959), 'Strangers in the Land: Social Relations in the Status Gap', *Social Problems*, 9, pp.253–60.

Rosen, B. C. (1959), 'Race, Ethnicity and the Achievement Syndrome', *ASR*, 24, pp.47–60.

Rowe, W. T. (1984), *Hankow: Commerce and Society in a Chinese City, 1796–1889* (Stanford, Stanford University Press).

Ryan, E. (1961), 'The Value System of A Chinese Community in Java', Ph.D. thesis (Harvard University).

Schooler, C. (1976), 'Serfdom's Legacy: An Ethnic Continuum', *AJS*, 81, pp.1265–86.

Schumpeter, J. A. (1934), *The Theory of Economic Development: An Inquiry Into Profits, Capital, Credit, Interest, and the Business Cycle* (Cambridge, Harvard University Press).

Schumpeter, J. A. (1951), *Imperialism and Social Classes* (New York, Augustus M. Kelley).

Seider, M. S. (1974), 'American Big Business Ideology: A Content Analysis of Executive Speeches', *ASR*, 39 (1974), pp.802–15.

Shanghai Economic Research Institute, Chinese Academy of Sciences, and Economic Research Institute, Shanghai Academy of Social Sciences (eds.) (1958), 南洋兄弟烟草公司史料 (*Historical Materials Concerning the Nanyang Brothers' Tobacco Company*) (Shanghai, Renmin Chuban She).

Shanghai Fraternity Association 上海聯誼會 (1978), 籌募福利基金國劇義演特刊 (*Chinese Opera In Mandarin for Raising Charity Fund*) (Hong Kong, The Association).

Shanghai Shi Shanghui (ed) 上海市商會 (1947), 紡織工業 (*Textile Industry*) (Shanghai, Shangye Yuebao She).

Shiba, Y. (1977), 'Ningpo and Its Hinterland', in G. W. Skinner (ed), *The City in Imperial China* (Cambridge, Harvard University Press, Press), pp.391–439.

Shiga, S. (1978), 'Family Property and the Law of Inheritance in Traditional China', in D. C. Buxbaum (ed), *Chinese Family Law and Social Change* (Seattle and London, University of Washington Press), pp.109–50.

Silin, R. H. (1976), *Leadership and Values: The Organization of Large Scale Taiwanese Enterprises* (Cambridge, Harvard University Press).

Singer, M. (ed) (1973), *Entrepreneurship and Modernization of Occupational Cultures in South Asia* (Durham, Duke University Press).

Sit, V. F. S., Wong, S. L., and Kiang, T. S. (1979), *Small Scale Industry in a Laissez-Faire Economy: A Hong Kong Case Study* (Hong Kong, University of Hong Kong, Centre of Asian Studies).

Siu, P. C. P. (1952-3), 'The Sojourner', *AJS*, 58, pp.35–44.

Skinner, G. W. (1957), *Chinese Society in Thailand: An Analytical History* (Ithaca, Cornell University Press).

Skinner, G. W. (1971), 'Chinese Peasants and the Closed Community: An Open and Shut Case', *Comparative Studies in Society and History*, 13, pp.270–81.

Skinner, G. W. (1977), 'Regional Urbanization in Nineteenth-Century China', in G. W. Skinner (ed), *The City in Late Imperial China* (Stanford, Stanford University Press), pp.211–49.

Smelser, N. J. (1963), *The Sociology of Economic Life* (Englewood Cliffs, Prentice-Hall).

Smith, C. (1972), 'English-educated Chinese Elites in Nineteenth Century Hong Kong', in M. Topley (ed), *Hong Kong: The Interaction of Tradition and Life in the Towns* (Hong Kong, Royal Asiatic Society Hong Kong Branch), pp.65–96.

Smith, H. (1966), 'John Stuart Mill's Other Island: A Study of the Economic Development of Hong Kong' (London, The Institute of Economic Affairs).

Solomon, R. H. (1971), *Mao's Revolution and the Chinese Political Culture* (Berkeley, University of California Press).

Soltow, J. H. (1968), 'The Entrepreneur in Economic History', *American Economic Review*, 58, pp.84–91.

South China Morning Post.

Speare, A., Jr. (1974), 'Migration and Family Change in Central Taiwan', in G. W. Skinner and M. Elvin (eds.), *The Chinese City Between Two Worlds* (Stanford, Stanford University Press), pp.303–30.

Spectre, S. (1958), 'The Chinese in Singapore', in M. H. Fried (ed), *Colloquium on Overseas Chinese* (New York, Institute of Pacific Relations).

Stigler, G. J. (1973), 'A Note on Potential Competition', in B. S. Yamey (ed), *Economics of Industrial Structure* (Harmondsworth, Penguin Education), pp.117–19.

Stites, R. W. (1985), 'Industrial Work as an Entrepreneurial Strategy', *Modern China*, 11, pp.227–46.

Stokes, R. G. (1974), 'The Afrikaner Industrial Entrepreneur and Afrikaner Nationalism', *EDCC*, 22, pp.557–79.

Stouffer, S. A. (1940), 'Intervening Opportunities: A Theory Relating Mobility and Distance', *ASR*, 5, pp.845–67.

Stouffer, S. A. (1960), 'Intervening Opportunities and Competing Migrants', *Journal of Regional Science*, 2, pp.1–26.

Sung, L. S. (1981), 'Property and Family Division', in E. M. Ahern and H. Gates (eds.), *The Anthropology of Taiwanese Society* (Stanford, Stanford University Press), pp.361–78.

Sutton, F. X., Harris, S. E., Kaysen, C., and Tobin, J. (1956), *The American Business Creed* (New York, Schocken).

Szczepanik, E. (1958), *The Economic Growth of Hong Kong* (London, Oxford University Press).

Taeuber, I. B. (1963), 'Hong Kong: Migrants and Metropolis', *Population Index*, 29, pp.3–25.

Tan, M. G. (1971), *The Chinese in the United States: Social Mobility and Assimilation* (Taipei, Orient Cultural Service).

Taylor, R. C. (1969), 'Migration and Motivation: A Study of Determinants and Types', in J. A. Jackson (ed), *Migration* (Cambridge, Cambridge University Press), pp.99–133.

Tang, Y. Y. 唐有庸 (1954), ' 棉紡工業向銀行借了多少錢？' ('How Much Has the Cotton Spinning Industry Borrowed From the Banks?'), *The Hong Kong Industry Monthly*, 1, p.23.

Textile Asia.

T'ien, J. K. (1953), *The Chinese of Sarawak: A Study of Social Structure* (London, London School of Economics and Political Science).

Ting, H. C. (1974), *Truth and Facts: Recollection of a Hong Kong Industrialist* (Hong Kong, Kader Industrial Company Ltd.).

Ting, S. J., 'Does Hong Kong's Textile Industry Permit Unlimited Investment?', *The Federation of Hong Kong Cotton Weavers 1961–62 Year Book*, pp.36–37.

Topley, M. (1969), 'The Role of Savings and Wealth Among the Hong Kong Chinese', in I. C. Jarvie and J. Agassi (eds.), *Hong Kong, a Society in Transition* (London, Routledge and Kegan Paul), pp.167–227.

Tu, Y. P, and Jiang, S. L. (eds.) (1940), 香港導遊 (*Travel Guide to Hong Kong*) (Shanghai, China Travel Service).

United Nations (1966), *Economic Survey of Asia and the Far East, 1965* (Bangkok).

United Nations (1970), *Economic Survey of Asia and the Far East, 1969* (Bangkok).

United Nations (1977), *Economic Survey of Asia and the Far East, 1976* (Bangkok).

United Nations Educational, Scientific, and Cultural Organization (1977), *Race and Class in Post-colonial Society: A study of Ethnic Group Relations in the English-speaking Carbbean, Bolivia, Chile and Mexico* (Paris, Unesco).

Walker, E. R. (1971), 'Beyond the Market', in K. W. Rothschild (ed), *Power in Economics* (Harmondsworth, Penguin Education), pp.36–55.

Walker, J. (ed) (1974), *Hong Kong Who's Who: An Almanac of Personalities and Their Comprehensive Histories, 1970–1973* (Hong Kong, Rola Luzzatto and Joseph Walker).

Wan, L. 萬林 (1947), '中國的「棉紗大王」「麵粉大王」無錫榮氏家族暴發史' ('A History of the Sudden Prosperity of the Rong Family of Wuxi in the Cotton Spinning and Flour Industries of China'), *Jingji Daobao*, 50, pp.1–7.

Wang, C. Y. 王楚瑩 (1947), 香港工廠調查 (*A Survey of Factories in Hong Kong*) (Hong Kong, Nanqiao Xinwen Qiye Gongxi).

Wang, L. 王齡 (1949), 香港潮僑通覽 (*A Compendium on the Chaozhou Sojourners of Hong Kong*) (Hong Kong, no publisher).

Ward, B. E. (1965), 'Varieties of The Conscious Model: The Fishermen of Southern China', in M. Banton (ed), *The Relevance of Models for Social Anthropology* (London, Tavistock Publications), pp.113–37.

Ward, B. E. (1972), 'A Small Factory in Hong Kong: Some Aspects of Its Internal Organization', in W. Willmott (ed), *Economic Organization*, pp.353–86.

Weber, M. (1930), *The Protestant Ethic and The Spirit of Capitalism* (London, Unwin).

Weber, M. (1951), *The Religion of China: Confucianism and Taoism* (Glencoe, The Free Press).

Weber, M. (1963), *The Sociology of Religion* (London, Methuen).

Weber, M. (1968), *Economy and Society* (New York, Bedminster Press).

Wertheim, W. F. (1964), 'The Trading Minorities in Southeast Asia', in W. F. Wertheim (ed), *East-West Parallels: Sociological Approaches to Modern Asia* (The Hague, W. Van Hoeve Ltd.), pp.39–82.

Wilhelm, R. (1947), *Chinese Economic Psychology* (New York, Institute of Pacific Relations).

Willmott, D. E. (1960), *The Chinese of Semarang: A Changing Minority Community in Indonesia* (Ithaca, Cornell University Press).

Willmott, W. E. (1966), 'The Chinese in Southeast Asia', *Australian Outlook*, 20, pp.252–62.

Willmott, W. E. (1967), *The Chinese in Cambodia* (Vancouver, University of British Columbia Press).

Willmott, W.E. (ed.) (1972), *Economic Organization Chinese Society* (Stanford, Stanford University Press).

Wolf, E. R. (1966), 'Kinship, Friendship, and Patron-Client Relations in Complex Societies', in M. Banton (ed), *The Social Anthropology of Complex Societies* (London, Tavistock Publications), pp.1–22.

Wolf, M. (1970), 'Child Training and the Chinese Family', in M. Freedman (ed), *Family and Kinship in Chinese Society* (Stanford, Stanford University Press), pp.37–62.

Wong, P. S. (1958), 'The Influx of Chinese Capital into Hong Kong since 1937' (University of Hong Kong, paper read at the Contemporary China Seminar).

Wong, S. K. (1966), 'An Interview with a Shanghai Capitalist', *Eastern Horizon*, 5, pp.11–16.

Wong, S. L. (1975), 'The Economic Enterprise of the Chinese in Southeast Asia: A Sociological Inquiry with Special Reference to West Malaysia and Singapore', B. Litt., thesis (University of Oxford).

Wong, S. L. (1983), 'Business Ideology of Chinese Industrialists in Hong Kong', *Journal of The Hong Kong Branch of the Royal Asiatic Society*, 23, pp.137–71.

Wong, S. L. (1984), 'The Migration of Shanghainese Entrepreneurs to Hong Kong', in D. Faure et al. (eds), *From Village to City: Studies in the Traditional Roots of Hong Kong Society* (Hong Kong, University of Hong Kong, Centre of Asian Studies), pp.206–27.

Wong, S. L. (1985), 'The Chinese Family Firm: A Model', *British Journal of Sociology*, 36, pp.58–72.

Wong, S. L. (1986), 'Modernization and Chinese Culture in Hong Kong', *The China Quarterly*, 106, pp.306–25.

Wong, S. L. (forthcoming), 'The Applicability of Asian Family Values to Other Socio-Cultural Settings', in Berger, P., and Hsiao, M. (eds.), *In Search of An East Asian Development Model*.

Wright, A. (1908), *Twentieth Century Impression of Hong Kong, Shanghai and Other Treaty Ports of China* (London, Lloyd's Great Britain Publishing Co.).

Xingdao Ribao. 星島日報 .

Xu, J. Q. 徐廣𡊑 (1932), 最近上海金融史 (*The Recent History of Finance in Shanghai*) (Shanghai, no publisher).

Xue, M. J. 薛明劍 , ' 辦理申新三廠勞工事業的經驗 ' ('My Experience in Handling Workers' Activities in the Shen Xin Third Mill'), *Jiaoyu Yu Zhiye*, 165 (1935), pp.333–9; 166 (1935), pp.411–20.

Yamamura, K. (1974), *A Study of Samurai Income and Entrepreneurship* (Cambridge, Harvard University Press).

Yancey, W. L., et al. (1976), 'Emergent Ethnicity: A Review and Reformulation', *ASR*, 41, pp.391–403.

Yan, Z. P. 嚴中平 (1963), 中國棉紡織史稿 *1289–1937* (*A Draft History of China's Cotton Textile Industry 1289–1937*) (Beijing, Kexue Chubanshe).

Yang, L. S. (1952), *Money and Credit in China* (Cambridge, Harvard University Press).

Yang, L. S. (1970), 'Government Control of Urban Merchants in Traditional China', *The Tsing Hua Journal of Chinese Studies*, 8, pp.186–209.

Yang, Y. P. 楊蔭溥 (1930), 中國交易所論 (*On Chinese Exchanges*) (Nanjing, National Central University Publications).

Yao, S. L.姚崧齡(1978), '民國人物小傳：榮宗敬(*1873–1938*)' ('Short Biographies of Personalities of the Republican Period: Rong Zhongjing'), *Chuanji Wenxue*, 33, pp.142–3.

Young, A. N. (1965), *China's Wartime Finance and Inflation, 1937–1945* (Cambridge, Harvard University Press).

Young, J. A. (1971), 'Interpersonal Networks and Economic Behaviour in a Chinese Market Town', Ph.D. thesis (Stanford University).

Young, S. C. (1969), 'The GATT'S Long Term Cotton Textile Arrangement and Hong Kong's Cotton Textile Trade', Ph.D. thesis (Washington State University).

Zhao, K., and Chen, Z. Y. 趙岡，陳鍾毅 (1977), 中國棉業史 (*A History of the Chinese Textile Industry*) (Taibei, Lianji Chuban Shiye Gongxi).

Zhao, Z. S. 趙鍾蓀 (1977), '訪中國大陸的民族資本家' ('Interviewing The National Capitalists in the Chinese Mainland'), *Qishi Niandai*, 91, pp.45–6.

Zhong, S. Y. 鍾樹元 (1948), '江浙財團的支柱─寧波幫' ('The Pillar of the Jiang-Zhe Financial Syndicate — The Ningbo *Bang*'), *Jingji Daobao*, 67, pp.6–8.

Zhongguo Shiye Bu, Guoji Maoyi Chu (ed) 中國實業部、國際貿易署（編）(1933), 全國實業調查報告之一：江蘇省 (*Industrial Survey of Jiangsu Province*) (Shanghai, Zhongguo Shiye Bu).

Zhongguo Wenshi Yanjiu Xuehui (ed) 中國文史研究學會（編）新中國人物誌 (*Biographies of New China*) (Hong Kong, Zhongguo Wenshi Yanjiu Xuehui, no date).

Zhonghua Renmin Gonghe Guo Fensheng Ditu Ji (*Provincial Atlas of The People's Republic of China*) (1974), (Beijing, Ditu Chuban She).

Zhongwen Da Cidian Bianzuan Weiyuan Hui, 中文大辭典 (*The Encyclopedic Dictionary of the Chinese Language*) (Taibei, The Institute For Advanced Chinese Studies).

Glossary

Ann, T. K. 安子介
Cha Chi-ming 查濟民
Chang Jye-an 張絜庵
Chaozhou 潮州
Chau Tsun-nin 周峻年
Chen, Eric L. C. 陳艮綱
Cheng Fu Textile School of Shanghai 上海市私立誠孚紡織專科學校
Chinese Democratic National Construction Society 中國民主建國會
Chinese General Chamber of Commerce of Hong Kong, The 香港中華總商會
Chinese Textile Industries Inc., The 中國紡織建設公司
Da Sheng Cotton Mill 大生紗廠
Da Yuan Cotton Mill 大元紗廠
dang laobang 當老板
Ding Li-fang 丁利方
fang 房
fenjia 分家
haipai 海派
Hankou 漢口
Heng Feng Cotton Mill 恆豐紗廠
Hong Kong Chinese Manufacturers' Union 香港中華廠商聯合會
Hong Kong Cotton Spinners' Association 香港棉紡業同業公會
Hong Kong General Chamber of Commerce 香港總商會
Hong Kong Jiangsu Residents' Association 旅港江蘇省同鄉會
Hong Kong Ningbo Residents' Association 寧波旅港同鄉會
Hong Kong Northern Jiangsu Residents' Association 香港蘇北同鄉會
Hu Ning Hang 滬寧杭
Hu Ru-xi 胡汝禧
Hua Bai-zhong 華伯忠
Hua Sheng Spinning & Weaving Mill 華盛紡織廠
ji 記
jia 家
Jiang Jun-qing 蔣涒卿
Jiangsu & Zhejiang Residents' (Hong Kong) Association 蘇浙旅港同鄉會
Jiangsu-Zhejiang-Shanghai Merchants' (HK) Association 旅港蘇浙滬商人協會
jiguan 籍貫
jingpai 京派
Kaifong association 街坊會

Koo, Wellington V. K. 顧維鈞
kuan-hsi 關係
Leung, Sally 梁王培芳
Li De-quan 李德鎵
Li Guo-wei 李國偉
Li Qi-yao 李啓耀
Li Shu-wen 李儲文
Liu Guo-jun 劉國鈞
Liu Hang-kun 劉漢塑
Liu Hang-tong 劉漢棟
Liu Hong-sheng 劉鴻生
Lu Zuo-lin 陸佐霖
Nantong College 南通學院
New China News Agency 新華社
pang 幫
Pao Hsing Cotton Mill 寶星紗廠
Pao Yuen Tung Hsing Yieh Co. Ltd. 寶元通興業股份有限公司
Po Leung Kuk 保良局
qianzhuang 錢莊
qinxin 親信
Rong De-sheng 榮德生
Rong Er-ren 榮爾仁
Rong Hong-ren 榮鴻仁
Rong Hong-san 榮鴻三
Rong Hong-xing 榮鴻慶
Rong Hong-yuan 榮鴻元
Rong Ji-fu 榮輯芙
Rong Ji-ren 榮紀仁
Rong Ju-xian 榮菊仙
Rong Mao-yi 榮茂儀
Rong Min-ren 榮敏仁
Rong Mo-zhen 榮墨珍
Rong Shu-ren 榮漱仁
Rong Shu-zhen 榮漱珍
Rong Su-rong 榮素蓉
Rong Wei-ren 榮偉仁
Rong Yan-ren 榮研仁
Rong Yi-ren 榮毅仁
Rong Yi-xin 榮一心
Rong Zhuo-ai 榮卓靄
Rong Zhuo-qiu 榮卓球
Rong Zhuo-ren 榮卓仁
Rong Zhuo-ru 榮卓如
Rong Zhuo-ya 榮卓亞

Rong Zong-jing 榮宗敬
sanwu 三吳
Shanghai Chartered Stock & Produce Exchange 上海證券物品交易所
Shanghai Fraternity Association 上海聯誼會
Shanghai Motoring Club 上海旅港汽車俱樂部
Shen Xin Cotton Mill 申新紗廠
Sheng Zuan-huai 盛宣懷
Shu Jun-zhang 束雲章
Song Mi-yang 宋美揚
Song, V. J. 宋文傑
Soong, T. V. 宋子文
Tang Hong-yuan 唐熊源
Tang, H. C. 唐翔千
Tang, P. Y. 唐炳源
T'ien 田
Tsao, Peter K. Y. 曹廣榮
Tsuen Wan Northern Chinese Sojourners' Welfare Association 荃灣北僑
  福利會
Tung Teh-mei 董德美
Tung Wah Hospital 東華醫院
Wang Yun-cheng 王雲程
Wing On Company 永安公司
Wong, C. Y. 王啓宇
Woo, Alex 吳中豪
Wu dialect 吳語
Wu Kun-sheng 吳昆生
Xu Jia-tun 許家屯
Xue Shou-xuan 薛壽宣
Yan Chai Hospital 仁濟醫院
Yang Dao-yi 楊道誼
Yang Sen-hui 楊勝惠
Yen Xing-xiang 嚴慶祥
Yin Shun-xin 應舜卿
yinhao 銀號
Zhang Jian 張謇

Index